PROUD BOYS
AND THE WHITE
ETHNOSTATE

PROUD BOYS
AND THE WHITE
ETHNOSTATE

HOW THE ALT-RIGHT
IS WARPING THE
AMERICAN IMAGINATION

ALEXANDRA MINNA STERN

BEACON PRESS
BOSTON

BEACON PRESS
Boston, Massachusetts
www.beacon.org

Beacon Press books
are published under the auspices of
the Unitarian Universalist Association of Congregations.

22 21 20 19   8 7 6 5 4 3 2 1

This book is printed on acid-free paper that meets the uncoated paper
ANSI/NISO specifications for permanence as revised in 1992.

Text design and composition by Kim Arney

Cataloging-in-Publication Data is on file at the Library of Congress.
ISBN 978-08070-6336-1

CONTENTS

INTRODUCTION The New and Old of White Nationalism ▪ 1

CHAPTER 1 Red Pills for the Masses: Metapolitical Awakenings ▪ 15

CHAPTER 2 Back to the Future: Reactionary Timescapes ▪ 33

CHAPTER 3 Whitopia: Ethnostate Dreamin' ▪ 51

CHAPTER 4 Cat Ladies, Wolves, and Lobsters: A Menagerie of Biological Essentialism ▪ 71

CHAPTER 5 Living the TradLife: Babies, Butter, and the Vanishing of Bre Faucheux ▪ 93

CHAPTER 6 Normalizing Nationalism: Alt-Right Creep ▪ 111

CONCLUSION Decoding and Derailing White Nationalist Discourse ▪ 129

ACKNOWLEDGMENTS ▪ 139

NOTES ▪ 141

INDEX ▪ 175

THE NEW AND OLD
OF WHITE NATIONALISM

In the summer of 2016, I was online doing some research on early twentieth-century eugenics and immigration restriction when I stumbled across the centenary edition of Madison Grant's *The Passing of the Great Race*. It was about one month after Donald Trump had won the Republican primary, and the prospect that someone who had called Mexicans "rapists," pushed "birtherism," and demanded a "massive border wall" would become the next president of the United States seemed remote, if not impossible.[1] As a scholar interested in the intersections of racial and reproductive politics, I was acutely aware of the history of white nationalism in America. I had studied and taught about organizations, old and new, such as the Immigration Restriction League, the Ku Klux Klan, and American Renaissance.

Now eugenics was rearing its bigoted head in a celebratory reissue of a racist classic brought out by Ostara Publications. This press was founded in 1999 to disseminate Arthur Kemp's *March of the Titans: The Complete History of the White Race*, its "flagship work," which appeared in its fourth edition in 2011. This massive text, which seems geared to homeschoolers, proposes that "a civilization 'rises and falls' by its racial homogeneity and nothing else. As long as it maintains its racial homogeneity, it will last—if it loses its racial homogeneity, and changes its racial makeup, it will 'fall' or be replaced by a new culture."[2] A little more online digging revealed that Ostara, with its commitment to "Eurocentric history," is one of a handful of publishing ventures that produces on-demand books with titles that scream Islamophobia and white supremacy, and glorify Western civilization. According to its website, Ostara is named after the Old High German goddess of spring, "Ēostre," who represents the "rebirth and fertility of ancient Europe"—a trope redolent of "blood and soil" nationalism.

Ostara easily fit the profile of a publisher that would make *The Passing of the Great Race* newly available to its readers. The first edition of this tendentious book aimed to rank "European races in history" as groups according to physical, mental, and personality traits, and proposed three European races—Teutonics or Nordics, Alpines, and Mediterraneans—anointing the first as the most advanced and comely. Beyond racist taxonomy, however, it sounded off eugenic warnings: of the degenerate immigrant masses, of impending white race suicide, and of the disharmonies of miscegenation. Alongside a plethora of early twentieth-century tracts about the biological inferiority of every racial and ethnic group save Northern Europeans, *The Passing of the Great Race* served as fodder for the 1924 Johnson-Reed Immigration Act, which set racial quotas on immigrants based on nationality. This legislation hardened existing bans on Asian immigrants, placed strict limits on arrivals from Southern and Eastern Europe, and facilitated the formation of the US Border Patrol.

On the back cover of the centenary edition, Ostara praises *The Passing of the Great Race* as a "sweeping and classic study of racial anthropology and history" that stands as a "call to American whites to counter the dangers both from non-white and non-north Western European immigration."[3] Today white nationalists are updating this Eurocentric and xenophobic script. Indeed, Richard Spencer, who coined the term "alt-right," is an adherent of Madison Grant.[4] In a lengthy essay, "Madison Grant and the American Nation," Spencer admires another one of Grant's books, *The Conquest of a Continent*, published in 1933, calling it a "great history" and a "grand vision of bio-cultural struggle and evolution, in which demography comes alive."[5] *The Conquest of a Continent* recounts the story of how America became a "Nordic country" through a combination of "individualism, Protestantism, uprightness, and the pioneer spirit." Unlike *The Passing of the Great Race*, which Theodore Roosevelt called a "capital book" and had a large following, *Conquest* was panned by reviewers, who by the mid-1930s were looking askance at such unbridled racism.[6] Now, more than eight decades later, Spencer wants to rescue Grant's later work, lamenting what he views as the unfair dismissal of the book as blunderheaded eugenic thinking associated with the Third Reich. He commends Grant's entire corpus as a guiding compass for assessing racial degeneration in twenty-first-century America and a masterful model of how to deploy science to promote white nationalism.

As it turns out, the rehabilitation of American eugenicists is a pastime of the alt-right. Four years earlier, in 2012, Palingenesis Press, based in the UK, published an edition (now out of print) of *The Passing of the Great Race*, with a forward written by Jared Taylor, the head of American Renaissance, an organization focused on so-called "race realism" and an entrenched pillar of white nationalism.[7] Grant and his contemporary Lothrop Stoddard, author of *The Rising Tide of Color Against White World Supremacy* (1920), are enduring darlings of the alt-right. The highbrow white nationalist webzine *Counter-Currents Publishing* (which also has a book-publishing arm) annually commemorates Grant's birthday, lauding his multipronged white advocacy. In the words of *Counter-Currents*, Grant was an "American aristocrat and pioneering advocate of white racial preservationism, immigration restriction, eugenics, anti-miscegenation laws, and the conservation of wildlife and wilderness."[8] *Counter-Currents* praises Grant as an exemplary environmentalist who, alongside Stanford University's first president, David Starr Jordan, and Sacramento philanthropist Charles M. Goethe, were "race realists and eugenicists."[9] *Counter-Currents* also memorializes Stoddard's birthday, extolling the virtues of his racist study of the Haitian revolution and his more widely known *The Revolt Against Civilization* (1922). Although *Counter-Currents* concedes that some of Stoddard's ideas seem trite today, it emphasizes the contemporary relevance of his contention that a "nation's breeding policy is at least as essential a factor in geopolitical strategy as trade policy or defense."[10]

Like many Americans, I was disconcerted and spooked by the alt-right's breakthrough into politics, media, and culture. Now it was surfacing in my research. I recognized its catchphrases, such as "white genocide," and its recycling of stereotypes about people of color, crime rates, and IQ scores. Struck by both the familiarity and the strangeness of the alt-right, I decided to bear witness to it in real time. Was the alt-right simply old wine in new bottles, the latest incarnation of American eugenics, racism, and anti-egalitarianism? Was it something novel, with the potential to reshape politics and discourse, abetted by a sympathetic Republican presidential administration, an upsurge in national populism, and a context of simmering "white rage"?[11] Could the alt-right appeal to younger generations of white Americans, who might be swayed by anxieties over demographic despair and tantalizing visions of racially homogenous homelands? What were the cultural and political implications of the circulation of the alt-right lexicon—as terms such as "ethnostate," "human biodiversity," "cuckservative," and "snowflake" entered the American vocabulary?

To answer these questions, I began to spend hours and hours online, taking deep dives in an ever-expanding sea of URLs, exploring sites such as *Counter-Currents*, *Radix Journal*, and that of Ostara Publications. Some of these sites had been actively posting without interruption for years, others distributing on-demand books and offering occasional posts, and some were moribund webzines with archived content. In order to mine the intellectual bedrock of the alt-right, I set out to read and analyze its quasischolarly work as a formidable form of knowledge production in an era of rising authoritarianism and ultranationalism across the globe. I began to amass my archive, concentrating on long-form essays, like Spencer's article on Madison Grant, as well as monographs, anthologies, and manifestos published by alt-right publishing enterprises such as Counter-Currents, American Renaissance, and the Budapest-based Arktos. Although unlikely to ever survive academic peer review, this sizable body of literature strategically adheres to scholarly conventions, reflecting the graduate training of a good many of the alt-right mandarins.

I knew that to unearth this history of the present, I also needed to get under—to excavate—the alt-right memes and tropes that had erupted online. Thus, I delved into virtual communities on Reddit, 4chan, and 8chan; visited the long-standing white nationalist message board Stormfront; read thousands of comments on YouTube and Twitter; and knocked around in the dark corners of the ugly, unmoderated virtual realms of Gab and BitChute. This unwieldy collection of sources—most born digital—constitutes the archive for this book. Drawing from this unconventional archive, I have written this book in tandem with the alt-right's crescendo before and after Trump's 2016 victory, its dispersal in the wake of Charlottesville in 2017, and its subsequent attempts to reassemble and normalize. Due to the ongoing if inconsistent wave of deplatforming of some white nationalists, like Jared Taylor, and alt-light conspiracy pushers, such as Alex Jones, some of the content that I accessed online has been blocked, removed, or suspended. Scattered fragments can be plumbed from the depths of the Wayback Machine, an internet archive that has captured digital materials since 1996.[12] This makes the screenshots I captured, and the video and audio content I transcribed, crucial and evanescent evidence of the alt-right's recent history.

The term "alt-right" dates to 2008, when paleoconservative Paul Gottfried, an emeritus professor of humanities at Elizabethtown College, used "alternative right" in a lecture to the H. L. Mencken Society. Since the 1990s, paleoconservatives, mostly affiliated with right-wing politician and pundit Patrick Buchanan, had roared about their abhorrence of liberals and distinguished themselves sharply from neoconservatives; a good many made up the right flank of libertarian Ron Paul's 2008 presidential campaign. After this electoral effort fizzled out, this contingent was eager for a political alternative outside the partisan mainstream. Gottfried channeled this yearning in his speech, declaring "we are part of an attempt to put together an independent intellectual right, one that exists without movement establishment funding and one that our opponents would be delighted not to have to deal with."[13] Soon after, Spencer, then an editor at *Taki's Magazine*, cleverly shortened Gottfried's talk title, "The Decline and Rise of the Alternative Right," to "alt-right."[14] Over the next few years, a motley crew of disaffected libertarians, paleoconservatives, racialists of varying stripes (white separatists, supremacists, nationalists, and ethnonationalists), men's rights activists and misogynists (like MGTOW—Men Going Their Own Way), neo-reactionaries, anti-Semites, and xenophobes with conspicuous animus against Latina/os and Muslims gravitated to the alt-right mantle, finding common cause in the fledgling movement's rejection of establishment conservatism and its antipathy toward feminism and multiculturalism. A notably decentralized movement, the alt-right was decidedly white, male, and aggrieved. Its key figures feuded about many things, but almost to a man, the alt-righters agreed that to have any modicum of success they would have to cultivate a fresh image and shed the Nazi insignias and KKK white hoods associated with white supremacy. As the popular vlogger RamZPaul (Paul Ramsey) explained in early 2016, the alt-right "was fundamentally identity politics for our people without the neo-nazi [*sic*] baggage."[15]

The accelerant for the alt-right was the internet. It is impossible to grasp the alt-right prairie fire leading up to the 2016 election without taking stock of the pitched volume of activity that unfolded in chat rooms, message boards, and tweet storms in those months.[16] Most notoriously, Pepe the Frog, once an anthropomorphized frat boy depicted hanging with his video-playing buddies in the "Boy's Life" comics, became corrupted in the digital corridors of 4chan and 8chan, claimed by Trump supporters, and later identified by the Anti-Defamation League as a hate symbol.[17] The alt-right was introduced on the national electoral stage in Reno, Nevada, in August 2016. At a campaign event, the Democratic Party presidential nominee Hillary Clinton decried the latest incarnation of the "vast right-wing conspiracy" she had assailed two decades earlier. After providing examples of fake news, racist remarks, and conspiracy theories emanating from the "dark reaches of the internet," Clinton asserted, "These are race-baiting ideas, anti-Muslim and anti-immigrant ideas, anti-woman—all key tenets making up an emerging racist ideology known as the 'Alt-Right.'"[18] She was absolutely correct, although in hindsight, this speech, along with her subsequent "basket of deplorables" jab, ended up galvanizing the Trumpian trollers and tweeters who took to the public square of the internet to amplify the alt-right's raucous, mischievous, and vicious memes and messages.[19]

Trump emboldened this amorphous online army further. And once he won the election, the alt-right gloated on a triumphant high. Even if the new commander in chief was not as extreme as many alt-righters would have liked, they heralded him as "a step towards this new normal" of white nationalism and the ineluctable demise of liberal America.[20] One proclaimed that Trump "may just unlock the future we have all been striving for."[21] And Spencer celebrated Trump's win as, "at its root, a victory of identity politics."[22] This high was deflated partially by the post-election "Hailgate" episode, when about two hundred attendees at a meeting held at the Virginia-based white nationalist think tank, the National Policy Institute, led by Spencer, raised their arms and shouted, "Hail Trump, hail our people, hail victory!"[23] While this spectacle, caught on video and spread with viral speed, might have sent shivers down the spines of most Americans, many on the alt-right shrugged it off as another ironic jest that "normies" just could not grasp. If Hailgate caused troublesome "optics" for the alt-right, the events that transpired at the August 2017 Unite the

Right rally in Charlottesville, Virginia, punctured the bubble. "C-ville" was a disaster that shattered a coalescing critical mass of white nationalists and tarnished the alt-right label.[24] It also proved that as the visibility of the alt-right increased, its ability to control its image decreased. The alt-right easily could succumb to its loudest, angriest, neo-Nazi denominator.

Today the alt-right is in an uncharted phase, facing media scrutiny, legal prosecution, and negative press, exacerbated by its penchant for eating its own, internecine backstabbing, and testosterone-charged power plays. Alt-righters themselves complain about the movement's tendency to "purity spiral," or insist on increasingly absolutist positions, usually related to the Jewish Question (JQ) or the Women Question (WQ), which induces paranoia and ideological claustrophobia. To a great extent, the fall-out from Charlottesville has forced a return to the alt-right's initial form of decentralization. At the same time, many sympathizers have become wary of the moniker "alt-right" and are now trying out labels such as "dissident right," "affirmative right," "ethnonationalist," and "identitarian," or simply opting for "nationalist." "Alt-right," however, has become a household term, used in media coverage and accepted, if begrudgingly, by nationalists on both sides of the Atlantic. Moreover, the prefix "alt" connects the term to a family of movements in Europe, such as Alternative for Germany and Alternative for Sweden, to which the alt-right is allied. There have been shake-ups in the alt-right pantheon too. Once atop his Hailgate high horse, Spencer has been sidelined and often is disparaged by prominent alt-righters and ideological allies. For example, in summer 2018 Gottfried roasted Spencer, saying that he "went off the deep end" trying to "become some kind of a guru to a white nationalist right which had no way of succeeding as an alternative to anything."[25]

Spencer's demotion bodes well for the future of the alt-right. Without him sucking all the air out of the room, the alt-right landscape is being populated by a growing cast of minor actors and activists who produce media content every day and are making efforts to build a white nationalist community in real life (IRL). Identity Evropa, rebranded in 2019 as the American Identity Movement, reports it is adding chapters and members at a fast clip.[26] The movement also has spread its international wings, forging and deepening ties with nationalist and identitarian groups across Europe.[27] At the ethnonationalist Scandza Forum in September 2018 in Copenhagen, the American and European speakers were sanguine about the future, noting an uptick in interest of people "waiting for a way for-ward" and reminding the audience that "the problems that are driving people towards us" are "not going away anytime soon."[28] On the five-hour Yule web TV marathon broadcasted by the alt-right channel Red Ice in December 2018, white nationalists voiced similar sentiments. During his cameo, James Edwards, host of the popular syndicated radio show *Polit-ical Cesspool*, exuded optimism, stating even though white nationalists in America might have to suffer a bit more, "our best days are ahead of us" and "tribalism is ascendant."[29] The regrouping of the alt-right is not hap-pening in isolation, and it benefits from a political and media environment hospitable to its message. Conservative media hosts like Tucker Carlson of Fox News parrot the alt-right's rhetoric, and Trump tweets white na-tionalist tropes.[30] Paradoxically, the intense criticism of the alt-right has encouraged the circulation of its icons and slogans.[31] Alt-right ideas that previously lurked in the shadows of the unspeakable have migrated into everyday discourse, becoming imaginable and utterable.

I am interested in these ideas, concepts, and frameworks. My approach is not biographical and does not dwell on personal motivation or organi-zational histories. Although names are mentioned for purposes of iden-tification, I have not attempted to suss out the actual identities of avatars and aliases, nor do I wish to engage in ad hominem attacks or doxing. My aim instead is to deconstruct the prevailing set of alt-right ideas, to trace their genealogies, flesh out their meanings, and explore how they endan-ger equality, diversity, and inclusion in twenty-first-century America. I neither trivialize nor sensationalize the alt-right, nor do I assume it is an aberration, even if it frequently inhabits the gutters of political discourse.

Some scholars and journalists interchange the terms "white suprem-acist," "white nationalist," "fascist," and "neo-Nazi." In this book, how-ever, I primarily use "alt-right" and "white nationalism." I have hewed closely to the written and multimedia production of self-professed alt-righters and white nationalists, which I seek to analyze with semantic veri-similitude. In addition, I want to avoid peppering the narrative with a dizzying array of descriptors. Understandably, there is significant overlap and slipperiness between white nationalism and white supremacy. The latter term often is understood as the more extreme and jolting of the pair. Assigning the labels of white supremacy and neo-Nazism to people and ideas has the advantage of shock value and attention-grabbing, but it often comes at the unfortunate price of sensationalism and hyperbole. Even if definitionally accurate, these labels can eclipse the more insidious aspects of white nationalism prone to mainstreaming. For example, it is essential to dismantle the claim made by white nationalists that they are more reasonable and compassionate than white supremacists because they merely want rights for white people or believe that "whites need[ed] to be protected within their own border, like an endangered species."[32] Increasingly white nationalists, as they tacitly take white exceptionalism for granted, contend that white supremacy is bad for all ethnoracial groups; it is a disharmonious arrangement of white domination over mixed-race populations that, given unfolding demographic patterns, will hasten white dispossession and extinction, and turn whites into shunned, persecuted minorities. White nationalists assert that they want a separate homeland not to reign with an iron fist over racial and ethnic minorities but to shore up and shelter their own. As Paul Ramsey has written, "Some people no longer want to be dispossessed from their homelands. And they also don't want to exploit or harm other races."[33]

This book seeks to expose the underlying logic and implications of white nationalism and its master plan of a racially exclusive patriarchal world. Each chapter of *Proud Boys and the White Ethnostate* explores a core dimension of the alt-right and white nationalism, highlighting what makes the alt-right new and old. I demonstrate how it adheres to quintessentially fascist ideas of patriarchy, hierarchy, victimhood, anti-egalitarianism, and racial and gender essentialism, manifesting them in the context of twenty-first-century America.[34] A potent representation of this is the white ethnostate, envisioned by alt-righters as a homogenous, pristine, orderly, and eugenically engineered utopia. I also explore how these ideas are torqued and spun, as they travel and ricochet around the digital playground of the internet, enabling the alt-right to mimic and appropriate mainstream popular culture to white nationalist ends. This can be seen in the alt-right's particular version of political awakening, red pilling, and in the case of white nationalist women, who have inserted themselves, despite patriarchal pushback, into the conversation, abetted by online cultures of DIY videos and digital storytelling.

Chapter 1, "Red Pills for the Masses: Metapolitical Awakenings," focuses on the idea of transformation or conversion, exploring the alt-right's conceptions of individual and collective transformation, often described as awakenings. "Red pilling," a term appropriated from the science fiction film *The Matrix*, represents the process by which someone comes to realize that things are not really what they seem, more pointedly that whites have been sold a bill of goods called diversity, inclusion, multiculturalism, and gender equality. Born in the toxic technoculture of the online "manosphere," where men blame women for their sexual failures and feminism for its destructiveness, red pilling migrated into the alt-right as the movement took shape and has become a staple expression for conversion.[35] The pill metaphor is so compelling that it has expanded to include white pills, which provide doses of optimism, and black pills, which cause despondency. This chapter moves on to examine "metapolitics," a term used to describe the pre-political approach of white nationalists who view winning the hearts and minds of white Americans as a necessary initial step toward massive social change. Originating in the French nationalist movements of the 1960s, the concept of metapolitics has become the alt-right's foremost way to explain how to bring about political transformation through cultural means. This chapter underscores the degree to which the alt-right's intellectual pedigree relies heavily both on European New Right thought leaders and the strategic appropriation of concepts from the Left.

Chapter 2, "Back to the Future: Reactionary Timescapes," explores the dimension of time and provides a philosophical rumination on the alt-right's approach to temporality, which is an integral if unacknowledged aspect of the imagined expansion of white nationalism. The alt-right's love affair with time is emblematic of the veneration of the mythic past characteristic of fascist movements, whether in the 1930s or in the current moment of heightening ethnonationalism across the globe.[36] Yet, the alt-right approach to time is about more than retrospective nostalgia; it is better understood as a timescape with its own tempo and beat. The alt-right projection of white demise incites a race against time—against demographic transition, the browning of America, and looming racial oblivion. Many alt-righters envision a present that is accelerating and a future marked by catastrophes, ruptures, and cyclical turnovers. Informed by scholarship that examines how fascist and authoritarian regimes have utilized temporality to rationalize their presence and message, this chapter uses the curious motto of Counter-Currents' publishing arm, "Books Against Time," to illuminate the Nazi and fascist antecedents of the alt-right's ideal cyclical emplotment of social change. I also address historical memory and amnesia in the context of the United States, elucidating why the alt-right has enshrined 1965 as the pivotal year of return. Overall, I argue that despite its seemingly abstract nature, upsetting white nationalist timescapes can be one of the most effective ways to push back against the alt-right vision of tomorrow.

Chapter 3, "Whitopia: Ethnostate Dreamin'," focuses on the ideas of place and belonging, looking closely at the paramount fantasy of the white nirvana: the ethnostate. I examine the genesis of the concept of the ethnostate, specifically how it has drawn on right-leaning fearmongering about racial degeneration and hopes for eugenic optimization as well as on left-leaning environmental notions of ecology such as the bioregion. I look closely at the Green and white nationalist literature that has influenced the conceptualization of the white ethnostate and its geographic attachment to the Pacific Northwest. Exploring the ethnostate opens up the Pandora's box of the criteria for whiteness and inclusion, which are contested issues among alt-righters. I examine the "vetting algorithms" for the ethnostate developed by one white nationalist, using his flow chart to gauge how whiteness is ascertained based on racial, moral, and political criteria. This chapter juxtaposes the alt-right's beneficent view of the ethnostate—a version of diversity that purports to respect races by separating them—with the harsh and cruel realities of the policies that would be required to enforce new territorial boundaries in multiracial America. I suggest that even if a remote possibility, the ethnostate is an idea that already is eroding the distinction between civic nationalism and ethnonationalism in ways that are particularly dehumanizing to Latina/os.

Chapter 4, "Cat Ladies, Wolves, and Lobsters: A Menagerie of Biological Essentialism," moves on to explore the ideas of difference and inequality. Specifically, I examine how biological essentialism undergirds the alt-right, anchored to rigid conceptions of gender binariness and natural hierarchies. Attention to essentialist logics helps to unveil the similarities between the alt-right and the alt-light. The former likes to portray the latter as sympathetic to core right-wing tenets of anti-feminism and anti-leftism but unwilling to abandon the safety of civic nationalism to embrace white nationalism. The latter likes to portray the former as obsessed with race and edging too closely to neo-Nazism and white power extremism. Despite these rivalries, the alt-right and the alt-light both posit that modern society is degenerating into chaos, that universality and egalitarianism are sham doctrines, and that political correctness and do-gooder leftists, dubbed social justice warriors (SJWs), are risible and absurd. For many online users, though, the turf wars between the alt-right and alt-light are an invisible and meaningless insider's game. There is steady traffic across the regions of the alt-verse, and red pills abound for those ready to scrap multiculturalism, liberalism, and feminism. I show that one of the bridges that spans the alt-light and alt-right is fathomless transphobia, undergirded by rigid paradigms of sex, gender, and biology.

Chapter 5, "Living the TradLife: Babies, Butter, and the Vanishing of Bre Faucheux," focuses on the dimension of traditionalism, explored through the online activities of alt-right women on YouTube, Twitter, Gab, and other platforms. Alt-right women promote traditionalism in a movement that sharply limits their maneuverability. Although several prominent alt-right men point out that women have the ability to normalize nationalism in significant ways and raise alarm bells about the threat of white genocide among possible white converts, women's presence is disparate and scant. This is explained in part by the overwhelming misogyny that saturates the alt-right and has fueled the harassment of some white nationalist women, like the pseudonymous Bre Faucheux. The alt-right is characterized by the dominance of its presumptive and actual patriarchal leadership and is inarguably male-centric. After all, a movement built on the premise of white male victimhood will concentrate on the rehabilitation of white men, on their metamorphosis from betas to alphas. Nevertheless, there is a nascent alt-right sisterhood that is vocal, uncompromising, and devoted to expanding the white nationalist community. Its members share stories of red pilling and the virtues of domestic life, and elaborate on the nefarious ways in which liberalism, globalism, and multiculturalism affect them and their families and ostensibly imperil their racial heritage. Focused mainly on digital forms such as vlogs (video blogs) and video interviews produced by alt-right women, this chapter explores how digital storytelling functions as a powerful modality for individual conversion narratives and the formation of alt-right collective identities.

Chapter 6, "Normalizing Nationalism: Alt-Right Creep," takes stock of the alt-right during the ongoing phase of concerted attempts at "normalization" of the movement. Many alt-right leaders strive to cast off any remaining vestiges of neo-Nazism and twentieth-century white power movements, and earn the badge of respectability. I review these attempts at normalization, which have unfolded alongside the continued tailspins from the 2017 Charlottesville rally and the meager turnout of white nationalists at the Unite the Right 2 rally in summer 2018 in Washington, DC. I also stress the conditions of possibility that exist for alt-right expansion today. Drawing from recent scholarship in political science, demography, and psychology, I examine the extent of alt-right political beliefs among white Americans. I also reflect on the demographic transition in the United States and how alt-righters exploit census numbers to incite fears of white extinction. In addition, I argue that the alt-right seeks to dismantle civic nationalism, which is chipped away at daily by Trumpian policies, and supplant it with ethnonationalism. I suggest that the appeal of alt-right discourse should not be underestimated during a moment when a widening phalanx of white men believe their rights and identities must be protected at all costs, when national politics include the extreme vetting of immigrants, and proposals are being floated to end if not revoke birthright citizenship for US-born children of undocumented parents and even of legal immigrants.[37]

While pundits on the right, left, and center are generally quick to condemn the alt-right and white nationalism, their ideas are being broadcast by Fox News and other media outlets, and by the Trump administration, and overtly endorsed or tacitly countenanced by Trump's wing of the Republican Party. As one journalist writes, together they are the "chief launderers of white-supremacist and white-nationalist ideas in America today."[38] It is not a foregone conclusion that the demographic transformation of America to racial plurality will lead to a semi-cohesive polity existing within the bounds of civic and multicultural nationalism. There are other, darker, pathways, on the near and far horizons, outlined by thinkers such as Timothy Snyder and Henry Giroux.[39] The contemporary moment is favorable to the alt-right in America. Populist movements are surging across the globe, moving not toward progressive grassroots democratization but toward the pernicious vortexes of ethnonationalism and xenophobia. The alt-right is not synonymous with national populism, but it can take advantage of these dynamics to advance its goals, bolstered by Trump's authoritarian predilections. Furthermore, the digital environments of social media, which afford instantaneous exchange on platforms such as Twitter, Gab, YouTube, and Facebook, not only serve as an imaginative cauldron for alt-right meme-making; they also enable the construction of a romanticized white tribal identity and of networks with flesh-and-blood counterparts that materialize in real-life nationalist meet-ups. Hannah Arendt cautioned in *Eichmann in Jerusalem* that "the unprecedented, once it has appeared, may become a precedent for the future."[40] This book seeks to offer a lens through which to detect and disassemble precedents of the alt-right that have gained traction in discourse and culture, and are anathema to the values of equality, justice, and democracy.

CHAPTER I

RED PILLS FOR THE MASSES

Metapolitical Awakenings

Europe Is Falling is the name of a British YouTube vlogger who posts short monologues about dystopia and decline in the West. He is one of many content producers on social media whose perspective is framed by ethnonationalism, and he labels himself and his growing gallery of videos as alt-right. Although Europe Is Falling is a minor avatar in the transatlantic movement, his ideas are representative of the larger alt-right world. Europe Is Falling melodramatically conveys the grave urgency evinced by many alt-righters about the desperate future of the West and white people. He also exemplifies a salient segment of the media landscape that encompasses not the big names of the movement, like Richard Spencer or Andrew Anglin of the Daily Stormer, but an ever-expanding ensemble of vloggers, podcasters, tweeters, and trolls. Several of his vlogs have been flagged by users as "inappropriate or offensive." Europe Is Falling describes poignantly and in a resounding voice what it feels like to swallow the red pill, that "perfectly crystallizing moment when a person lets go of what was has been and what was and realizes, with a sense of pure clarity and calm, that the place they have known their entire life, the place their parents and grandparents inhabited, that place is gone. The world generations of Europeans have lived, loved, and lost in for hundreds if not thousands of years is leaving us, and it can't ever return."[1]

Europe Is Falling's description of red pill conversion was inspired by off-script remarks given by the Scottish ethnonationalist Millennial Woes at an alt-right conference held in Europe, when he expressed intermingled astonishment and remorse at the prospect of white Europeans being replaced irrevocably by brown and black interlopers. In this instance, red pill awareness came packaged as anxieties about the supposed slow grind toward white European extinction. For Europe Is Falling, this awakening was so emotionally intense that it generated "a deep, profound amount of cognitive dissonance and grieving," sensations common among many alt-righters who alternately bewail and boast about their status as heretics, dissidents, and victims in the multicultural era.[2]

Now a prevalent metaphor, the red pill made its debut in the cult science fiction film *The Matrix*. Toward the end of the movie, Morpheus holds out his hand and offers Neo, the (anti)hero, the choice between the red pill and the blue pill. Morpheus tells him, "After this there is no turning back. You take the blue pill, the story ends. You wake up in your bed and believe whatever you want to. You take the red pill, you stay in Wonderland, and I show you how deep the rabbit hole goes."[3] Neo, famously, takes the red pill. This iconic moment, of choosing raw reality over the Matrix has become a ubiquitous meme and shorthand for alt-right conversion. To be red pilled is to accept the cold, hard truth about the foundations of individual and collective existence, and to radically shift one's parameters of reality in accordance with this newfound knowledge. It symbolizes a bold exit from mainstream society, corrupted as it is by liberals and conservatives alike, and an alternative approach to making distinctions between what is and what ought to be.

The red pill might lead to an epiphany about the rightness of white nationalism and/or the repudiation of feminism, multiculturalism, leftism, liberalism, and globalism, followed by the embrace of traditionalism, hierarchy, and inequality. There are thousands of red-pilling stories, each one slightly different, yet they all pivot around transformation. As conversion stories characterized by a near-religious fervor, they interweave information, feeling, exhibitionism, and solipsism, betraying the extent to which the internet is an affective mediascape that enables personal and cultural meaning-making.[4] Sharing these testimonies, as Europe Is Falling does, with anonymous and vast online congregations makes red pilling a communal experience and helps construct a shared language of social transformation. The alt-right pines for an interlinked transatlantic community of awakened whites who will reverse their impending minority status and reclaim the West before it is too late.

RED-PILLING STORIES

Ryan Lenz, who gathers information on hate groups for the Southern Poverty Law Center and edits its *Hatewatch* blog, claims that the red pill is "a new label for an old idea," namely one of white superiority, employed by white people trying to convince their kin that "we're better than others."[5] Researchers at the Data & Society Research Institute in New York City found that the red pill has been instrumental in catalyzing online radicalization and illustrates how the "alt-right, white nationalists, and men's-rights activists manipulate the mainstream media to amplify their ideas and shape news narratives to their advantage."[6] Even if it's a well-worn prejudice encased in new-fangled coating, how the red pill is swallowed matters. It is an internet drug with unique properties that can induce personal transformation and collective conversion. In the words of Jazzhands McFeels, host of the Daily Stormer's *Fash the Nation* podcast, "There is no going back once you go down that route." Once a libertarian and conventional conservative, McFeels was always searching for something more, and the red pill unlocked that possibility: "the red pill is in and of itself a quest for truth."[7] The stark before-and-after is a Manichean worldview in which principles are unequivocal and there is no room for ambiguity. Even the latest rejoinders to the red pill/blue pill dyad, the black pill and the white pill, are but change supplements. The black pill represents the nihilism and defeat that some men experience when post–red pill life turns out to be drearily anticlimactic.[8] The white pill symbolizes a peppy infusion of optimism, usually related to perceived personal and political achievements.[9]

The red pill metaphor first gained traction in the manosphere in the early 2010s, as men's rights activists Men Going Their Own Way (MGTOW) and Pick Up Artists (PUA) sought out virtual communities where they could interpret their romantic, physical, and erotic lives without the irritating interference of feminism and gender egalitarianism.[10] Blogs like *Return of Kings* and *Chateau Heartiste* emerged as forums for unfiltered discussions of sexual prowess, warrior culture, and female conquest among straight men who "believe men should be masculine and women should be feminine" and that "testosterone is the biological cause for masculinity."[11] These sites are bustling today, and posts and discussions frequently veer into pornographic and gruesome depravities about women's bodies and their sexual objectification.[12]

In the manosphere, swallowing the red pill meant not only the crowning of masculinity but the erasure and evisceration of feminism and its beguiling companions of liberalism, leftism, and "cultural Marxism." Rather than blindly accepting modern gender relations, which had turned men into wimpy betas or, worse yet, frustrated and despondent incels (involuntary celibates), the red pilled turned to a version of "evolutionary psychology," which posits that "men and women are genetically different, both physically and mentally."[13] The nasty, brutish, and short upshot was that men had evolved to dominate women and women had evolved to be dominated. Howard Dare, a MGTOW vlogger, assures his audience that after ingesting the red pill they will no longer let themselves be controlled by women or harmed by the distortions of a society held hostage by third-wave feminism.[14] Comments to his posts bear out these eureka moments: "2017: The year of enlightenment. The year I woke up. The year I stopped being thirsty. The year I took the red pill. The year I stopped putting other people ahead of me and put myself first."[15] One user connects his self-actualization to the (re)imposition of a strict gender order: "A society must have a gender that is more dominant. It has always been Men just like the animal kingdom. Man has always been expected to hunt and woman to care for the family (cooking and cleaning)."

The premier chat room of the manosphere is subreddit r/The Red Pill (TRP), launched in 2012, when it broke away from sub-reddit r/seduction to concentrate more directly on "game," or how to vanquish women and maintain traditional relationships. TRP advised its users that "the frame around public discourse is a feminist frame, and we've lost our identity because of it," and that the "key to developing a good sexual strategy" was to adhere to sexist interpretations of evolutionary psychology.[16] TRP became the go-to site for men to compare notes about dating and sex, discuss diet regimes and workout routines, and offer philosophical reflections on gender and sex differences.[17]

Subreddit r/TRP remains enormously popular, with over 280,000 subscribers and around 2,500 users online at any given moment.[18] Morpheus Manfred, whose handle was inspired by *The Matrix*, is one of the TRP's head moderators and describes its mission as providing "a place where men could discuss masculine topics without facing the same public shaming outcry that happens on social media sites. . . . Feminists are quick on the trigger to try to take down anything they consider wrong."[19] At r/TRP, men learn self-reliance and how to solve their own problems, which "encourages strength" and diminishes dependency on others. They also learn that women are untrustworthy flirts who possess no insights about men or male-female relationships: "Having a vagina does not afford your words special weight or wisdom, or give you any inside understanding of how men should deal with women."[20] Particular animosity is directed at feminists and assertive women in threads such as "Feminism is a Cancer that is Metastasizing everywhere," "How feminism has fucked society," and "Women are entitled, spoiled brats."[21] Advice for controlling undesirable female behavior, setting boundaries, and conveying male preferences abound in threads such as "Training Your Woman: Subliminal."[22] In fall 2018 Reddit placed TRP in quarantine status, advising visitors that this online community "is dedicated to shocking or highly offensive content," a depiction that its moderators vehemently deny. They have appealed the quarantine and complain that Reddit never provided any reasoning for their action.[23]

Appropriating the lingo of the Left, manospherers called their virtual forums "safe spaces," constructed as exclusionary male sanctuaries freed from the tone and content policing of feminists. The masculinist origins of the red pill help to explain why it appealed to alt-righters, overwhelmingly white men, who felt aggrieved and victimized, and resented that their entitlement and privilege was no longer necessarily the default position in society. The Manichaean logic of the red pill migrated easily to the emerging alt-right, which bundled the ideas of innate gender roles into understandings of racial and ethnic differences as biological and fixed.[24]

Red pilling often begins through exposure to the so-called alt-light. For example, social media personality Stefan Molyneux shies away from overt advocacy of white nationalism and thus is dubbed alt-light, but his ideas open up the side door of the alt-right. Molyneux's YouTube channel, Freedomain Radio, which has over eight hundred thousand subscribers, is a superstar red piller, raising awareness of the putative destructiveness of feminism and incontrovertible genetic associations between race and intelligence.[25] In one of his vlogs, Molyneux asks his viewers what red pilled them, recounting his experience of waking up to the hypocrisy of so-called feminists who supported President Bill Clinton during the Monica Lewinsky affair.[26] His users offer hundreds of responses. Alt-right female media personality Bre Faucheux shares, "The biggest red pill for me was realizing that feminism had a connection to communism and that having a job and income wouldn't fulfill me in the end."[27] An anonymous user writes, "My biggest red pill moment was realizing White Europeans had distinctive qualities, and not just physically, and deserved protection and to keep their ethnic bastions." Others mention being red pilled by the presidential campaigns of Ron Paul or Bernie Sanders, as well as by Brexit and by reading *The Bell Curve* by Charles Murray and Richard Herrnstein.

If red pilling was happening on the DL (down low) and mainly in the manosphere in the early 2010s, it mushroomed after Donald Trump's presidential victory in 2016. One recent study identifies Trump, whose Twitter megaphone is stamped with the imprimatur of the White House, as a red piller of colossal proportions.[28] In the days leading up to Thanksgiving 2016, the media was awash with warnings about the likelihood of irreconcilable political rifts erupting around turkey and apple pie. To prepare its readers, *Vice* published "How to Tell If Your Alt-Right Relative Is Trying to Redpill You at Thanksgiving."[29] Part serious advice, part tongue-in-cheek, the piece warned that "things will really take a turn if" your uncle "decides he wants to redpill you after you pass him the gravy." While *Vice* was trying to counter the red pill, alt-right websites were actively encouraging proselytizing. A sub-thread appeared in TRP on "Strategies to RedPill Your Family over the Holidays." On Infowars, the now-banned conspiracy-laden site run by Alex Jones, guest host Matt Dubiel primed the "Resistance" on how to red pill skeptical relatives at Thanksgiving dinner without scaring them away. He paternalistically advised fathers to orate the poem "If" by Rudyard Kipling, the unabashed British racist and imperialist fawned over by alt-righters.[30] Rigidly composed, "If" celebrates obduracy in the face of uncertainty. One poetry scholar calls it "a classic of righteous certitude."[31] Dubiel assures his viewers that Kipling's verse will allow fathers to "show"—not "tell"—family and friends the right way forward. Stanzas like "Yours is the Earth and everything that's in it, And—which is more—you'll be a Man, my son!" stress the necessity of fighting through adversity and will prompt relatives to reflect on what they've endured as Americans and appreciate Trump for persevering despite being pilloried by the liberal media. Evidently, mansplaining poetry from the playbook of "The White Man's Burden" can anchor core alt-right tenets while making the Resistance family-friendly.[32]

In addition to serving as an accessible device for self-narration and a beacon for cultivating group identity, the red pill encapsulates the alt-right's love affair with culture. The red pill was offered by a cinematic hand; its magnetic message has circulated far and wide. It signals the alt-right's desire to become the hip counterculture of the twenty-first century. As a catchphrase, it has helped spawn an inventive glossary that includes "cuckservative/cuck," "normie," "fashy," "snowflake," and "Overton window."[33] As the most colorful entry in the alt-right glossary, the "red pill" is also a metaphor that relies on and seeks to shape culture.[34] As a sign in a semiological hall of mirrors that careens from righteous militancy to misanthropic irony, it signifies how alt-right vocabulary has insinuated itself into the American imagination and helped create alternate myths.[35]

Alt-righters expend a lot of energy reflecting on red-pilling strategies, particularly those that might turn someone. *Fash the Nation* offers a series of Red Pill 101 tutorials such as "Multiculturalism, Equality, and Race."[36] Before her 27Crows Radio YouTube videos disappeared from the internet in 2018, Bre Faucheux devoted much time to red pilling, including "Alt Right 101: How to Red Pill Loved Ones," which she coproduced with British nationalist Mark Collett. Tweeter Alba Rising expresses a common viewpoint, "Want to 'redpill' someone? Don't say the edgiest shit you can say. Say the small thing that they're thinking but don't have the courage to say. You'll have a disciple for life."[37] In a podcast conversation, Richard Spencer and his former collaborator at the National Policy Institute, Gregory Conte, mull over the hope that alt-righters, presenting as "normies," can infiltrate institutions, then start "implementing red pilled positions" and enact a stealth take-over of society.[38] In the ideal scenario, alt-righters will engineer a "mass seduction of society." This fantasy of mass conversion, of thousands of Neos swallowing the red pill, connects the red pill metaphor directly to metapolitics, one of the alt-right's core concepts.

If the red pill represents the individual conversion from darkness to light, then metapolitics is white nationalist consciousness-raising at the collective level. Unearthing the history and meaning of metapolitics illustrates the peculiar evolution of the alt-right at the fraught nexus of the manosphere, paleoconservatism, white supremacism, anti-Semitism, and xenophobia. However, tracing the genealogy of metapolitics leads not to white hoods carrying torches or swastika-filled rallies but instead to Western Europe in the mid-twentieth century.[39] Surprisingly, it also leads to the theories of the Italian Marxist Antonio Gramsci and to a group of Jewish intellectuals and exiles that founded the Frankfurt School to critically study authoritarianism and capitalism in the aftermath of the Holocaust.[40]

Metapolitics and the European New Right

At a press conference in September 2016, soon after Trump had won the Republican primary, Spencer offered a definition of the alt-right: "I don't think the best way of understanding the alt-right is strictly in terms of policy. I think metapolitics is more important than politics. I think big ideas are more important than policies."[41] For the alt-right intellectuals who draw on theory and philosophy, the concept of metapolitics undergirds and guides their agendas. Privileging cultural intervention over institutional political change, metapolitics distinguishes the New Right from older conservatives, whether neocons, libertarians, or the Religious Right. Alt-righters view metapolitics as the intellectual key that can unlock massive social transformation, bewildering the Left and liberals along the way.

The hosts of the *Interregnum* podcast, produced by Arktos, encourage the conspicuous use of metapolitically coded language to reform the Right. Like most European identitarians, they want to jettison the clumsy nationalist rhetoric attached to Nazism.[42] They attest that using a metapolitical vocabulary will make the New Right "unique and radical and revolutionary. . . . It's fresh. . . . These are ideas that have never been put in practice into politics before. . . . These are metapolitical ideas."[43] The Arktos brain trust claims that metapolitics is the "thing that they [the Left] don't understand," namely, that "we are reformulating the right, and we are doing that by altering what is the left/right paradigm. . . . By changing the political paradigm, we are bringing with us the ideas that will reformulate the right."[44] For European and American white nationalists, metapolitics is interwoven into proposals for pervasive social change. Assessing the continued fallout from Charlottesville in late 2018, Conte was interviewed on *Interregnum* about the status of the alt-right. He interpreted setbacks in the legal and online realms as par for the course for a dissident movement that is "playing for all the marbles," clarifying that "you can't expect to fight an asymmetrical metapolitical war if you are not able to take the blows as they come." This transatlantic podcast conversation emphasized that the alt-right's primary objective is the conversion of whites-in-waiting to their side, a prospect facilitated by the current "late stage of disintegration, of social disintegration," which is dissolving bonds of "kith and kin." In this maelstrom, ideas are the only glue that can build and unite white nationalist communities. Arktos's editor in chief, John Bruce Leonard, reminded listeners "our ideas have to be stronger means of binding us than anything else in today's world, because we don't have anything else to fall back on."[45]

Metapolitics, however, was not formulated during the alt-right's recent rise but has a much longer and more circuitous trajectory. Originally coined by German thinkers such as Gottlieb Hufeland, August Ludwig von Schlözer, and Carl von Rotteck in the nineteenth century, metapolitics initially referred to a philosophical exploration of principles of rights and of the state independent of politics. French thinkers picked up the term in the late 1800s, proposing that metapolitics was to politics as metaphysics was to physics—the "meta" implied an overarching supra-philosophical approach to the subject at hand. To study the "meta" required forays into the transcendental and religious dimensions of politics, which in turn often translated into a foregrounding of "sacred roots, mythic symbols, and eschatological values."[46] Metapolitics was distinct from, if not antithetical to, materialism; it rejected classic Marxism or structuralism and was outside the epistemological margins of empirical disciplines such as sociology or history.

Since its initial coinage in the nineteenth century, metapolitics has taken many shapes, meaning different things to various intellectual and political coteries. For example, the French philosopher Alain Badiou published a book in 2012 titled *Metapolitics*, which seeks to reinvigorate militant politics through a theoretical rumination on the fiction, if not vacuity, of the modern state. Badiou employs the lenses of Marxism, reserving ample room for the revolutionary theories of Lenin and Mao. Politically, this approach contrasts to that of the alt-right. It does share, however, a focus on culture as the staging ground for political change. It aligns with the pithy adage articulated by *Breitbart News*: "Politics is downstream from culture."[47]

The American alt-right's foregrounding of metapolitics owes a large debt to the European New Right (ENR). Indeed, the rise of the alt-right is inextricably linked to the new nationalist movements that surged in Europe, especially France, in reaction to the political radicalization of the 1960s generation. Across the globe, a generation that had come of age in the aftermath of World War II and during the height of the Cold War began to question conventional power relations and rigid social structures and norms. From Buenos Aires to Prague, the New Left blossomed, seeking to change society through reform and revolution. In May 1968, French students protesting changes to the educational system (ironically associated with Americanization) took to the streets, and a brutal police response ensued.[48] Against this backdrop, the ENR was coalescing around an aversion to such radicalism and to liberalism, a rebuke of globalism, and angst about societal decay. The lettered intellectuals of the ENR were unnerved by what they witnessed unfolding around them as mores were broken and traditions ripped asunder. Yet this group averred that the answer was not the organization of another political party but the control of ideas and culture.

To formulate its intellectual program, the ENR eyed the Frankfurt School, a loose group of exiled—mainly Jewish—intellectuals who had established a school of critical thought starting in the 1930s. The Frankfurt School included thinkers such as Theodor Adorno, Max Horkheimer, and Herbert Marcuse, who developed a cultural Marxist critique of authoritarian societies and the strictures of capitalism that distinguished it from economic analyses of capital and labor.[49] Its intellectual projects ranged from deconstructions of authoritarian personalities using sociological and psychoanalytic techniques to analyses of films and novels, often with close attention to aesthetics. For the Frankfurt School, form and style were as, if not more, important as function and content; the epiphenomena of culture merited a kaleidoscopic exploration that could unveil the deeper, bleaker dynamics at play in modern society, like those that allowed national socialism to take root in Germany. The ENR fashioned itself as the Frankfurt School of the new radical Right.

Elitist in make-up, the ENR distanced itself both from conservative establishment politicians and armed insurrectionary cells with neo-Nazi inclinations. Expressing its affection for socialist European thinkers, the French Right spearheaded the articulation of "metapolitics," infusing it with a heavy dose of Gramscian theory. The Italian Marxist Gramsci wrote his magnum opus, *The Prison Notebooks*, under the watchful eyes of prison guards in Italy, developing a vocabulary of political theory including terms such as "hegemony," "war of position," and "organic intellectuals." He theorized political struggle as a long game that required significant engagement with culture, through which the Left could eventually reign by consent not force. This vision held great appeal to the ENR. During the tumultuous year of 1968 in Paris, the philosopher Alain de Benoist gravitated toward the Group for the Research and Study of European Civilization (GRECE), which had been formed by nationalist student organizations active in the 1950s and bestowed a name whose acronym nodded toward Hellenic mythology.

Benoist and the French New Right followed in the footsteps of the political non-conformism associated with the Ordre Nouveau, a group founded in France in the 1930s as an alternative to communism and capitalism, and which had provided an intellectual space for anti-egalitarian, patriarchal, and quasi-mystical ideas.[50] As the next incarnation of this variant of contrarian French politics, GRECE offered a home and a hub for the most radical Far Right intellectuals and for the exposition of right-leaning metapolitics. Benoist christened the date of "the birth of the New Right" as March 11, 1968, which marked the publication of the first issue of the magazine *Nouvelle École*.[51] Tellingly, GRECE's inaugural seminar was called "What Are Metapolitics?," and this "Gramscianism of the Right" cemented its commitment to culture and to fighting on the "battlefield of ideas."[52] As scholars of the New Right have noted, the *Manifesto per una rinascita europea* (Manifesto for a European Rebirth), edited by Benoist in 2000, implies that one of GRECE's leading achievements was "without a doubt its metapolitical bent and the subsequent decision to abandon all militant or activist ambitions."[53] GRECE devoted itself "exclusively to the vast and complex realm of culture, establishing, in the first decade, an ideological structure that was held up primarily by two fundamental themes: anti-egalitarianism and the definition of an authentically European identity." As historian of fascism Roger Griffin has explained, GRECE didn't want to "shoot politicians and seize power" but "take over book clubs."[54]

GRECE flourished, commandeering the editorial page of the noted magazine *Le Figaro* in the 1970s and 1980s. Benoist received the Grand

Prize of the French Academy for his book *The Way of the Right*.[55] According to historian John Hellman, like its precursor Order Nouveau, by "focusing on the meta political and ignoring the democratic political processes" GRECE "infiltrated political parties, public administration, universities, and the mass media" and has had a lasting cultural influence in France.[56] Inspired by GRECE, metapolitics became a watchword of thinkers throughout Western Europe who gave "primacy to the struggle for cultural power over and above any concrete policy making, or politics as usual."[57] A corollary of metapolitics was identitarianism, which also has a distinctly French flavor and gestated out of the intellectual milieu of the French New Right. Identitarianism was spearheaded by writer Guillaume Faye, who published in 2001 the "key work for Twenty-first century Identitarians," *Why We Fight: Manifesto of the European Resistance*.[58]

During the period from the genesis of GRECE to the advent of identitarianism, these European movements would not have mapped neatly on to white nationalism in America, which from the 1970s to 1990s was the province of neo-Nazi and right-wing Christian groups like Aryan Nations, National Alliance, and the World Church of the Creator.[59] American and European nationalists might have shared straitjacketed gender ideologies and loathing of liberalism and Jews, but the American movement in the late twentieth-century was dominated by white supremacists who conspired about race wars and were distant from bookish discussions of theories of culture.[60] They likely would have been perplexed and dismissive in the 1990s, when the French Right adapted the slogans of diversity and ethnopluralism, which sound eerily in sync with multiculturalism. Of course, this identitarian version means "diversity in isolation: all Frenchmen in one territory and all Moroccans in another." [61] And it was a forerunner of the alt-right's euphemistic idea of human biodiversity, which postulates that cultures and racial groups maintain their integrity through a "separate but equal" policy that disallows interchange and mixing. In tandem with the rise of the alt-right, the theories of Benoist and his contemporary Faye have become the intellectual bedrock of ethnonationalists and identitarians across Europe and North America. Many of Benoist's and Faye's books have been translated into English and are distributed by both Counter-Currents and Arktos. Benoist and, to a lesser extent, Faye make regular appearances in alt-right webzines, podcasts, and on other online forums.

One of the myriad intellectual ironies of ethnonationalist and identitarian movements is that their desire to develop an edgy think tank prompted them to emulate the Frankfurt School, in which Jewish intellectuals played a crucial role. Today the alt-right at every turn excoriates so-called "cultural Marxism," naming it as an enormous danger to Western civilization and linking it to Jewish conspiracies. In 2014 one alt-righter went so far as to venture that Herbert Marcuse, who was affiliated with the Frankfurt School, was the "father of the blue-pill."[62] This honor was due to Marcuse's intellectual dismantling of America's repressive sexual regime in the 1960s and his calls for upending the strictures of monogamy and patriarchy, which he dubbed the "great refusal."[63] According to this alt-righter, postwar excessive sexual liberalization misled men with spurious enticements of libidinal freedom, only to find that the doors to gratification had been shut purposefully by women, who invariably were irrational and spiteful. The sexual counterculture of the 1960s was thus a great deception, obfuscating the truth of gender hierarchies: "True red-pillers know that all the betas marching around in berets were the first to lose out on the sexual bonanza promised by the 'sexual revolution' as they found out that, much to their horror, women's unrestrained sexual nature is hypergamous."[64]

Metapolitics, American Style

In the early 2000s metapolitics began to cohere as a framework for the nascent alt-right in the United States, becoming a conceptual anchor for the webzine *Counter-Currents Publishing*, established in 2010 by Greg Johnson for an elite audience, which he believes is one whose members possess an IQ of 120 or higher. With its academic patina, *Counter-Currents* views metapolitics as pivotal to dislodging the Left's control of culture, in all of its facets, fomenting white identity politics and installing the alt-right brand. In *Counter-Currents* Johnson explains that "our enemies have carefully laid the metapolitical foundations for the power they enjoy. They control academia, the school system, publishing, the arts, the news and entertainment media, and they have remade the American mind to their liking." The aim of Counter-Currents, both the webzine and book publisher, is to "change people's sense of what is politically desirable and right, and their sense of what is politically conceivable and possible."[65] As with the ENR, Gramsci's theories of hegemony loom large. In Johnson's words, "The concepts of metapolitics and hegemony are the keys to understanding the differences between the Old Left and the New Left."[66] The alt-right's "war of position" will unfold on cultural terrain. As one comment posted to *Counter-Currents* stated: "The medium of metapolitics is culture."[67]

However, the alt-right could not shake off good old American pragmatism. Whereas the French New Right was uninterested in political power, American white nationalists often see metapolitics as pre-political. Writes Johnson: "It is too soon for White Nationalist politics. So in the meantime, we need to focus on metapolitics, which will lay the foundations for the pursuit of political power."[68] Alt-righters espouse two prongs for building and expanding "soft power." The first is propaganda or "articulating and communicating our message"; the second is community organizing or "creating a community that lives according to our philosophy today and will serve as the nucleus of the new political order we seek to build tomorrow." Identified strategies for effective messaging and community building are negative and disruptive tactics like trolling; the creation of cultural spaces like publishing houses, websites, and musical bands; and the reclamation of "turf from the Left" such as unions, environmental organizations, and media. With this plan of engagement on various levels, the alt-right wants to build up a rivaling "soft power" exclusively for white people that will permeate all the contours of daily life.[69]

Before Trump's win, the intellectual camp of the alt-right viewed its work occurring in the margins and focused on shaping belief systems about what was politically and ontologically possible.[70] A small cadre affiliated with *Counter-Currents*, *Taki's Magazine*, *Occidental Quarterly*, and *Radix Journal* interpreted films, movies, and music through alt-right lenses, producing a constant output of books, articles, blog posts, vlogs, podcasts, and more. They commonly employed the analytical and expository tools they had learned at "leftist" universities: "Using what they taught me, I deconstructed the deconstructionists. I saw what a fighting politics could be: Left-wing techniques and social analysis mobilized for Right-wing ends."[71]

Around 2010, as alt-righters were evincing equal alienation from Republicans and Democrats, and flirting with paleoconservatism and libertarianism, metapolitical change solidified as the Holy Grail. Alt-righters were devising strategies to convert white minds, one at a time, to the allure of a racially homogeneous society guided by traditionalism and anti-egalitarianism, whether by coaxing or willing it into being: "If White Nationalists attain complete hegemony in the metapolitical realm, that means that white interests will be sacrosanct, and anti-white ideas will be anathema."[72] In keeping with an interest in reporting on and influencing culture, alt-right publications and blogs feature reviews of movies, books, music, even clothing. Topics have included the implicit white nationalist leanings of Taylor Swift, based on her phenotypic characteristics as a desirable white woman, and the fact that she never condemned her white nationalist fandom and appeared on Instagram once with a fanboy wearing a T-shirt with a spray-painted swastika.[73] She recently disappointed alt-right admirers by endorsing women's and LGBTQ rights and asking her fans to vote for Democrats in the 2018 midterm elections.[74] Blog posts have explored the world of Hogwarts, from the Harry Potter series, praising its whiteness, rituals, and occult dramas but criticizing Harry's boarding school for upholding tenets of meritocratic education.[75]

Concern with slow metapolitical uptake prompted *Radix Journal* in 2014 to complain that "our friends in Europe seem to be having a bit more success than us in popularizing White advocacy" and attributed this to their more appealing aesthetics.[76] Alt-righters were urged to make hipper choices in clothing, photography, and design, fashioning themselves on their identitarian brothers in France and Germany. Dashing "fashy" apparel for men was recommended, including T-shirts ordered from the official Generation Identitaire website and Fascist Crew Love. Metapolitics extends to sports. A recent post on *Counter-Currents* contends there is a strong affinity between skateboarders and alt-righters given that the sport "is undeniably a White innovation," even as it undergoes "multiracialization." As with many manifestations of American culture, this writer asserts that white boarders need to become "conscious of their sport as an expression of their ethnic heritage."[77] At the same time, the alt-right has claimed affinity with elite cultural and literary forms, including the poetry of imperialist Rudyard Kipling, neofascist modernist Ezra Pound, and even the socialist writer Jack London.

One arena that has received special attention in metapolitics is music, above all heavy metal, which offers a bridge from the neo-Nazism of the 1980s and 1990s to the alt-right counterculture of the 2000s. As one writer asserts in *Radix Journal*: "I can say with confidence that heavy metal music has done far more to advance authentic right wing aesthetics, values, and yes, even philosophy, than all the failed institutions of the Beltway Right put together."[78] Metal is right wing because "it's very un-Black in its rhythm and structure" and stresses "White masculinity and utilizes the mythology and history of Europe for lyrical inspiration" as well as highlighting themes of "conquest, self-overcoming, strength, and conflict."[79] As Kirsten Dyck has shown, white-power music worked to create community and forge "interpersonal relationships among European-descended individuals."[80] In the United States, it has a long lineage in white nationalism, dating back to Reb Rebel Records, founded in Louisiana in the late 1960s, which distributed racist country music that condemned racial integration and denounced black civil rights.[81] In the 1980s white power skinhead groups appeared on the punk scene, and in the 1990s bands like RaHoWa (short for Racial Holy War) were promoted to "transcend national boundaries and reach out to our racial brothers and sisters around the globe."[82] Since the 2000s, there has been an increasing turn to neofolk music, which draws on paganistic themes, invokes Nordic and Greek iconography, and pays tribute to the metaphysical writings of the Italian neofascist Julius Evola. In Europe, metal and hardcore music is popular among many identitarians.[83] The Swedish group Arditi, for example, celebrates the warrior ethic and calls for a return to traditional white Europe.[84] Arditi writes that its "torch was set alight in 1997, inspired by the Italian Futurist Movement of the early 20th century."[85] The band name is taken from a World War I Royal Italian Army elite special force known for being on the front lines of assault and for its interwar associations with nationalists and protofascists.

The biggest blessing, and to some extent curse, for alt-right metapolitics has been the advent of cyberspace. Metapolitics found its medium online, merging with digital culture. The digital engagement of white nationalists dates back to the Aryan Nations' development of the Aryan Liberty Net, a computer-to-computer network created in the 1980s using first-generation Macs and PCs.[86] The advent of the World Wide Web took this to the next level, exemplified by the launch of the trendsetter message board Stormfront in 1995, followed by websites such as Infowars (1999), Red Ice TV (2003), the Right Stuff (2012), Daily Stormer (2013), and a slew of webzines, such as *Occidental Quarterly* (2001), *Taki's Magazine* (2008), the short-lived AlternativeRight.com (2010), *Counter-Currents* (2010), and the now-folded *Radix Journal* (2013). Since the mid-2000s, white nationalists and misogynists have flocked to the internet, creating websites and blogs, and launching YouTube channels, which run the gambit from David Duke's poisonously anti-Semitic website to the almost cult-like vlogs of Vox Day, VertigoPolitix, and Sargon of Akkad, to the misogynist blogs *Chateau Heartiste* and *Return of Kings*. Platforms like Facebook, utilizing plug-ins such as Google Chat, have birthed virtual communities, as have the nasty online arenas of 4chan and 8chan. Even in a context of deplatforming, there is a steady proliferation of alt-right and alt-light YouTube channels, Twitter accounts, websites, and blogs, of which that run by Europe Is Falling is but one recent example.

These sites are visited by thousands of users, many of whom offer comments or participate in live chats. For example, Stormfront counts over 800,000 monthly visits and close to 1,800 interlinked websites; the Daily Stormer nearly 600,000 monthly visits and over 1,000 interlinked websites; and the more academic American Renaissance gets 350,000 monthly visits with just under 1,500 interlinked websites. *Counter-Currents* reports that in its eighth year, ending in summer 2018, they received 150,000 unique visitors per month, uploaded 43 podcasts, and produced 18 interviews.[87] For the most part, the combination of a legal landscape characterized by stalwart support for free speech, limited precedents for regulating hate speech, and a virtual infrastructure characterized by decentralization, anonymity, and unaccountability has been conducive to the forging of an alt-right "wild west" that has grown dramatically over the past two decades. This extends to the microblogging platform Twitter, which, with its lax moderation, "unwittingly gave white supremacists an ideal venue for their hatred."[88]

Since Charlottesville, the alt-right's internet presence has been tested. To give several examples: the Twitter, Facebook, and YouTube accounts of Jared Taylor (who is suing Twitter for First Amendment violations), Richard Spencer, Vox Day, Millennial Woes, and the Mormon nationalist Wife with a Purpose have been temporarily or permanently suspended.[89] Some alt-righters claim to have been shadow-banned on Twitter, meaning that their posted comments are not visible on others' timelines. Facebook uploads have been removed, reported, and/or flagged as offensive. Most notably, InfoWars was deplatformed, with blanket removals of video content on YouTube, and absented from Facebook and Spotify.[90] On the eve of the first anniversary of the 2017 Unite the Right rally, Twitter suspended the account of Gavin McInnes, founder of the Proud Boys, a fraternal organization sporting the motto "The West Is the Best."[91] In addition, PayPal stopped payment processing for Red Ice TV, Identity Evropa, and the Canadian nationalist Faith Goldy just as she launched her failed bid to be Toronto's "Canada First" mayor, prompting one alt-right organization to tweet that "payment processor deplatforming is one of the most pressing issues we face."[92] Many on the alt-right are reduced to asking for handwritten checks sent to PO boxes or a growing roster of cryptocurrencies. Yet this wave of deplatforming has been inconsistent, and for the purposes of shutting down the alt-right, too little too late. The interventions have been done haphazardly and with scant transparency, so that it is not clear why one person is blocked and another person is not. Moreover, the feedback circuitry so instrumental to alt-right amplification is firmly in place, as tweets and retweets flash among alt-righters, alt-lighters, and right-wing pundits and politicians. As long as they can maintain online footholds, the alt-right will continue to propound its metapolitical messages, hoping to dispense red pills and transform American society from outside in. [93]

Metapolitics has taken a nonlinear journey from its initial formulation by nineteenth-century European philosophers, to its espousal by the European New Right in the 1960s, to its consolidation as a staple intellectual concept of the alt-right in America today. It would be easy to shrug off "metapolitics" as just an opaque word of the alt-right lexicon—such as "incel" or "cuck"—but progressives do so at their own peril. Metapolitics is essential to understanding the ideological genealogy of revamped nationalism, as well as its discourse, approaches, and strategies. The cultural domain is the primary site for the alt-right's Gramscian "war of position," which revolves around an incessant quest to win the hearts and minds of the white majority. As Greg Johnson, founder and editor of Counter-Currents, puts it, "Actual politics comes later, once we have laid the metapolitical groundwork."[94] Laying this groundwork through red pilling and raising white consciousness is a redoubtable project that began long before Trump's election and certainly will outlast his presidency.

CHAPTER 2

BACK TO THE FUTURE

Reactionary Timescapes

In spring 2018, Identity Evropa held its inaugural conference, with the theme "Leading Our People Forward," at a secluded venue in Tennessee.[1] The newest alt-right organization, Identity Evropa defines its mission as building European-style identitarianism and ethnonationalism in America. It links white identity politics to grandiloquent visions of Western history and heritage: "We are a group of patriotic American Identitarians who have realized that we are descended from the great traditions, history, and people that flowed from Europe."[2] Identity Evropa specializes in actions such as banner drops, community service, and targeted protests, including a demonstration with flash cards spelling out "Build the Wall" in front of the Mexican consulate in New York City and "Make America Great Again" chants.[3] Identity Evropa cultivates a clean-cut look and distances itself far from the "yahoo" stereotypes associated with twentieth-century neo-Nazis and white supremacists.[4]

Identity Evropa's leader, Patrick Casey, who took over in 2017 from founder Nathan Damigo, opened the spring 2018 conference with an overview of the organization's philosophy and objectives. He delivered predictable alt-right talking points about white identity and destiny, yet his talk was also a rumination on perceptions and interpretations of time. Casey implored the audience to "dispense with the dangerous linear view of history that defines liberal notions of progress. Instead we must view things cyclically."[5] Despite its newness, Identity Evropa was tapping into ultranationalism's tendency to repudiate unilinear narratives rooted in the Enlightenment and the revolutionary independence struggles of the eighteenth and nineteenth centuries. In this sense, Identity Evropa sidles up closely to fascist ideologies, deprecating the pretense of liberal progress and its accompanying teleological timescape, which are seen as corrupt modern impositions.

Alt-right groups like Identity Evropa contend that conventional conservatives have been "cucked" by buying into America's myth of civic nationalism: cuckservatives are mere spectators standing outside of time "yelling stop," taking no serious action to turn back or block the train of progress.[6] Identity Evropa, conversely, is throwing itself into the mosh pit of time, consciously pushing back against the temporal tide, disrupting its chronologies and flows, all in the name of harnessing and jumpstarting the Golden Age. Although it might seem abstract and opaque, the alt-right's imagined timescape—how it remembers the past, envisages the future, and grapples with the present—is one of its most insidious and alarming dimensions. In more concrete terms, understanding these reactionary timescapes sheds light on the alt-right's contempt for equality and individualism, which it views as deracinated principles designed to unfold in sequential and analog time.[7] In distinction, alt-right temporality is anchored to hierarchies and blood and soil collectivism; it moves in cycles, through catastrophe and grandeur, always with its finger on the eternal. Repeating the eloquent words of Timothy Snyder, alt-righters can be considered "eternity politicians" who "bring us the past as a vast misty courtyard of illegible monuments to national victimhood, all of them equally distant from the present, all of them equally accessible for manipulation."[8]

Time, then, is of the essence for alt-righters. Fueling their anxiousness about the dire need for a temporal course correction is the ticking of the demographic clock. Affixed on the alt-right calendar is the rapidly approaching mid-twenty-first century, when, according to the narrowest interpretation of US Census projections, America will become an ethnoracial plurality. Indeed, Richard Spencer's National Policy Institute suggests that temporal compression might mean that "2050 is coming sooner than we thought." In a study produced by NPI, one of the few recent outputs of that alt-right think tank, based on selected census and voting data, 2031 is pinpointed as the dreaded Rubicon when whites will lose their hold on America as a political majority.[9]

In addition to my interest in the alt-right's admiration of long-maligned eugenic ideas, its fixation on time piqued my curiosity about the intellectual underpinnings of contemporary white nationalism. In the fall of 2016, racist flyers appeared at my university, offering lies about the relationship between race and IQ, and demonizing black men as intellectually inferior and criminally predisposed. These unsettling images, which upset students and faculty alike, were plastered in the buildings where I teach. They included flyers from Identity Evropa, which targets college campuses in the hopes of finding recruits and to puncture holes in what they see as the totalitarian environments of politically correct universities. The Identity Evropa flyers were carefully designed and printed, featuring a classical statue of a young man in profile, all marble locks and draped cloak, and bold sans serif type proclaiming "Our Future Belongs to Us." I pondered the visual coding of the statuary: clearly, it was meant to evoke the superiority of Western civilization, and the superiority of men. But it was the word "Future" that caught my attention. How was this future being imagined and how did Identity Evropa hope to arrive there?

I soon ascertained that the alt-right, and its biggest intellectual influences, many European, are enraptured with time, temporality, and historical narrative. This is illustrated by the mottos of the flagship purveyors of alt-right books and media. For instance, Counter-Currents' publishing tagline is "Books Against Time."[10] Ostara Publications' website reminds viewers that its name refers to the "concept of the rebirth."[11] The motto of Red Ice TV is "the future is the past."[12] And the podcast produced by Arktos Media is called *Interregnum*, signaling "a period of time connecting the end of one era to the beginning of a new one," enveloping the ongoing time that is "the end of modernity."[13]

Alt-right timeframes reach back to pasts dripping with nostalgia and electrified by dire foreboding, and stretch forward to futures that oscillate from apocalyptic to magnificent. Whether the characterization of any one moment or era is negative or positive, the timescapes of the alt-right are emphatically nonlinear. They have multiple genealogies, including the philosophies of Friedrich Nietzsche and Martin Heidegger, but they are tied most palpably to several esoteric philosophers who consorted with fascist ideas and enshrined traditionalism and tribalism, whether nationalistic or ancestral.[14] Foremost among these influences are René Guénon, Savitri Devi, and Julius Evola. Their ideas were incorporated in various configurations and to varying degrees by the leading thinkers of the European New Right, such as Guillaume Faye and Alain de Benoist, who are idolized by the American alt-right. In fact, Casey's rebuke of linear narratives and his own website, Reactionary Futurism, draw from the temporal conceptions of Faye, who coined the term "archeofuturism" and warns that "linear history, like progressive ideology, is a trap."[15]

Consider that the "against time" portion of Counter-Currents' publishing motto derives from *The Lightning and the Sun*, written by Savitri Devi, a Greek-French author (née Maximine Julia Portaz) who converted to Hinduism, allied herself with Indian nationalism and fascism, and merged ideas of Eastern occultism and Nazism before and after World War II.[16] As her biographer has explained, Devi "elaborated an extraordinary synthesis of Hindu religion and Nordic racial ideology involving the polar origin of the Aryans, the cycle of the ages, and the incarnation of the last avatar of Vishnu in Adolf Hitler."[17] She was an unrepentant devotee of Nazism and the Führer. She wrote *The Lightning and the Sun*, her most well-known and far-fetched work, from 1948 to 1956, as a fugitive moving from city to city in Western Europe, and while imprisoned in Germany for distributing Nazi leaflets and posters. More a mystical treatise than a narrative interpretation of the rise and fall of the Third Reich, *The Lightning and the Sun* identifies three types of men: those who are rag dolls in time, buffeted by historical forces with no agency or conviction; those outside of time, who watch things unfold from the safety of the sidelines (like the men "yelling stop," mentioned by Casey); and, most importantly, men against time. In Devi's scheme, "men against time" fight during times of social disintegration, the greatest among them Hitler himself. Devi believed that Hitler was an avatar of Vishnu materialized on earth to bring transcendence to the chosen. The book's dedication reads "To the god-like Individual of our times; the Man against Time; the greatest European of all times; both Sun and Lightning, ADOLF HITLER, as a tribute of unfailing love and loyalty, forever and ever."[18]

"Men against time" are associated with both "the Sun" and "the Lightning." To be "against Time" is to fight for the Golden Age against immeasurable odds, and men who take up this struggle are "absolutely sincere, selfless idealists, believers in those eternal values that the fallen world has rejected, and ready, in order to reassert them on the material plane, to resort to any means within their reach." Devi also venerated the S.S., Hitler's bodyguards, as "against Time" and a "perfect organisation and a perfect aristocracy of character and deeper intelligence" made up of "a brotherhood of real supermen."[19] Devi believed that Hitler himself or another Übermensch "against Time" would return at the next cyclical aperture to unlock the Golden Age.

Devi's greatest influence on Nazism did not occur during the Third Reich but after World War II. In addition to *The Lightning and the Sun*, she published several other books that melded Eastern esoterica with ultranationalism, deep ecology, and, always, an undying fealty to Hitler. By the 1960s she had a fervent following of Nazi revanchists in Western Europe and the United States. She died in 1982 in England, en route to America, where she had been invited by Nazi groups to give a series of lectures. Once she was cremated, her ashes crossed the Atlantic, and her funerary urn was placed at the American Nazi Party shrine, where the faithful "held a formal New Order memorial service replete with memorabilia and Nazi bathos," and her photo was draped with a sash that ostensibly belonged to Hitler.[20]

On first glance, Counter-Currents' tagline "against time" seems anodyne. It is anything but, instead gesturing to the deep-rooted metaphysical facets of fascism and racial nationalism of the twentieth century. Even the late hard-core British nationalist Jonathan Bowden, who wrote an entire book extolling right-wing extremists, classified Devi as "extraordinarily radical" and "one of the most *extreme* and militant individuals that I've ever discussed."[21] Counter-Currents appears to be captivated by Savitri Devi; it is publishing many of her writings and books, and has become the home for the planned centennial edition of Devi's works. Notably, Devi is the only female author whose books are distributed by Counter-Currents' publishing.

The alt-right is neither the first nor the last movement to fixate on time and temporality. Many political, social, and cultural movements and their representative thinkers—liberal, conservative, authoritarian, revolutionary—perform complex dances with time in order to write themselves into the present and stake out a path for the future. National and collective histories are invented through plotlines of progress and decline, which can be continuous or discontinuous. Whiggish histories, associated with eighteenth- and nineteenth-century British political history, come in the form of marching-forward progress narratives, whereas the degeneration narratives penned in the late nineteenth and early twentieth centuries, often informed by the pessimistic evolutionism of criminologists like Cesare Lombroso, present downward slides into disarray.[22]

The favored timescapes of fascist and authoritarian regimes, which usually insist on a dramatic break from the past, are characterized by cyclical, recurrent, and eternal rhythms. These lend themselves to grandiose conceptualizations of resplendence and rebirth. Historian Roger Griffin offers a one-sentence definition of fascism as "a genus of political ideology whose mythic core in its various permutations is a palingenetic form of populist ultranationalism."[23] This definition, which portrays fascism more as an assemblage of ideologies than a particular set of political or institutional structures, pivots around the idea of rebirth from a mythological past, and helps explain why nostalgia, restoration, and awakening are quintessential features of fascist formations.[24] We can split definitional hairs about whether or not the alt-right is fascist. It certainly is not a political movement or party like the Romanian Iron Guard or the Estado Novo in Brazil under Getulio Vargas, and its wannabe intellectualism and desire for normalization distinguishes it from the neo-Nazi groups that the watchdog organization Southern Poverty Law Center identifies as "focused on the revolutionary creation of a fascist political state."[25] Yet if we rely on Griffin's definition, with its emphasis on palingenesis (the reproduction of ancestral characteristics), then the alt-right has marked fascist elements, which, moreover, are deeply linked to their conceptions of time.

KALI YUGA: THE PRESENT

The slogan "against time" not only gestures toward Hitler and National Socialism; it also connects to notions of time proposed by European esoteric thinkers. The "About" page of Counter-Currents.com announces an allegiance to a patently nonlinear version of history.[26] It explains: "History is cyclical, and its prevailing current is downward, declining from a Golden Age through Silver and Bronze Ages to a Dark Age." This cyclicity is drawn from the writings of the French metaphysical philosopher René Guénon.[27] Most people have not heard of Guénon, or they had not until the flurry of articles probing the right-wing reading list favored by Steve Bannon, Trump's chief campaign strategist and short-lived special advisor.[28] Guénon elaborated his abstract and metaphysical worldview in the early twentieth century as he fashioned himself an iconoclast opposed to modernity and rationality. After surveying a range of religious movements such as Masonry, Sufism, and Tao, he adapted the tenets of Hinduism (Vedanta), namely the cyclical concept of the kalpa, an eternal time that is divided into fourteen manvantaras, each lasting 64,800 years, which are subdivided further into four yugas. For Guénon, these yugas translated into the Western traditions of gold, silver, bronze, and iron as described by the ancient Greeks, and map on to four cycles that adhere to the golden ratios (4:3:2:1) such that the Golden Age lasts four times as long as the Iron Age. Following this formula, Guénon posited a distant Golden Age when man (and he speaks only of men) existed in a glorious, primordial state. This utopia was disrupted by mundane forces that have accelerated exponentially through the Silver, the Bronze, and, finally, the current Iron—or Dark—Age, known in Sanskrit as the Kali Yuga. People in the twenty-first centuries are living through the last gasps of this Dark Age, which will devolve into utter chaos or luminous transcendence.[29]

A corollary of Guénon's thought is that during these Big Bang moments of hyperacceleration it is imperative to stress quality over quantity, so as to be prepared for the return of a "primordial state" that will be more radiant than the last. Guénon believed that the modern preoccupation with quantity worked to distort deeper human values and attributes, sacrificing them to the superficiality of measurement and numeration. Moderns were too intent on reducing time to uniform sequences and squashing the "modern spirit." For Guénon, anything that resembled the Swiss-like quest for precision in time measurement was anathema to a more genuine apprehension of time: "The correct representation of time is to be found in the traditional conception of cycles, and this conception obviously involves a 'qualified' time."[30] To quantify is to rob substances and experiences of their essence: "Quantification is seen as emptying the world not just of what makes it meaningful to man, but of what makes it human."[31] For the alt-right elite, these ideas, of speeding up, quality over quantity, and cyclical return, provide the conceptual scaffolding for a kind of palingenesis that will culminate with paroxysms of the Kali Yuga and the nascence of the Golden Age.

The European New Right was attracted by Guénon's ideas, which provided scaffolding for GRECE's multipronged antiliberalism and fledging identitarianism.[32] As the American alt-right began to build its brand of white nationalism and identity politics, often looking to the ENR for a philosophical canon, it heartily absorbed Guénon's cyclical frameworks. Concomitantly the alt-right also seized upon a companion, and now more visible, set of ideas elaborated by the Italian philosopher Julius Evola.

Both Guénon and Evola were traditionalists; they abhorred modernism and liberalism as reprehensible forces of disordering. Although Guénon looms large on the *Counter-Currents*' webzine and in the publishing company, Evola has the broader reach on both sides of the Atlantic. Born at the cusp of the twentieth century, Evola lived through World War I (serving in the Italian army) and World War II (during which he was left paralyzed by a Soviet bomb attack in Vienna in 1945), and into the 1970s, and he left a prolific mark with books including *Introduction to Magic*, *Men Among the Ruins*, *The Path of the Cinnabar*, *Fascism Viewed from the Right*, and *A Handbook for Right-Wing Youth*. Starting largely in the 1990s, his works were translated into English and published by houses like Inner Traditions that specialize in esoterica. By the early 2000s, the nascent alt-right's fascination with Evola was growing, and his books were reissued by both Counter-Currents and Arktos.

Evola has been labeled a protofascist, and if we evaluate him according to Griffin's definition of racial rebirth, then the definition fits. Yet he had a tempestuous relationship with fascism and with Mussolini, who liked some of Evola's notions but not others.[33] Notably Evola was one of the few to criticize fascism from the right, assailing it as a misguided incarnation of nationalism that undervalued traditionalism.[34] Evola's viewpoints were eccentric, complex, and often evinced distrust of political formations; like Guénon's, Evola's outlook was morose and gloomy: "Evola felt a deep affinity with Guénon's esoteric pessimism."[35]

Evola's contentions about the racial superiority of white Europeans generally allied him with Nazism. However, he disdained the biological theories of racial superiority favored by the Germans and racial hygienists. For him, eugenics was excessively materialistic and disregarded the spiritual aspects of race and civilization. Evola articulates these perspectives in *Revolt Against the Modern World*, which has achieved mythic status among the alt-right.[36] Mirroring Guénon, Evola discusses the Four Ages, fleshing out the contours of the Golden Age: "This era corresponds to an original civilization that was naturally and totally in conformity with what has been called the 'traditional spirit,'"[37] which did not express itself in "linear, 'historical' time." This spirit occupied the "polar seat" (i.e., Northern European and Arctic) and also was embodied by Indo-Europeans (i.e., Aryans), but as the ages unfolded it was displaced and destroyed.

Racial purity and male dominance defined Evola's "Arctic Cycle of the Golden Age," which occurred about six thousand years ago. Each coming cycle degraded and upended this racial and gender order. Societies either became too feminized, run by a "priestly gynecocracy" (like the Egyptians and Mayans), or improperly masculinized (like the Titans and Demetrians). In *Revolt*, Evola lays much of the blame for this retrogression on women who sullied the warrior and priest castes, making them too weak to exert anything resembling true masculine vigor. Indeed, *Revolt* seethes with revulsion for women and the feminine, and endorses gender essentialism: "Man and woman are two different types." Men are innately superior in spiritual and humanistic terms, and in their ideal form embody two types of "pure virility": the warrior or the ascetic. Although it is impossible for women to attain such sublimeness, they can approach greatness in the prescribed roles of lover or mother. A woman's fulfillment comes from "totally giving of herself and being entirely for another being," whether that being is her lover or her son. The masculinization of women is the quickest road to civilizational downfall. But men also are culpable; if they fail to exert their virility and maintain order, then women, slaves, and other inferiors can become emancipated. In Evola's eyes, the twentieth century "emancipation" of women was "infecting the rest of the world faster than a plague." With this gendered imbalance, it was "no wonder the superior races are dying out before the ineluctable logic of individualism." The only hope for the future was to retain, however tenuously, a grasp on a lineage of a "civilization of heroes," which could "restore the tradition of the origins on the basis of the warrior principles and of membership in the warrior caste."

Alt-righters are fond of invoking Nietzsche's adage that "the future belongs to those with the longest memory." This framing aligns with the works of Guénon and Evola. The alt-right knocks on various doors of the past trying to build an everlasting memory that reaches back to an exalted yesteryear.[38] These contortions around time, which anticipate the cyclical return of an ancestral past in a fated future, can lead the alt-right to bizarre, sometimes conspiratorial, sometimes nearly hallucinogenic places. At its most trippy, for example, the "longest memory" rubs up against quantum physics, where the past, present, and future commingle in an "eternal metamorphosis" that is never-ending. As described by alt-right author Michael O'Meara, perhaps the most schorlarly of the bunch: the "Eternal Return is thus nostalgic not for the past, as it is with primitive man, but for the future."[39] In these time warps, if the future is the past, and the past is the future, then an alt-right now is plausible. The alt-right swims in these turbulent and potentially mesmerizing temporal tidepools, which allow Identity Evorpa to pronounce pompously that "Our Future Belongs to Us."

The timescapes of Evola, Guénon, and their acolytes can be characterized as metanarratives. They are abstract, void of materialism, and feature no tangible human actors. There is little room even for the default male subject born out of the Cartesian principles of the Enlightenment. The Four Ages constitute a sweeping cyclical saga that replaces sequentiality and causation with symbolically laden and spiritual metamorphosis. The only viable protagonist is a nearly godlike European male warrior vitalized by his Nordic or Aryan lineage. The end-time will be spectacular and all-changing. When this moment arrives, only those bestowed with innate primordial knowledge, Devi's "men against time," will emerge unscathed and ready to rule.

The Archeo-Future

The alt-right expends much energy entertaining projections about an irresistible future, auguring the white ethnostate or supermajority and the reassertion of a strict gender order. If the temporal bedrock of this future is a primordial past, what happens to modern technologies, which the alt-right contends are overwhelmingly white European and American innovations? Many on the alt-right, it turns out, do not dismiss modern technologies as excesses of the current state of disorder but see them as indispensable instruments (over which they presume inherent ownership) for the realization of the Golden Age. They have thus formulated some interesting approaches to their incorporation into the future. These possibilities are most vividly captured by Guillaume Faye's concept of archeofuturism, which depicts a future of technologically enhanced primordialism. Faye's ideas resonate with a longer intertwining of fascism and futurism that some scholars consider emblematic of the contested modernity of the twentieth century.[40]

Faye, who paints with a catastrophic brush, posits in *Archeofuturism* that "the present civilisation cannot endure," largely because egalitarianism and progress have proven themselves to be nothing more than fairytales. Moving to the next civilizational phase requires "an archaic mindset," one that harks back to the ancestral. Yet this will be "a future society that combines techno-scientific progress with a return to the traditional answers that stretch back into the mists of time." Linear temporality, associated with the Enlightenment, must be dismantled to reach an eternal transfiguration. In this temporal vortex, "the Ancients must be associated not with the Moderns but with the Futurists."[41]

Faye's twist is to propose that "archaic and ancestral values" can be maximized by technology and, indeed, that they will enable man to survive the "century of iron and fire" intact. In this rendition, the future is not simply the sequential unfolding of the present into the beyond; rather it heralds a sharp break from modernity. The twenty-first century might witness "a huge, universal techno-scientific regression," followed by upheaval and the installation of a high-tech archaism. In this scenario, technological enhancement can extrude even more naturalness out of nature.[42] Faye, for example, ardently supports genetic technologies—including reproductive ones—which paradoxically "do not fight against nature: they go further than nature does and accelerate nature itself by attempting, in a risky manner, to substitute human choice for evolutionary chance." In this way, technoscience becomes a means to realize what is good and right about the ancestral past. In short, reproductive technologies can be deployed to save the white race in Europe. They can promote "a rehabilitation of the stable traditional couple and the encouragement of strictly European natality," a process supported by "biotechnologies, genetic manipulation, artificial intelligence, and incubator births."[43] In the archeofuture, marriage and birth rates of whites will rise; if accompanied by harsh immigration control, there will again be white demographic predominance in Western societies.

Many American alt-right thinkers draw inspiration from Faye, even though they have to contend with his stereotypically French anti-Americanism, a feature not uncommon in antiglobalist European ethnonationalism.[44] Some alt-righters see examples of Faye's vision in cultural forms like film and fiction. For example, Greg Johnson of Counter-Currents publishing appreciates the science fiction classic *Dune* because of its "combination of futurism with archaic values and social forms which is basically what Guillaume Faye talks about in his book *Archeofu-turism* as the way forward."[45]

Alt-right futurism also is hinged to the self-described neo-reactionary movement of the Dark Enlightenment, another albeit shadowy strand of the alt-right that slams egalitarianism and progress as the two great evils of the twenty-first century. This movement is connected to the internet and trolling culture, and was coined around 2007 by a blogger who published the Dark Enlightenment series as an online book. This treatise aims to expose the incompetent and retrograde thinking of democracy and rationality: "Where the progressive enlightenment sees political ideals, the dark enlightenment sees appetites. . . . Setting its expectations as low as reasonably possible, it seeks only to spare civilization from frenzied, ruinous, gluttonous debauch."[46] The alternative is some form of autocratic rule, not dissimilar to monarchism or feudalism. The logic at play is that unlike elected officials, who deal in short time horizons and do not want to invest in the future, kings and dynasties look out for the long-term welfare of their families and vassals.[47] This criticism of the short-sightedness of democracies, which prioritize immediate gratification over forward-thinking sustainability, has been developed by the German philosopher Hans-Hermann Hoppe, a thinker cited in the more cerebral quarters of the American alt-right.[48]

ALT-RIGHT AMNESIA

In the American context, cyclical ages and eternal returns become reactionary futurism, the philosophy elaborated by Casey on his own website and found in allusions to Evola and the Kali Yuga. The alt-right literati are beholden to the ideas of Guénon and Evola, which foreground the Iron Age and insist on the inevitability of dramatic change. Some are partial to the title of one of Evola's books, *Ride the Tiger*, which describes men who, instead of becoming martyrs of the final spasms of the Golden Age, which might obliterate them or simply be a losing battle, grab the mane of the beast and endure the bumpy ride.[49] These men are keenly aware of what they are doing and stand poised to act during the interregnum when the Kali Yuga comes to a calamitous close. This explains why Alex Witoslawski, an alt-righter affiliated with America First Media who is interested in mapping out political strategies has dubbed his (protected) Twitter account "Surfing the Kali Yuga"—where Evola and Guénon meet the Beach Boys and adventure sports.[50] In a talk about Evola at the New York Forum (styled after the London Forum, started by British nationalists), one alt-righter said, "The idea that we are living in Kali Yuga and that everything is inevitably doomed to collapse may seem like quite a black pill. But . . . I think it does accurately describe our situation."[51] Beyond their immersion in the alt-right speak that spans both sides of the Atlantic, these concepts have helped spawn interest in the motifs of horizons and windows. They also have fostered an alt-right brand of selective amnesia, which is most apparent in relation to the topics of the Holocaust and the civil rights movements of the 1960s.

The trope of horizons has emerged as an alt-right device for viewing the near future and pushing the envelope of change. Horizons are spun off by the increasing velocity of modernity. Following Evola and Guénon, as time accelerates, horizons shrink: "Look, democracy is a failure and undermines civilization because it shrinks time horizons down, and that means you can't pursue grand strategies and civilizational goals," says Greg Johnson.[52] Thus, the alt-right needs to pry open horizons by bending time, most pragmatically by popularizing "long time horizon" philosophies that can induce distinct (meta)political possibilities.[53] Given the prevalence of horizons in alt-right timescapes, it is not surprising that the "Overton window" metaphor has gained much traction recently. This obscure expression was coined by libertarian conservatives in Michigan, and then picked up by Trump and advisors during the 2016 election campaign, to suggest that there is a "relatively narrow range of public policy ideas that are considered politically acceptable."[54] The alt-right wants to jam open this window so that ideas that seemed unthinkable become viable, even implementable in the near term.[55]

Whatever it does, the alt-right cannot escape time if it wants to imagine a future and grapple with the present. In this sense, the present is at once an obstacle and an opportunity, a festering moment that needs to be radically overhauled. Jared Taylor, who defines himself as a "race realist," outlines this predicament in *White Identity: Racial Consciousness in the 21st Century*. From his viewpoint, America has failed because it is biologically and culturally impossible to mix ostensibly discrete racial types in any virtuous or productive way. His list of ailments are typical white nationalist laments: white interests have been diluted and are under attack, crime rates are skyrocketing, fatherless families are on the rise, and, disturbingly, the demographic transition is bringing about the browning of America.[56] These, not surprisingly, reflect the collapse of the "American Dream," which was sold to the American people as a vehicle of equality and liberation but has served to imprison them. As Gregory Hood, a regular contributor to the American Renaissance website, retorts with an alt-right declaration in his book *Waking Up from the American Dream*: "We hold these truths to be self-evident: that all men are created unequal, that a natural aristocracy has been endowed among them by their Creator, and that the purpose of human existence is the upward development of the individual, the ethnic community, and the race."[57] In a nod toward Devi and Evola, Hood writes, "We are the sons of the North, the race of Europa, the People of the Sun." From the vantage point of Hood and other alt-righters, the American Nightmare is synonymous with egalitarianism and diversity run amok. The result is that "the American Dream is over—and it has to be replaced with the waking vision of the White Republic."

Trump's "MAGA" slogan—"Make America Great Again"—thus holds particular resonance for the alt-right. "Again" summons and invents the memory of an idealized past and encourages nostalgia for an earlier era in America, certainly before 1965, or before the adoption of the Fourteenth Amendment in 1868, or better yet as far back as the 1790 Naturalization Act, when only "free white persons" of "good character" qualified for citizenship. On the ground, at rallies, repeating this mantra worked to Trump's favor in unleashing populism into a reactionary, angry emotion, wrapped up in calls for the restoration of whiteness and manhood.[58]

Nevertheless, slogans like "MAGA" also engage in historical distortion and amnesia. The coveted future can only be enacted by hitching to a plotline that lunges across a timescape in which certain aspects of history are remembered and others are forgotten. Among alt-righters, to be remembered are the white founders of the original US colonies; the hard-working, "hale stock" of British and German immigrants who populated the country in the eighteenth and nineteenth centuries; and anyone whose "root ancestry" is white. Also to be remembered are the great exploits, conquests, and crusades that unfolded in Europe before the

Enlightenment and that many of us read about in grade school textbooks, as well as the glories of Manifest Destiny and westward expansion, and Hollywood-esque tales of the taming of the frontier. To be forgotten are popular and revolutionary struggles for equality and liberal democracy such as the French Revolution, with its motto of Liberty, Equality, and Fraternity, and the Haitian Revolution, even more disliked given its calls for racial equality. The alt-right views such plotlines as fallacious linear narratives that pimp equality and multiculturalism under a loose banner of political correctness. Moreover, these narratives have been contaminated by feminism and diversity-stamped by legal, corporate, and educational institutions. From the white nationalist perspective, they are instruments of SJW-indoctrination that hinder possibilities for red pilling and effective metapolitics.[59]

One of the chronological flashpoints for the alt-right is the Holocaust, which is sometimes discussed and sometimes negated but serves as a powerful if resented pivot for white nationalist ideas. Given the alt-right's cognizance of the risk of overt association with swastikas, Holocaust denialism, and the Ku Klux Klan, the neo-Nazi repertoire does not figure prominently in many white nationalist narratives. One alt-righter warns that Nazi symbols divert potential converts from American patriotism and, moreover, can incite sympathy for victims and the vulnerable, a "cucked" attitude common among liberals. These tendencies are counterproductive to saving the white race. Richard Spencer has suggested that alt-righters abandon white supremacist symbols and instead promote tried-and-true emblems of Americana like the Stars and Stripes and Uncle Sam.[60] Rather than getting tied up in knots about neo-Nazism, "we white nationalists today must reach for the power that lies within ourselves and bring forth the future our Founding Fathers would have wanted us to have," writes Ward Kendall.[61] In a similar vein, Kevin MacDonald, associated with the online publication *The Occidental Quarterly* and known for his strident anti-Semitism, recommends that the Holocaust (which he intentionally spells with a lowercase "h") be "stepped over" because it is not pertinent to whites today and serves as a distraction from propagating alt-right ideas.[62]

Providing strategies for this disavowal, Johnson, in *New Right Versus Old Right*, describes the Holocaust (he also uses a lowercase "h") as an unavoidable topic, a demanding annoyance in history's march forward that must be tackled in some form, namely, by underplaying its relevance to the contemporary moment. Johnson states that the Holocaust has been the mega-producer of "white guilt," which has weakened prospects for white nationalism by turning many potential white converts into liberal lost causes and unreachable SWJs. Johnson does not indulge in overt Holocaust denial but instead wants to mold history to enable white nationalist consciousness, "because mere historical facts—no matter what they are—should never deter us."[63] Like many alt-righters, Johnson casts his mission in bold terms that are emplotted toward the future and selectively interact with the past. As he admonishes, "Make no mistake, White Nationalists are not just struggling to save the white race, since the welfare of the whole world depends upon our triumph. If we perish, the other races will breed recklessly and despoil the planet unchecked, and the one place in the universe where we know there is life will end up nothing but a burnt-out cinder in the vastness of space."[64]

As alt-right authors devise ways to sidestep and downplay the Holocaust, they also latch on to 1965 as the decisive year when the White Republic was lost. As one participant said on a recent Identity Evropa podcast, "1965, MLK, all that, that's year zero."[65] Not only was the Hart-Celler Act, which liberalized immigration laws and ended racial quotas, passed in 1965, so was the Voting Rights Act, which sought to counteract decades and decades of legalized and vigilante disenfranchisement of African Americans. The fixation on 1965 encapsulates the alt-right's belief that unchecked immigration has ruined America, a sentiment echoed by best-selling author Ann Coulter, who has written, "It was Teddy Kennedy's 1965 immigration act that snuffed out the generous quotas for immigrants from the countries that had traditionally populated America—England, Ireland, and Germany—and added 'family reunification' policies, allowing recent immigrants to bring in their relatives, and those relatives to bring in *their* relatives, until entire Somali villages have relocated to Minneapolis."[66] In short, the alt-right espouses the idea that the hardy seeds for white genocide were planted in 1965. Significantly, the opening of the multicultural gates in 1965 is laid directly at the feet of Jews, the supposed culprits behind the formulation and passage of the Hart-Celler Act. As Kevin MacDonald has written, "The organized Jewish community was the most important force in enacting the 1965 law which changed the ethnic balance of the country, ensuring that Whites will be a minority in the US well before 2050."[67]

For some alt-righters, a critical look at 1965 can become a red pill. "1965 Red Pill" is the title of one of the YouTube videos produced by Lacey Lynn, a white nationalist and traditional housewife. In this vlog she debunks diversity: "We have been sold the lie of assimilation," she says, adding that this "lie . . . began with the immigration act of 1965."[68] In these chronologies, milestones in American history that occurred in 1965, such as the massive civil rights march from Selma to Montgomery to protest racism and police brutality against blacks, are glaringly absent.[69] If examples of the civil rights and feminist movements of the 1960s are mentioned, it is to reproach them as conjurers of the falsehood that diversity is good and racial equality is an achievable and desirable goal. To upstream a white nationalist future, alt-right writers somehow must downstream the past, one that is not in sync with mainstream, let alone progressive, renditions of American history.

Alt-righters employ nonlinear conceptions of time when interpreting current political events and the viability of white nationalism going forward. In summer 2018, for example, Patrick Casey of Identity Evropa interviewed the veteran white nationalist Paul Kersey, author of *Whitey on the Moon* and a regular companion of Jared Taylor on American Renaissance podcasts. Kersey was undeniably hopeful about "the cataclysmic events of 2017" and talked gleefully about intensifying polarization and civil unrest in American society. He saw the unexpected victory of Alexandria Ocasio-Cortez, a Democratic Socialist from the Bronx who won a US congressional seat, as evidence that "the future has arrived too early." This political shakeup was another salvo in a speeded-up temporality in which "Trump has accelerated things" through his border policies of family separation and detention camps, which Kersey praised as being pursued with "ruthless efficiency at its finest." Kersey and Casey's entire conversation was framed in temporal language and metaphors, of a pounding velocity, characteristic of the final stages of the Kali Yuga that would force unrest and disarray; they agreed that "things are moving in the right direction."[70] On New Year's Eve 2018, Casey tweeted confidently, "If we are lucky, 2019 will be 2015 on steroids."[71] The obsession with time is a crucial dimension of the alt-right imagination. As the temporal horizon closes in and speeds up, white nationalists want to push a primordial past and a techno-utopian future into a present they feel is both slipping out of their hands and perhaps within close reach.

CHAPTER 3

WHITOPIA

Ethnostate Dreamin'

Ozarkia, New Albion, Hyperborea, Cascadia, Gulflandia. Welcome to the future homelands of the alt-right. They are homogenous territories with vigilant borders and populations that never dip below 90 percent white. They are reincarnations of America's apartheid past and waking dreams of purity, community, and belonging. No star burns brighter for white nationalists than the ethnostate; it is the alt-right's most outlandish and most chilling idea. The white ethnostate is the hallowed destination that beckons on the horizon. Mostly it is a mirage, but it also is a bell-wether of the alt-right's treacherous effacement of the line between civic nationalism and racial nationalism. The ethnostate is a wedge idea that alt-righters hope to make thinkable and plausible.

The ethnostate's foremost mission is to protect and fortify whiteness; it is a faithful proof of concept of the palingenetic ultranationalism that historian Roger Griffin identifies as foundational to fascism.[1] While progressive Americans from abolitionists to LGBTQ activists have sought to make society more inclusive and diverse, and to expand the beneficiaries of the Declaration of Independence's promise of life, liberty, and the pursuit of happiness, white nationalists aim for contraction—back to a nation composed predominantly of "free white persons" of "good character." White nationalists frequently repeat these key phrases of the 1790 Naturalization Act as proof that the Founding Fathers wanted the American republic to be a perpetual white ethnostate.

When seeking prototypes for "Whitopia," alt-righters look backwards, abroad, and to popular culture. They find inspiration in the eclectic list of American utopian experiments, from the Oneida Colony of the 1850s in upstate New York to the Farm in rural Tennessee in the 1970s. They can drink at the historical trough of Confederate secession and savor the sight of Dixie flags across America. White nationalists are motivated by Poland, Japan, and, especially, Estonia, a heritage nation "founded on the legal principle of restorationism."[2] They find unexpected models in Liberia, an independent nation established by repatriated American slaves, and Aztlán, the mythic homeland envisaged by Chicanx activists as a recovered and thoroughly decolonized Southwest.[3] Most recently, alt-righters have seized on Wakanda, the African diasporic homeland in the movie *Black Panther*, as a possible paradigm.[4]

If the thirteen colonies provide the original template for the white ethnostate, the more recent and recollectable 1960s is the demographic sweet spot. As one white nationalist writes, "The USA of 1960 was more of an ethnostate than the USA of 1790, when Americans of African or part-African ancestry were nearly 20 percent of the population."[5] This decade, above all, symbolizes the "peak of American civilization," when this country "was sending a man to the moon, when our cities were clean and vibrant in a good way."[6] An alt-right injunction is that a sizable swath of the country needs to return to the pre-1965 "status quo," when whites made up 90 percent of the population, desegregation was in its infancy, and racial quotas kept a tight lid on immigration from most of the world. In the alt-right fantasy world, this was an unsullied time before multiculturalism, feminism, and globalism became juggernauts of "white genocide," when white families lived in bubbles of security and traditionalism.[7]

Across Europe, ethnonationalists hope to halt the "Great Replacement," turn back multiculturalism, and recover white dominance.[8] Some European nationalists express doubt about the likelihood of reversing demographic trends in Europe, but others are buoyed by the successes of Brexit, the French National Front and Alternative for Germany, and the hardening of immigration policies in Italy and Hungary. In the United States, the prospects for white restoration are complicated by the sheer size of the country, the presence of Native Americans, the centuries-old roots of African Americans, the entrenched expanses of ethnic and immigrant communities, and an increasingly multiracial population. Thus, from the alt-right's vantage point, an autonomous white ethnostate is the only solution. As a blogger for *Fash the Nation* asserts: "Anything short of ending all non-White immigration tomorrow and bringing in millions of Europeans into America will fail to fix our demographic issues." These trends lend the pursuit of the ethnostate further urgency and necessitate that any solution "will necessarily have to include separation and secession from the United States of America and the majority non-White hordes within it."[9]

"ETHNOSTATES FOR ALL"

Greg Johnson of Counter-Currents publishing has produced extensive written and audiovisual content on the white ethnostate. Johnson's fans describe him as a "great ambassador to normies," and many of his writings are outward-facing as he strives to make the alt-right legible and alluring to the curious and the skeptical.[10] He acknowledges that the notion of the ethnostate might be unnerving and downright scary, and wants to mollify these anxieties. In the essay "The Slow Cleanse," Johnson contemplates how to create "homogeneously white homelands where our people can reproduce and fulfill our destiny, free from the interference of others."[11] Reflecting the sanitized approach of the alt-right elite, Johnson rejects the bellicosity of Aryan insurgents drawn to schemes like the four-phase Butler Plan, which exhorts that "acts of insurrection and guerrilla warfare must take place, actual and serious physical damage must be inflicted on the enemy."[12] He disdains groups like the Northwest Front, based in the white nationalist hotbed of rural Washington, which abides by the Butler Plan and adheres to the Fourteen Words, devised by the late David Lane of the white power group the Order: "We must secure the existence of our people and a future for white children."[13] Race wars are déclassé; the alt-right should not be "seduced by these apocalyptic scenarios about race war and cataclysm."[14] The road to the ethnostate runs not through Aryan Nations compounds like Ruby Ridge or Hayden Lake in Idaho but through Lake Wobegon, once denuded of liberals, Jews, and lingering nonwhites.[15]

Johnson is confident that a "well-planned, orderly, and humane process of ethnic cleansing" can bring about the ethnostate with relatively little Sturm und Drang.[16] He presumes that whites and nonwhites alike, while perhaps not thrilled with the turn to ethnostates, ultimately will, by force or incentivization, repopulate along racial lines in an orderly fashion. The video montage "White Nationalism Is Inevitable," posted on the *Counter-Currents* webzine, visualizes these ideas, stressing that when the stakes are as high as extinction, "whites will fight back when we feel we are being attacked."[17] Johnson, who despairs of the messiness of race wars, believes that whites will wake up and begin to enact policies and inducements that create racial boundary lines across America, which he thinks can lead to the consolidation of a white ethnostate in less than fifty years. As Johnson likes to say, "We need to return to status quo 1965 by 2065."[18]

Although Johnson delivers these tutorials with smooth prose and a euphonic tone, the implications of Ethnostate 101 are disquieting to say the least. The multipronged endeavor would begin with closing borders to nonwhites, followed by the deportation of "illegal aliens," hastened by the termination of welfare and benefits to noncitizen immigrants. Birthright citizenship would be retroactively repealed, requiring children born of nonwhite foreign parents to return to their parents' country of origin.[19] White nationalists would capitalize on those occasions when, moving for reasons of family or work, nonwhites would exit permanently. Propelled by racial "in-group" preferences, blacks would relocate to an ethnostate in the South, perhaps even induced by monetary reparations since "the ethnostate discussion can include that issue."[20] These expulsions would be accompanied by pronatalist policies for whites, such as an abortion ban, subsidized maternity leave, and tax bonuses for married couples, all geared toward stimulating the birth rate.[21] Lana Lokteff of Red Ice TV lays out this plan in her vlog on ethnostates, which would "need to have laws in place to protect the nation's founding demographics, to protect the white majority, to stop the invasion, to start deportations."[22] Johnson suggests that most whites would find such a gradual plan of "ethnic cleansing" morally acceptable. He also believes it would work: "Such policies would create entirely white homelands within a few decades" and be "consistent with the human rights of all parties."[23] This plan, according to white nationalists, is not delusional or unrealistic. In the words of one particularly enthusiastic white nationalist, ethnic cleansing is as "well-tested and well-proven as automobile transportation."[24]

For the alt-right, the White Republic's virtues would benefit everyone on the ethnoracial spectrum. White nationalists frequently claim that ethnostates are predicated not on white supremacy but on respect for each race as a distinct cultural and biological entity: the "central rationale for ethnonationalism is that it is the political philosophy that best allows different races and nations to live in accordance with their own identities."[25] As such, white nationalists argue, the race realism behind the ethnostate exemplifies compassion, not bigotry. In a twist of logic, the white ethnostate would displace the impulse toward dominion over racial minorities, absolving whites of the burden of this oppressive arrangement. According to a white nationalist writing for American Renaissance, the ethnostate idea can be presented in such a "positive and forward-looking way" that the African American writer and reparations proponent Ta-Nehisi Coates would get on board.[26]

The potential emotional appeal of the white ethnostate should not be underestimated. It taps into longings for group solidarity, self-determination, and sustainable communities. As a construct soaked in ultranationalism, the ethnostate arouses romanticism, sentimentality, and the promise of comfort and fellowship. For its designated denizens, the white ethnostate symbolizes a "place where everything is familiar, where everything is intelligible, and where you don't feel alienated."[27] It would be a geographical sanctuary for the preservation of "ancient phenotypes that we know and love" and a barrier against "newly arriving DNA" of "lower quality."[28] If any conflict arises, "it will be a family quarrel," not tribal warfare.[29] At its most maudlin, the idea of the ethnostate arouses heartache and homesickness among those who hunger for such comforts: "We find ourselves lost and alone, searching for that homeland that never was, one which is unified, advanced and racially aware."[30] Once arrived to the sanctified destination, white nationalists would rest assured in a place where racial kinship would "bind us all together" and people would "plant trees so that future generations can enjoy shade."[31] This Eden appears in the final pages of the speculative novel *Victoria*, in which, after engaging in protracted and graphic bloody battles, the victims become victors, seizing an ethnostate in the Northeast. After white renegades recapture the land from a multicultural and leftist totalitarian regime, "our rocky New England soil" experienced a "revival of literature, music, and art and the recovery of beauty."[32]

For everyone who rejects or would be rejected by the white kingdom, the ethnostate is an aggressor that would remove millions of people, enact extreme racial and ideological vetting, and balkanize multiracial America. Even the most unruffled white nationalists, like Johnson and the Scottish YouTuber Millennial Woes, admit that a "little bit of social oppression" and "compulsion" would be necessary. Building ethnostates seems utterly unfeasible for so many reasons that it would be an exercise in absurdity to list them all. To start, it would require massive transfers of human and financial capital to one part of the country. It would treat regions and peoples as blank slates and moveable parts, and it could not be realized without recourse to blunt force and bloodshed. But for the alt-right, such sacrifice, disruption, and pain are justifiable when the goals are so righteous, the yearning so great, and the scenario so dire: "We have got a greater than 99% chance of extinction."[33]

The premise of the white ethnostate—that racial nationalism is better, fairer, and more logical than a multicultural society necessitates the unraveling of the civic and constitutional values that hold the national fabric together. The alt-right hopes to hatch ethnonationalism out of a weary civic nationalism by persuasive meme-ing, metapolitical projects, and molding discourse so that the ethnostate becomes just another matter-of-fact idea. As American Renaissance contributor Gregory Hood writes, making "race the defining difference" is the "precursor to the formation of an ethnostate, the great dream of the White Republic."[34] Toward this end, alt-righters stress the importance of discerning when to "push the envelope" with ideas like the ethnostate so it goes "over a little bit" but not far enough to scare away possible white sympathizers.[35]

While the materialization of an outright ethnostate might seem implausible, national boundaries are not set in stone and have been redrawn from the top down and bottom up during times of geopolitical ferment. In the current American context, the horrifying rub is that the Trump administration's policies are lifted from a manual sitting on the alt-right shelf. Refugee bans, zero tolerance, family separations, and prolonged detention are strategies implemented under the thinly veiled guise of "law and order" with pointed demographic intent and racial animus. Trump's comments in summer 2018 about Europe "losing its culture" due to immigration, as well as previous offhand remarks comparing "shithole countries" like Haiti and El Salvador to desirable Norway are nothing if not starkly ethnonationalist.[36] The political and discursive environment in the late 2010s is conducive to ethnostate thinking, which intensifies divisive dichotomies and encourages the dehumanization of an expanding roster of others and outsiders. For white nationalists, the wistful nostalgia for an unrequited homeland has red-pilling potential, and these affective dimensions should not be overlooked.

IMAGINING THE ETHNOSTATE

The standard-bearing *Oxford English Dictionary* does not include an entry for "ethnostate." However, the related term "ethnonationalism" made its etymological debut in 1959 in connection to politics in fascist Italy. The Oxford dictionary defines "ethnonationalism" as "advocacy or support for the interests of a particular ethnic group, esp. with regard to its national independence or self-determination." This term was cited in reference to independence movements in Africa and Asia when tribalism and regionalism tested efforts at postcolonial governance. According to the dictionary, its lesser-known companion "ethno-state" first surfaced in a 1969 article in *Africa Quarterly* analyzing ethnonationalist pressures on emerging independent governments. The term made the leap to right-wing nationalism, acquiring a more explicitly racial framing in 1992 with the publication of Wilmot Robertson's *The Ethnostate: An Unblinkered Prospectus for an Advanced Statecraft*.[37] Robertson was the pen name for Sumner Humphrey Ireland, who, twenty years earlier, wrote *The Dispossessed Majority*, which became an underground classic in white supremacist circles; David Duke pronounced it "one of the most brilliant books of this century dealing with the weakening of the American majority."[38]

The Dispossessed Majority contended that whites were being overtaken in their country by the "presence of 'unassimilable minorities,'" including "blacks . . . Asians, Hispanics, Greeks, Southern Italians, Arabs, Amerindians, and Jews."[39] Robertson argued that nonwhites should be denied constitutional protections because of their racial and cultural inferiority. He reserved sharp condemnation for "Jewish hegemony," which he said had perverted America and opened the doors to the havoc of multiculturalism and unrestrained immigration.[40] Robertson's anti-Semitism surfaced as Holocaust denialism in *Instauration*, a monthly journal he published from 1975 to 2000 that sought to cultivate an academic tone for racism. *The Dispossessed Majority* forecasted most of the ills that preoccupy the alt-right today and foreshadowed an alt-right lexicon of terms describing what they see as the rotting symptoms of liberal multiculturalism: "white dispossession," "xenophilia," and "ethnomasochism."[41]

The Ethnostate was the second installment of Robertson's white nationalist work. While he was optimistic about an approaching "sharp white backlash to minority racism and cultural degeneration" when he published *The Dispossessed Majority*, two decades later, Robertson had become despondent: "America, as we have known it, is beyond saving." Writing against the backdrop of the breakup of the Soviet Union, the waning of Communism, and nascent post–Cold War globalization, Robertson rued the predicaments of Europe and America. The darkest storm cloud was modernization, under which churned the deleterious forces of globalism, feminism, and multiracialism. The sole salvation would be a "new form of government that would transform socially destructive forces into socially constructive forces."[42] Race and race alone would be the organizing principle behind this transformation; the renewal of order would depend on "devolution," or the reemergence of natural human hierarchies predicated on inherent differences among racial groups and communal connections to place and ancestry. In this configuration "men and women of similar biological and cultural background" would thrive among their own.

A dedicated homeland would allow whites to stave off extinction and eventually retake their spot atop the racial apex, on their own territorial terms. Ethnostates would be "lifeboats to keep whites alive until they recover their spirits and morale." Robertson reminded his readers that, by definition, "an ethnostate has room for only one race." As self-sufficient, insular units, ethnostates would avoid chaos and fractiousness. They would be streamlined and contained: "The history of an ethnostate will be the history of one people in one chronological and one geographic frame." The perimeters around the white ethnostate would need to be firmly guarded, with "heavy restrictions on immigration. Xenophilia should not be the order of the day." Robertson did recognize that "the relocation of 30 million American Negroes . . . would present massive logistical problems," and like his alt-right successors, he pictured them moving to a black ethnostate in the South. Conversely, the Jewish problem was easier to solve: they could move to Israel. The geographical dispensation for Jews who opted out was an enclave "across the East River from Manhattan." *The Ethnostate* gilded alt-right doublespeak. On the one hand, if whites wanted to salvage their superlative civilization and "again take their place in the vanguard of the Great Evolutionary Trek," draconian measures of exclusion, removal, and displacement were imperative. On the other hand, the ethnostate was pitched as a magnanimous plan with universal appeal: "The beauty of the ethnostate is that, although it rests solidly on race, it promises great benefits to all races. In no way does it suggest the superiority of any one race, subrace or population group."

Robertson conceived of the ethnostate as a eugenic laboratory, and indeed, he had a great deal of experience with the American eugenics movement. For decades, he was closely connected to the Pioneer Fund, an organization founded in 1937 by the textile magnate and Nazi sympathizer Wickliffe Draper to support projects "tailored to meet his goals of immigration restriction and racial separation."[43] It was established to ensure that the nativist priorities of the American eugenics movement could continue to be promoted at a time when prominent geneticists and anthropologists were criticizing that movement's crude racism. The Pioneer Fund was so extreme that its first president, Frederick Osborn, a eugenicist who eschewed racial hierarchies in favor of a broader understanding of the distribution of genetic traits, resigned. Yet hardline eugenics resonated with Robertson; he published *The Dispossessed Majority* thanks to financial support from the Pioneer Fund.

Although there is no visible money trail from the Pioneer Fund to the publication of *The Ethnostate*, this manifesto is a decidedly pro-eugenics project that underscores the relevance of race to intellectual capacity and white women's social mandate to propagate hearty alabaster babies. The implementation of eugenic policies inevitably would produce a "bumper crop of gifted children," and the environment would foster the rearing of "top-of-the-line statesmen." Given the ethnostate's homogeneous whiteness, accusations of racism would be moot, and "both positive and negative eugenics programs can be put in place in an ethnostate without the necessity of imposing harsh and seemingly inhuman rules and regulations."[44] Robertson's ethnostate eerily resembles the Big Brother world in the science fiction film *Gattaca*, in which parents are required to meet with a genetic advisor to review the advantageous and deleterious traits of their children. Writes Robertson, "What is the harm of a 'genetic report card' that lists the inborn and inherited qualities and capabilities of every infant?"[45] Robertson thought the tools of genetic testing would allow the leaders of the ethnostate to measure natural aptitude, inborn abilities, and predispositions to disease with precision, and use scientific tools for predictive purposes. Mimicking Aldous Huxley's *Brave New World*, the Alphas, Betas, and Omegas would be assigned genetically appropriate functions in the ethnostate and reproduction would be scientifically managed.[46]

If eugenic surveillance would lead to biological enhancement, eco-consciousness would encourage an organic and fruitful relationship to the homeland. Anticipating the alt-right, Robertson arrogated ideas from the Left: his prototype for the ethnostate was the bioregion, "part of the earth's surface where there is a more-or-less distinct geographical, biological, horticultural and climatic identity."[47] Robertson was keenly aware of the first bioregional congress, held in Missouri in 1980, where Ozarkia and Cascadia were discussed. The eco-consciousness of the Green Party, with its focus on local sustainable communities, greatly appealed to Robertson. But he wanted to apply a "racial angle," so that the bioregion would be a refuge from white genocide and a cradle for racial revitalization.[48] The appendix of his book includes a list of "probable and improbable ethnostates in North America" for whites and nonwhites.[49] They include Cumberland, Aztlán, the Nation of Islam, Indian territories, and Dixie, as well as Ecotopia, which extended from Northern California to the Canadian border.

Robertson's ethnostate had an intertwined eugenic and environmentalist parentage that dated back to early twentieth century, when racialists like Madison Grant, author of *The Passing of the Great Race*, compared the extinction of the white race to the endangerment of redwoods and various animal species, and espoused the protection of native-born Americans against swarthy, undesirable "new immigrants" hailing from southern and eastern Europe.[50] After World War II, this preservationism morphed into a strain of environmentalism alarmed by immigration and overpopulation, and which was championed by vocal segments of the Sierra Club.[51] The Pioneer Fund connects the financial dots between these population-control efforts, the activities of the Federation for American Immigration Reform (FAIR), and American Renaissance.[52] Following this trajectory, the concept of the ethnostate slides into alt-right thinking, furthered by affinities with eco-fascism and deep ecology, both of which consecrate the relationship between European man and nature, tethered to the tenets of "inegalitarianism, hierarchy, and order."[53]

CASCADIA AND THE LURE OF THE WEST

There is no dearth of schemes for partitioned lands in America, most advocated by ethnonationalists. One plan turns Alaska into New Europa to receive "persecuted whites."[54] Another aggregates Maine, Vermont, and New Hampshire and "places nearby" into New Albion, a "preserve for western culture first and foremost" that capitalizes on the tri-state's 95 percent white population.[55] Ozarkia would be an ethnostate with forty counties in Arkansas and Missouri that exceed 95 percent white residents, and Gulflandia would stretch from the Atlantic coast of Florida to Brownsville, Texas.[56] Dependably blue California is not immune to such bids. Twenty-one counties in inland Northern California, which are less diverse and more conservative than the Blue Coast, want to extricate themselves to form the 1.7 million-person-strong state of Jefferson.[57] Other proposals abound, such as Calexit (turning California into three or six states), Texas secession (a persistent scheme most recently called Texit), and a convoluted attempt in the early 2010s to establish the Second Vermont Republic (the first was in the late 1700s), which illustrates that in overwhelmingly white regions like the upper Northeast, liberal pipedreams of breakaway states are a hair's breadth away from becoming neo-Confederate models.[58]

If the South deals the full secessionist deck, the Pacific Northwest is the wildcard. No region is a more powerful magnet for dreams of geographical separation, across the political spectrum, than Cascadia, the verdant bioregion conjoining Oregon, Washington, and Northern California.[59] So named in the 1820s by a Scottish naturalist, Cascadia has been the beloved subject of eco-poets, like Gary Snyder and Denise Levertov, and has inspired quixotic plans for regional autonomy.[60] For instance, the Cascadia Independence Party advocates for a "free and sustainable" bioregion detached from the United States and committed to sustainability and self-sufficiency. Its platform is "inclusive, welding residents of the USA, British Columbia, First Nations and Native Americans into a strong and dynamic regional community . . . outside the current liberal/conservative paradigm."[61]

Cascadia's standing as a countercultural utopia was elevated by a signature novel of the environmental movement. Published in 1975 by Ernest Callenbach, *Ecotopia: The Notebooks and Reports of William Weston* recounts the visit of the first journalist permitted to enter the fictional

Ecotopia and chronicle its way of life, nineteen years after its secession in 1980.[62] Weston finds a lush land, where Ecotopians live in harmony with nature, which has reverted to a sprawling, bounteous, and unruly garden. Ecotopians lead simple and fulfilling lives and are liberated from the bourgeois distractions of modernity. Weston initially feels very much an outsider, but he soon falls in love with a woman with whom he has a carnal bond. Weston's communion with his Ecotopian lover culminates in a spiritual and epiphanous homecoming: "I heard my own voice saying: 'I am going to stay in Ecotopia.'"[63]

Tapping into utopian dreams of Cascadia, Callenbach's Ecotopia is green in politics and foliage, and possessing a female president, tilts toward feminism. Nevertheless, Ecotopia is a white ethnostate: "There are surprisingly few dark-skinned faces on San Francisco streets." After independence, blacks desired separation in response to white domination. They were joined by the Chinese, and eventually the "black areas" and Chinatown became "officially designated city-states within Ecotopia."[64] This novel often is celebrated as a utopian reverie of the Green counterculture of the 1970s; however, it indulges heavily in the narcissism of one white man's metaphysical awakening proxied through feminized and sexualized nature. Strikingly, if the region's matriarch were replaced by a patriarch, Ecotopia would become an ethnostate satisfactory to many white nationalists. Moreover, Ecotopia envisions a future of geographical fragmentation, "away from the former greatness of America, unified in spirit 'from sea to shining sea'" to a patchwork of "small, culturally homogeneous groupings."[65]

That Ecotopia would be uniformly white is not that surprising given the Pacific Northwest's demographics. Four decades after the publication of this novel, and even with increasing racial diversification, approximately 87 percent of Oregonians are white and 80 percent of Washingtonians are white.[66] Moreover, the Cascadian stronghold of Oregon carries the distinction of being the "only state ever admitted with a black exclusion clause in its constitution."[67] This helps explain why the alt-right wunderkind James Allsup, raised in eastern Washington, could nonchalantly call the Pacific Northwest a "proto-ethnostate" in a talk delivered at an ethnonationalist forum in spring 2018 and why Greg Johnson could indulge in visualizing "West-Coast white nationalism."[68] The irony is that even the most politically progressive platforms for Cascadian independence would, by demographic default, grant white nationalists "their wish to create a white ethno-state."[69]

The contestation over the racial and political direction of the Pacific Northwest is illustrated by the short-lived white nationalist True Cascadia, organized in 2016 "to promote a white ethnic consciousness in the Pacific Northwest," foster traditionalism, and stop nonwhite immigration.[70] True Cascadia emerged as a discussion group on the Right Stuff website, evolving into an in-person organization based in Seattle. Evincing little originality, its emblem was the triangular logo developed previously by lovers of Cascadia but now stamped with the token words "Heritage, Tradition, and Solidarity" on the outer bands. Red Ice TV got wind of these efforts, and Lana Lokteff of *Radio 3Fourteen* interviewed three True Cascadia representatives. They reported activity in Oregon, Washington, Northern California, and Idaho, boasting that they were bringing "new people entirely" to the cause.[71] Despite these plans for expansion, YouTube comments indicate that True Cascadia did not respond promptly if at all to membership requests. At the same time, this group's mission did not sit well with their co-Cascadians, as antifa commandeered their website, rebranding truecascadia.com as "your foremost anti-hate, anti-fascist, anti-capitalist group in the Pacific Northwest."[72]

True Cascadia fizzled out. It is but the latest in a long procession of real and metaphorical white homelands in the Northwest. Indeed, the "Great White Northwest" has been a notorious epicenter of white power groups. The Southern Poverty Law Center currently counts over twenty hate groups operating in Washington alone. In the late twentieth century, the Order and Aryan Nations hunkered down in Idaho and Washington, feverishly prepping for race wars and federal raids.[73] They were joined by the Northwest Front, "a political organization of Aryan men and women in the United States and Canada, of all ages and social backgrounds, who recognize that an independent and sovereign White nation in the Pacific Northwest is the only possibility for the survival of the White race on this continent."[74] Its late founder, Harold Covington, was resolute, declaring that the survival of the white race on Earth is non-negotiable and that homosexuality, miscegenation, and gambling would be outlawed. He posted online charter documents for the Northwest American Republic (which would include Oregon, Washington, Idaho, and western Montana), including a constitution and "Principles of Migration." Appropriating the color scheme often associated with dreams of Cascadia, Covington riffed a tricolor flag to convey the nationalist message: "The sky is the blue, and the land is the green. The white is for the people in between."[75] From 2010 until his death in summer 2018, Covington hosted a weekly radio show, delivering a hodge-podge of political commentary and folksy rambling, prefaced by Celtic music.[76] He assured listeners, not very persuasively, that whites were quietly moving to the region and that a homeland would one day prevail.

Covington wrote four novels, each of which depicts a race war culminating in an America purged of people of color. *The Brigade*, his first book in the quartet, "encompasses all of the elements of the first three novels jammed into one."[77] It chronicles a small group of men as they journey from being the sorry victims of enforced cultural diversity, feminism, anti-hate speech, Jewish influence, and unemployment to valiant rebels with a cause: to incite warfare against a broken system and a government that unjustly persecutes them. Replete with gratuitous and grotesque scenes of shocking violence, delivered in clunky sentences, this book revels in the murder of multitudes of nonwhite people and degenerate whites like "lesbo bitches."[78] It also pays homage to the Pacific Northwest region. In addition to its 80-plus percent white population, the terrain is conducive to waging attacks. One of the characters (and the coordinator of the burgeoning Northwest Volunteer Army brigade) lays out the benefits of the topography: "I don't know if it's hit you guys yet, but you're sitting right in the middle of perfect guerilla country here. Huge expanses of heavy forest, mountains, and ravines where you could hide an army, and where maybe we will someday." Like the frontiersmen of yesteryear, white men can reach their natural fighting potential in the Northwest. Rugged nature becomes an ally to white liberation; their enemies will never beat "the white man of the Northwest in his pickup truck, his blue jeans and his baseball cap, with a pistol stuck in his belt and a backpack full of Semtex, on the rainy streets of Seattle."[79]

This novel illustrates the lure of the Pacific Northwest in the white nationalist imagination. Jam-packed with jerky Rambo-esque enactments of white masculinity, it offers a crash course in how white nationalism scapegoats, dehumanizes, and dismembers its way to the White Republic through the bullets and bombs of its vindicated martyrs. It is pornographic fantasy literature that captures the fury and frustration of some misanthropic white men. However, it also is a fading genre that has moved largely to live-action role playing (LARP) video games and is scorned by the college-educated alt-righters who have no room for LARPers, "Hollywood Nazis," and stormtroopers in their movement. Among the alt-right today, there are barbed debates about who should embody, literally and symbolically, the alt-right. These manifest in the possessive policing of whiteness, which is conceived in genetic, ideological, and existential terms.

WHITE ENOUGH?

There is a lot of hand-wringing among alt-right patricians and plebeians alike about the mechanics of creating and maintaining the white ethnostate. A search for "ethnostate" on Reddit r/DebateAltRight yields a plethora of questions: Where would the white ethnostate be located? Would outsiders be incentivized to leave or forcibly deported? Would church attendance be mandatory? Would mixed-race people have any place in the ethnostate? What percentage of whiteness is the threshold? What about Jews and white liberals who want to be part of such a territory?[80] While Reddit users discuss the terms and scope of the ethnostate, a contingent of alt-right thinkers, building on the legacy of Robertson's *The Ethnostate*, have been entertaining possible answers.

Most designs imagine distinct territories for blacks and Latina/os, and assume that Native Americans will stay on their reservations and that Jews will emigrate to Israel. The fate of Asian Americans, who receive scant consideration in ethnostate planning, is uncertain, as is the whereabouts of millions of mixed-race Americans, white liberal defectors, and the multitudes disqualified due to gender, sexuality, or politics. The mechanics of such ethnoracial geographical reshuffling usually are glossed over, although one white nationalist suggests the passage of a Minority Relocation Act and the formation of an agency called HEARTLAND (Helping Euro-Americans Reclaim their Land and National Destiny) to oversee repatriations. As for the polyglot contingent, they will reside alongside "homosexuals and gamblers" in the "Alternate Culture Zone."[81]

The consensus threshold for whites would correspond to the 1950 US census: "I believe that a white ethnostate that is 90% white, 8% part-white-half-not black, and 2% other will be sufficient."[82] This 90 percent solution begs the questions "Who is white?" and "According to what criteria?" Even though white nationalist rhetoric is beholden to the idea that race is encoded in biology, and that racial and gender differences are innate, they shy away from exact genetic formulas. Perhaps this reflects the surprise and dissatisfaction experienced by some white nationalists when DNA and ancestry testing reveal unexpected results, such as African or Asian heritage, which would exclude them perforce from the white ethnostate.[83]

Perhaps, however, alt-right conceptions of whiteness can be better explained by the groupthink assumptions about racial differences and belonging that characterize white nationalism. Beyond the baseline definition that "white people are the aboriginal peoples of Europe and their unmixed descendants around the world," the alt-right leans toward a vague doctrine of tacit and intuitive recognition of one's own people.[84] Using Johnson's go-to analogy, just like a grocery shopper can distinguish between lettuce and a cabbage, "we know whites when we see them."[85] Endowed with a white-dar, future ethnostaters can differentiate among the white, nonwhite, and almost white. This acute racial perception itself is an artifact of historical context and the white identity politics the alt-right longs for; as America becomes browner, white people necessarily will become more cognizant of their racial identity. If white identity politics gains more traction, the alt-right will be waiting, with red pills in hand, hoping to convert the awoken. If they get lucky, they will manage to sway a few white liberals wallowing in white guilt, caused by some combination of multiculturalism, feminism, and whites' own misguided penchant for altruism and kindness. Encased in this construction of whiteness is the alt-right's wish for metapolitical awakening: "Our people need to *think* that we are a distinct race, with a distinct white identity and interests."[86]

However, white nationalists also indicate that this visceral art of recognition will not suffice for determining insiders and outsiders, particularly when it comes to "edge cases" that test the boundaries of belonging in the white ethnostate. To address this thorny classification problem, the *Counter-Currents* webzine writer Spencer J. Quinn developed "vetting algorithms" to evaluate admittance to the ethnostate and be prepared "ahead of time." Striving for scientific metrics, his three-part series includes a flow chart with possible pathways; a table delineating rights for those with full, partial, and minimal citizenship; and an Excel spreadsheet with weighted calculations for "racial vetting."[87] Quinn concedes this is an imperfect exercise that will leave some feeling as though he has been too harsh and others jeering him as a "cuck" who did not go far enough.

The upshot of this vetting schema is predictable—it replicates white supremacy's annhilation of blackness. The one-drop rule reigns: almost without exception, being more than one-sixteenth black bars people from the white ethnostate. To wit, the three core criteria for inclusion are 1) having at least three white grandparents and no black grandparents; 2) not having a black spouse; and 3) being of "good character" (cue the 1790 Naturalization Law). Only people who meet these requirements with no questions asked can proceed through the portal and claim full citizenship; as percentages indicate, this group will constitute the vetted 90 percent of verified whites. This does leave wiggle room for ethnostaters with, for example, an Asian or Latina/o grandparent. There is less concern for purging nonwhite ethnostate residents who are past reproductive age—they will be allowed to stay since their days are numbered. The implication is that the children born of these vetted parents, each of whom is three-quarters white, will comfortably meet the racial litmus test and perpetuate whiteness over time. Indeed, one of the strictest rules relates to children: "It's cruel, certainly, but non-white children simply cannot stay in a white ethnostate."[88] This pertains to white parents of adopted nonwhite children, who will have to find another homeland.

The remaining 10 percent will be judged on a case-by-case basis, and only the "pick of the non-white litter" will pass through the door.[89] The non-white spouses of white ethnostaters would be required to undergo such scrutiny. In many cases, these superlative outliers would bring skills, knowledge, and wealth to the white ethnostate. Demonstration of good character, specifically high marks in behavior, patriotism, and ideology, is critical. For instance, if someone has supported Black Lives Matter, La Raza, or the detested Southern Poverty Law Center, it is almost guaranteed that person would not pass ethnostate muster. While "homosexuals" would not be banished, they would not be able to marry, and the preference would be for heterosexuals expected to wed and procreate. Whites who had served time in prison or were drug addicts might qualify albeit with probationary status. But the individuals in this group, by virtue of standing outside the perimeter of whiteness, would only qualify for partial or minimal citizenship, meaning they could not hold leadership positions or bear firearms, and would pay higher taxes. The privileges of whiteness would be baked into this tiered system with no possibility of climbing up a notch in citizenship status (although everyone, even the 90 percent, would be subject to demotion for character violations).

Although no estimates are given, the bottleneck for the 10 percent is narrow. The vetting flowchart maps a direct sequence to full citizenship only for whites with good character; about fifteen additional criteria, which range from "security risk" to "voluntary military service," in just a few scenarios, lead to partial or minimal citizenship. More likely outcomes are removal to the reservation (for American Indians), repatriation, rejection, and deportation. The contorted dynamics of evaluation, which fluctuate from drastic to arbitrary, are on display in the consideration of a handful of real-life scenarios. For instance, conservative commentator Michelle Malkin, a "full-blooded Filipino who is married to a full-blooded Jew," would not make the cut despite her anti-immigration sentiments; "to make an exception for Malkin would simply undermine the entire vetting process and the very point of an ethnostate."[90] Milo Yiannopoulos would not be undone by his "flamboyant gay man schtick" but because he trashed the alt-right. Even though the ethnostate would need residents with talents in science, technology, and engineering (STEM), who could build and innovate, an Asian engineer would be barred due to his race (fewer than three white grandparents) and lack of English. However, "a Hispanic military general with impeccable service and pro-white credentials" would receive a .53 on weighted scores for nonwhites and thus be allowed into the ethnostate, only, of course, as a partial citizen.[91]

The most complicated and fraught "edge case" is the Jewish Question, or JQ. Despite their intricacies, Quinn's vetting algorithms do not tackle the fraught JQ. It is common alt-right knowledge that some well-known nationalists like Paul Gottfried, who coined "alternative right," are Jewish. A minority of alt-righters begrudgingly accepts Jews with proven credentials. For instance, the well-known white nationalist Jared Taylor maintains that Jewish allies who have attested their commitment to the cause can be granted entry into the sanctum of whiteness. Others equivocate on the JQ, punting the issue by invoking Israel as the go-to Jewish ethnostate. The bottom line, however, is that the anti-Semitic blade of the alt-right is sharp and tipped for blood. In fact, most white nationalists see a Jewish stranglehold on American society that fuels multiculturalism and feminism and hence accelerates white extinction, constituting the largest obstacle to the white ethnostate. As one blogger asserts, "It is the Jew and the Jew only that stands in the way," adding, "Without first formulating a plan to remove these subversives from their positions of control," such a plan is "100% pointless. It is, without question, putting the cart before the horse."[92] Anti-Semitism is a ferocious black hole in the alt-right cosmos, and no conversation about the ethnostate can proceed very far without the demonization and dehumanization of Jews. At the same time, alt-right whiteness revolves around the eradication of blackness and the perpetual policing of intraracial differences, ascertained by phenotype, personality, and political beliefs.

Alt-right leaders hope to attach a dignified image to the ethnostate. The impossibility of creating an actual "homogenous homeland" should not induce a sense of complacency among those who find the proposal frightening or ludicrous. The ethnostate's premise of cleansing and separation, which fuels calls for intensified deportations, the revocation of birthright citizenship, and the annulment of naturalization of those lacking "good character," is running roughshod over America. The impulse of ethnic cleansing underlays the dispatching of thousands of troops to the Southwestern border and the heartless cruelty enacted on undocumented migrants and their children and families. For alt-righters the ethnostate is the envisioned outcome of their metapolitical efforts, reaped after extensive red pilling and the mobilization of masses of enlivened whites intent on returning to the demographic makeup of 1965 America. In this schema, the white ethnostate would be the new normal. Consider, for example, the well-groomed boys of Identity Evropa, who embody a hip identitarianism that aims to extirpate every last vestige of diversity and multiculturalism.[93] As one Identity Evropa member explained at a recent gathering: "I think there's a better way to sell it than explicitly saying 'ethnostate,'" namely a "white supermajority."[94]

CHAPTER 4

CAT LADIES, WOLVES, AND LOBSTERS

A Menagerie of Biological Essentialism

"The West Is the Best!"[1] That's the motto of the Proud Boys, a men's group launched in 2016 by Gavin McInnes, controversial cofounder of Vice Media and a jester-provocateur who hovers on the outer rings of the alt-right. "Proud of Your Boy," a song from the musical *Aladdin* inspired the group's name. The Proud Boys bemoan that men are falling behind, becoming depressed and marginalized, and have nostalgia for a time when "girls were girls and men were men."[2] The main culprits of this desolation are feminism and leftism, which, according to the Proud Boys, spur women to assume ill-fitting male roles based on the specious logic of gender equity. The cure for this malaise is the full restitution of the male/female "biological binary."[3]

To fulfill their half of the binary, Proud Boys man up through bonding rituals—hanging out and drinking beer—and undergoing a three-phase initiation. Declaring oneself a Proud Boy is, in their lingo, the "first degree" of this fraternal hazing. The second degree has two steps. The first is you "get the crap beaten out of you by at least five guys until you can name five breakfast cereals."[4] The second is #NoWanks, or restricting porn to "once every 30 days" and having permission to "ejaculate [if he is] within one yard of a woman with her consent." The third degree is branding with a Proud Boy tattoo. These frat boy antics and exercises in sexual abnegation are meant to inculcate "adrenaline control" and to get single men "off the couch and talking to women" and married men off their screens and "back into bed" with their wives. The Proud Boys' jocular form of confidence building strives to make fathers out of slackers; it pushes its members "to settle down and have kids." McInnes boasts that their veneration of the housewife has earned them a "big female following," dubbed the Proud Boys' Girls, who crave such cocksure and dependable men.[5]

The Proud Boys is a staunchly antifeminist group. As demonstrated by its motto, it also is unabashedly pro-Western. Its members describe themselves as "Western chauvinists" who "refuse to apologize for creating the modern world." These #NoWankers once were "ashamed of themselves" and accepted the "blame for slavery, the wage gap, ableism, and some fag-bashing that went on two generations ago." But now they have shed that white guilt and chest-thump about the "greatest culture in the world."[6] Yet, according to McInnes, "the greatest fraternal organization in the world" is not prejudiced; it welcomes all races, religions, and sexual preferences. The Proud Boys walk a fine line—professing to be anti-SJW (social justice warrior) "without being alt-right."[7] As one Proud Boy put it, "We're like the alt-right without the racism."[8]

Despite these punchy proclamations of inclusivity and anti-racism, most of the men who joined the Proud Boys when it was formed in 2016 were white, straight, and aggrieved. They embodied the profile fleshed out in Michael Kimmel's study of the contemporary crisis of masculinity in America: white men of overlapping generations with faith in the American Dream who came of age "believing they would inevitably take their places somewhere on the economic ladder, simply by being themselves." They never realized or had to comprehend the extent to which the "deck was stacked in their favor for generations." They are hostile to notions of equality and diversity, which promise not to improve their lot but to humiliate and displace them. This nagging sensation of dispossession and impotence, Kimmel argues, "is the source of their rage."[9]

For this demographic, the internet is the go-to place to blow off steam, usually in the form of unbridled sexism and racism.[10] In cyberspace, the anonymity and ephemerality of avatars and message boards enable perpetual re-tweeting and re-meming of hateful posts with no accountability.

Even if users are LGBTQ-friendly millennials in real life, their online activity, especially in nameless forums, frequently follows hackneyed homophobic scripts, excoriating betas on the left, right, and center.[11] Great contempt is held for "cucks," particularly those on the conservative side of the aisle, who are viewed as the epitome of traitors to vigorous white manhood. An alt-right neologism, "cuckservative," derived from the Old English "cuckold," was devised to describe establishment Republicans who are selling out to diversity speak and civic nationalism; being "cucked" is represented, often visually, by their wife having sex with another man, usually a black man, while the cuckservative raptly watches.[12]

Mike Wendling, a British journalist who explores the heterogeneous typology of alt-righters in his book *Alt-Right*, spent a lot of time on 4chan and Reddit's r/The_Donald, reaching out to American alt-righters. Rather than encountering "a cool posse of young intelligent kids," the self-image aggrandized by many on the alt-right, the decidedly unscientific sample of men Wendling interacted with online was "older—in some cases old— and skewed working class."[13] Wendling suggests that many angry white men online "might be internet-savvy, but they're not particularly young, or countercultural. Mostly they seem to just harbor lingering resentments against political correctness, and their actions tumble forth from there."[14] Although its members slant toward the younger crowd, and their modus operandi includes meeting off-screen to drink beer and stir up trouble, the Proud Boys fit this profile of male embitterment.

It is ironic that Dante Nero, an African American comedian friendly with McInnes, devised #NoWanks. He wanted to encourage men to be less self-obsessed and more empathetic in their encounters with women. As Nero's novelty became the group's hallmark, he observed a troubling trend that flew in the face of its message of inclusivity. As the Proud Boys grew in numbers during the 2016 presidential campaign, it swelled with Trump supporters who plastered Facebook walls with racial epithets directed at blacks and Jews. Nero was taken aback by the intense racism and the "perception of being disenfranchised" expressed by the white guys flocking to the Proud Boys.[15]

After he learned about this, McInnes spanked his acolytes for their wrathful and off-color remarks, and vocally defended his buddy Nero. Nevertheless, white nationalists found the Proud Boys to be a receptive and raucous haven for their angst about male victimhood and cultural dispossession. Indeed, Jason Kessler, who co-organized both Unite the Right rallies, was a member of the Virginia chapter, and several Proud Boys marched in Charlottesville with him in 2017.[16] Proud Boys have joined the pugnacious Patriot Prayer, a loud far-right and pro-Trump group founded in Portland, Oregon, for pitched skirmishes against antifa in the streets of their hometown and Seattle.[17] The Southern Oregon Proud Boys chapter Facebook page features a pastiche celebrating gun culture, condemning sanctuary cities, and blasting Mexican immigrants.[18] More recently, men of color are joining the Proud Boys, where they can vociferously exclaim their macho contempt for leftists, immigrants, and Muslims.[19] Given the rank and file's adherence to Western chauvinism, and McInnes's previous collaborations with organizations such as the anti-immigrant VDARE and American Renaissance, the Southern Poverty Law Center added the Proud Boys to its roster of hate groups.[20] The antics of its members, which on a dime turn from boisterous to bloody, often foist the Proud Boys into the news. In August 2018, on the eve of the second Unite the Right rally, Twitter suspended the account of McInnes and the Proud Boys based on its "policy prohibiting violent extremist groups."[21] In fall 2018 a riled-up posse of Proud Boys brawled on the Upper East Side of Manhattan after leaving a speech given by McInnes at the Metropolitan Republican Club.[22] Supposedly a plastic bottle thrown their way by protestors who had staked out the event prompted the Proud Boys, who were joined by the local skinhead group 211 Boot Boys, to beat up three people.[23] New York governor Andrew Cuomo called for an FBI investigation, and the NYPD arrested five Proud Boys for their role in the incident.[24] Soon after these legal developments, McInnes announced in a YouTube video that he was leaving the Proud Boys, a maneuver orchestrated as "100% a legal gesture" intended to help "alleviat[e] the sentencing" of the nine men ultimately arrested for the brawl.[25]

McInnes, who glibly calls the Proud Boys a latter-day "Elks Lodge," has decried its characterization as Far Right and fascist, and blames this ostensible exaggeration on leftists and the liberal media, who, he says, hysterically associate every group that extols the West with neo-Nazis and the KKK. After Charlottesville, which he did not attend, McInnes tried to distance the Proud Boys from that debacle. On his YouTube channel, McInnes chastised Proud Boys who participated in Unite the Right, declaring that "all white nationalists/anti-Semites are banned from Proud

Boys" whether they express racial ideas or not. "We Are Not Alt-Right" was splashed across media platforms to insist that the group diverges from the alt-right on "the 'JQ' [Jewish Question] and racial identity politics," the implication being that this dual repudiation ipso facto disqualified the Proud Boys from the alt-right.[26]

McInnes might be naive, calculating, or duplicitous. He certainly resorts to the ruse of asserting plausible deniability and offering up excuses of irony or ignorance.[27] But the motives behind his inconsistent approach are difficult to ascertain and not ultimately relevant to understanding the Proud Boys phenomenon. The bigger and more interesting question is the nature of the relationship of the Proud Boys' masturbatory and hypermasculinist obsessions to the alt-right-verse. An Escherian stairwell built on the ideological affinities of anti-feminism, xenophobia, and racial othering connects the Proud Boys to the alt-right. Moreover, these prejudices are anchored to a rigid dogma of innate biological differences and natural hierarchies, and a corollary belief that the sacrosanct order of Western society is being dismantled at a vertiginous pace, rushing toward several possible endpoints, all of them tragic for white men and European peoples.[28] From this vantage point, the future of "white well-being" hinges on the (re)imposition of natural hierarchies and biological differences.[29]

Race might be the master switch of the alt-right circuit board, but it does not operate at full capacity without the currents of gender and sexuality. When men carrying tiki torches through the streets of Charlottesville chanted, "You will not replace us," they were referring to the perceived takeover of white America by Jews and immigrants. However, the gendered implications of "The Great Replacement" were not trailing far behind. From the white nationalist viewpoint, it is incumbent upon white women to take on their ordained roles as mothers and breeders to forestall white genocide, which could be a mere few generations ahead. Motivated by these concerns, a small contingent of white women, such as the Canadian Faith Goldy, in 2017 a rising star at Rebel Media (but who subsequently was fired after appearing on a Daily Stormer podcast), and Lana Lokteff, who runs Red Ice TV with her Swedish husband, attended the Charlottesville march to represent the TradLife (traditional life) flank of white nationalists.[30] Ayla Stewart, aka Wife with a Purpose, whose webpage tagline is "the restoration and preservation of traditional values," had planned to join them, but ultimately did not attend, citing security concerns, and she blamed the violence on the local police. Stewart delivered the speech she had prepared on her YouTube channel.[31]

Alt-right men and women alike concur that a massive roadblock to the restoration of the White Republic is feminism, which is the archenemy of natural hierarchies and gender binaries. As the late British nationalist Jonathan Bowden, an intellectual maharishi among the American alt-right, asserted in a 2011 lecture titled "Feminism: Lilith Before Eve," feminism has "turned the world upside down in 50 to 60 years."[32] It has emasculated men and masculinized women. To right the ship, new movements must advance one of the "most powerful political discourses that can ever be enunciated"—the biological truth of "traditional male and female role models." The alt-right certainly is not the first movement to enshrine "differentiation as the key to advancement."[33] Conservatives and fascists in a variety of sociohistorical contexts have foregrounded the gendered idea that "roles and identities are essential" and "are fixed in biology and spirit."[34] Moreover, feminist scholars have elucidated how in Europe and the Americas nationalist ideologies are intertwined with deep-seated concerns about the fortitude of white masculinity.

The Alt-Light Turnstile

The alt-right and so-called alt-light are engaged in low-intensity warfare that periodically flares with verbal firebombs. Yet these sparring camps share the same gender politics, characterized by deep-seated anti-feminism and transphobia. Until he became persona non grata after the discovery of a YouTube video in which he countenanced pedophilia, Milo Yiannopoulos, who had capitalized on his own brand of flamboyant queerness, was a lightning rod for the alt-light. He titillated, astounded, and red pilled audiences with his incessant recitation of the provocation "Feminism is cancer" and his tirades against women and trans folks.[35] In typical alt-fashion, Yiannopoulos responded to criticism of his gross sexism with the favorite retort of trollers, namely that his detractors could not grasp a joke.

The alt-light is prone to dog-whistling, promoting conspiracy theories, and spreading disinformation, and its roster of media personalities include the now de-platformed bombastic Alex Jones of Infowars and provocateur Mike Cernovich, who is fixated on twisted tales of Democratic Party cabals and clandestine child sex-trafficking rings.[36] Much to the dismay of alt-righters, despite noticeable similarities, alt-lighters hedge and deflect, refusing to explicitly advocate white nationalism. For this reason, many alt-righters view Jones, Cernovich, McInnes, the politically incorrect YouTuber Stefan Molyneux, and others as menaces to the movement, "sopping up money and energy that could be used to liberate our people."[37] Nevertheless, the alt-light's retrograde gender politics make it an unfailing turnstile into the alt-right.[38] It dispenses legions of red pills and primes the pump of us-versus-them thinking, which is so central to white nationalist thinking.[39] The Southern Poverty Law Center recently conducted a study of social media patterns to explore the "pipeline between the alt-lite and racist 'alt-right.'" Gathering information from users on the Right Stuff website, they found that the most common introduction "to hardcore, veteran white nationalists" was via alt-lighters like McInnes and Molyneux. About 15 percent of respondents specifically "mentioned McInnes as a step in their path to white nationalism or recommended using his videos and writing to convert others."[40] Although the two top converters are 4chan's "Politically Incorrect" /pol/ forum and Jared Taylor, the doyen of race realism and head of American Renaissance, Molyneux ranked third and McInnes ranked fifth (of twenty-four total) in their influence, higher than Richard Spencer and Red Ice TV.

The alt-light/alt-right convergence is starkly captured by their indistinguishable panic over gender fluidity and gender nonbinariness. Several years before founding the Proud Boys, McInnes wrote a blog post titled "Transphobia Is Perfectly Natural," in which he contends that "trannies" and their SJW enthusiasts suffer from a collective delusion, and that they are destroying natural gender norms and manufacturing people with mutilated bodies.[41] Posted on thoughtcatalog.com, this rant was "reported by the community as hateful or abusive content" and removed, although it can be retrieved online with a Google search.[42] Greg Johnson of Counter-Currents indulges in similar trans-bashing in his book of essays *Truth, Justice, and a Nice White Country*.[43] Although these days Johnson derides McInnes as obnoxious and "coke-addled," he concurs with him that transphobia is "a perfectly natural feeling" of revulsion.[44] Transitioning from a cisgendered body to a transgendered body is tantamount to ontological sacrilege: "'Sex changes' do not change anyone's sex. They merely transform a man into a butchered simulacrum of a woman, or a woman into a butchered simulacrum of a man."[45] For Johnson and many alt-righters, "trannies" are the categorical destabilizers of biological binaries and gender roles. As the Scottish nationalist Millennial Woes, who travels in international alt-right circles, pronounced in one of his Ask Me Anything (AMA) videos on YouTube, "the trans thing is the most fundamental attack on a civilization."[46] For the alt-right, then, "trannies" provoke monumental dread. According to Johnson, they are scarier than antifa: "Like the lesbians of Berkeley, they can reduce a man to a skeleton in under 30 seconds."[47] To be trans is synonymous with the destruction of existential and embodied maleness, eliciting fears of castration: "I love my penis, and the thought of losing it fills me with horror."[48]

The same antipathy to gender nonbinariness propelled Jordan Peterson, the Canadian psychologist and best-selling author of the self-help book *12 Rules for Life*, into the media spotlight. Peterson made headlines in 2016 by announcing his vehement opposition to C-16, a bill in the Canadian parliament prohibiting discrimination on the basis of gender identity and expression.[49] Peterson claimed this legislation would obligate him to use alternative gender pronouns, which amounted to "compelled speech" imposed by the totalitarian Left, with its army of "social justice warrior, left-wing radical political activists" and "radical social constructionists."[50] Like McInnes and Molyneux, Peterson is scorned by the alt-right (although not without a tinge of envious admiration), which likes to cast him as a celebrity-hungry demagogue. In turn, he has criticized the alt-right as misguided and flirting with authoritarianism. Yet Peterson is the Pied Piper of red pills, reeling in thousands of young men and women through his sold-out book tours and Twitter (over 900,000 followers) and YouTube (more than 1.5 million followers) accounts. In his Canadian cadence, he enthralls them with lectures on the virulence of feminism and leftism and his exhortations for the imposition of order—coded as male—over chaos, coded as female.

On media venues such as the popular podcast hosted by Joe Rogan, Peterson dexterously employs alt-right lingo, throwing out terms such as "enforced monogamy" and "incels."[51] He combines calm and collected rhetoric with select empirical evidence to support the biological basis for natural hierarchies, which he attests are good for both women and men: "The thing that makes them [women] miserable is having weak partners." Women, he says, "want deeply men who are competent and powerful."[52] His preferred analogy for natural hierarchies are lobsters: "I use the lobster as the example.... We diverged from lobsters in evolutionary history about 350 million years ago, common ancestry. And lobsters exist in hierarchies. They have a nervous system attuned to the hierarchy. . . . And it's part of my attempt to demonstrate that the idea of hierarchy has absolutely nothing to do with sociocultural construction, which it doesn't."[53] In *12 Rules for Life*, Peterson writes that in the lobster universe, the female gravitates toward the alpha male, to whom she becomes "irresistibly attracted," and proceeds to exhibit her feminine charms. She "will disrobe, shedding her shell, making herself dangerously soft, vulnerable, and ready to mate."[54] Projecting his interpretation of the mating behavior of a lower order species that has existed since the age of dinosaurs to humans, Peterson paints with a primordial brush, driving home the point that evolutionary biology is destiny.

Peterson's pop psychology appeals to a wide spectrum and exemplifies the powerful role that ideas about gender, especially about masculinity, can play in politics, sometimes in unexpected ways. For example, a researcher who embedded herself within the alt-right after Trump's election was surprised to find that half (fifteen of thirty total) of the young white men she interviewed had campaigned for Bernie Sanders in the 2016 presidential election.[55] In a similar vein, on one of Identity Evropa's podcasts, one former "Bernie Bro" explained why he did a "total 180 in a few months."[56] As "antimale" and "antiwhite" rhetoric began to feel all pervasive to him, it simultaneously dawned on him why he had enjoyed living in Vermont (Sanders's home state), which is 95 percent white, earlier in his life. Young white male progressives are not immune to red pilling; in fact, their familiarity with progressive identity politics makes the identitarian politics of the alt-right legible to them.

Restoring the Biological Binary

The alt-right refers to many white women as "Cat Ladies." The stereotype is not one of spinsters living with a bevy of felines but of vapid women who want to rescue all creatures, including those from the "Parasite Class," such as undocumented immigrants and "African boat people."[57] Cat Ladies have been indoctrinated to foolishly accept and even coyly beckon Islam despite its patriarchal tendencies. The French New Right author Guillaume Faye, who is highly regarded among the alt-right literati, links Islam and feminism, viewing them as fire-breathing twins that are irretrievably enfeebling and wrecking European society. Alt-right authors also often collapse what they see as the dual destructive effects of feminism and Jewish influence, both of which sanction race mixing and unchecked immigration. According to long-time white nationalist Kevin MacDonald, the strong in-group preferences of Jews, coupled with their high intelligence, has resulted in their successful manipulation of resources and capital to control Western societies. His book *The Culture of Critique* features the age-old conspiracy theory of Jewish dominance (à la *The Protocols of the Elders of Zion*) masked in a scholarly facade.[58] MacDonald sees the Jews' conscious promotion of race mixing, immigration, and feminism as part of a concerted plot to leverage their media and financial power to hasten America's transition from a white-majority country to a nonwhite-majority country.

Locked arm in arm, feminists, Jews, and liberals have cemented the pathological altruism and ethnomasochism that dooms white society. They have self-righteously disrupted the gender binary and show no signs of abating; worse, they have created a world in which "cuckservatives" attend gay pride marches and might even praise Caitlyn Jenner. From the alt-right perspective, Western countries that should be preserving their heritage instead are Pollyannas rolling out the welcome mat for aliens and credulously engendering the conditions for demographic change. Liberal white women are the most culpable of this capitulation, acting as brainwashed gatekeepers who spent a lot of time "virtue signaling"—making sanctimonious proclamations to win moral brownie points in diversity-drunk American society.

The novel *The Camp of the Saints*, by the French novelist Jean Raspail, is integral to the alt-right canon and can be read as a harbinger of anxieties about hyperfeminization. Many Americans first heard about this book when Steve Bannon touted its prescience in speeches and media interviews that betrayed his strident xenophobia.[59] Yet *The Camp of the Saints* was known in nationalist and right-wing circles long before Bannon's rise to prominence during the 2016 Trump presidential campaign. Since its publication in 1973 (and translation into English in 1975), Raspail's novel has provided the narrative template and pathos for stories about immigrant invasions and the subsumption of the white race. The pretense of the story is that Hindus from the Ganges River region are invading France. Raspail demonizes these interlopers with a barrage of animalistic terms: they are "swarming all through," "spreading through cities," "worming their way by the thousands," and "slithering in."[60] Ultimately, they overrun French shores: "a million poor wretches, armed only with their weaknesses and their numbers, overwhelmed by misery, encumbered with starving brown and black children, ready to disembark on our soil, the vanguard of the multitudes pressing hard against every part of the tired and overfed West."[61] France succumbs to their onslaught, forfeiting its venerable culture and tradition. The desperate migrants, however, are only partially to blame. This foreign inundation would not have transpired without the softening of French society, without younger generations gripped by a "morbid, contagious excess of sentiment."[62] Alt-right YouTuber RamZPaul (Paul Ramsey) has referred to *The Camp of the Saints* as prophetic. He heralded this book when retweeting an image of a white European woman handing "bottled water to a migrant," with the caption that "helping an invading army used to be known as treason, but our enemies have rebranded it as 'humanitarian aid.'"[63] A post on the webzine *Chateau Heartiste*, a pivotal node in the manosphere, echoes RamZPaul. The caption under an image of African migrants arriving on Spanish shores reads the "Camp of the Saints happening right before our eyes."[64] Raspail is a hero among European identitarians, who have produced visual memes that feature a portrait of his face accompanied simply with the word "Saints," which serves as ethnonationalist code for the near inescapability of the Great Replacement.[65]

Some alt-right authors admit that the feminist movements of the 1960s unfolded for understandable reasons. Yet they are hypercritical of what they see as feminism's subsequent disruptive trajectory: "Deviations and excesses began to appear and feminism, from being a movement promoting equality of the sexes before the law, was transformed into an emotional ideology with egalitarian and extremist overtones."[66] Once past this tipping point, ever-hungry feminists launched into a vampire-like crusade to skew the gender order and violate basic principles of biology and nature. This narrative of overspilling and oozing feminism is repeated over and over by alt-righters. From their perspective, white women are afflicted with psychosexual complexes of massive proportions. They despise men, yet in an act of quintessential transference want to become them. For this reason, white women can easily become barren and unfulfilled. In the words of a *Counter-Currents* blogger: "I can pretty much guarantee you that these women aren't happy—childless and sucking down their

Diet Cokes at 47."[67] Moreover, this ravenous urge is leading to the evisceration of masculinity: "In practice, since the feminist can never be the equal of men at the male role, she concentrates her efforts upon sabotaging that role."[68] The alt-solution for gender disorder is to put women back in their "natural" place—to reestablish the biological binary through the formation of hypermasculinized tribes, patriarchal control of hypergamous women, and pronatalist incentives, as well as dating apps for white women to mate and propagate the race. The alt-right, and the alt-light for that matter, engages these approaches on a continuum that ranges from sentimental to punitive.

In its benevolent form, anti-feminism manifests in "gender complementarity," a construct in which men and women have different but equal roles to play. Once freed from the shackles of feminism, white women can return to reproduction and mothering. The British nationalist Mark Collett often takes to YouTube to expound on this vision. According to him, feminism has yanked white European women away from their natural motherly and nurturing instincts, and is impeding the coalescence of traditional families.[69] In addition to abetting demographic suicide, feminism demeans men, who are not embraced as loving partners, fathers, and husbands, merely as oppressors. Collett, more than most alt-righters, regularly broaches the topic of gender relations and has cohosted programs, such as "This Week on the Alt-Right," with women. He also has criticized the Men Going Their Own Way (MGTOW) and men's rights contingents of the alt-right for banishing women.[70]

Romanticized notions of white heterosexual relationships are another thread of the alt-right gender narrative, espoused by a handful of women, like Empress Wife, who, until her Twitter account was suspended, unapologetically praised white women who wanted to "preserve your people" while displaying nostalgic images of white families and gesturing to Nazi iconography.[71] To encourage white matchmaking, one alt-right woman started WhiteDate for European singles. With the tagline "We Have Woken Up," this service seeks to put "like-minded" white singles in contact in Europe and anglophone countries, sponsoring meet-ups and virtual groups.[72] Its website features a panorama of smiling couples enjoying romantic dinners and snuggling, chastely clothed, and informs searching singles that they can find mates with the same cultural heritage, assuring them that "we follow classic roles, where strong men take the lead, and graceful women play the game." Intermittently blocked on Twitter, WhiteDate nonetheless has over 1,500 followers, and its #White Family messaging about courtship and etiquette has a dedicated crowd on its website and on the microblogging platform Gab.

More often than not, however, alt-paternalism has an unforgiving dictatorial edge, and rather than being idealized, white women are trashed as devious sluts who deserve to be disciplined by daddy. According to men's rights activist F. Roger Devlin, author of *Sexual Utopia in Power: The Feminist Revolt Against Civilization*, women are programmed for hypergamy. While men are wired to spread their seed, given their endless supply of semen and ability to impregnate from puberty until senescence, women, with their finite ova, are much more selective about their mates. Hypergamy compels women to find the fittest genetic male specimen and the strongest protector; this pursuit of alphas makes women untrustworthy and fickle. In one of his podcasts, Molyneux derides a woman who supposedly poked holes in the condom of an unsuspecting guy because she wanted to have his baby and later extort him for child support. Hypergamous instincts motivated this incidence of "sperm jacking," a female trick to deceive unsuspecting men and potentially leave them in a state of "indentured servitude."[73]

In the view of the alt-right, managing hypergamy requires "enforced monogamy," most often in the form of traditional marriage, an arrangement advocated across the alt-light to alt-right continuum. Mandatory monogamy channels "female hypergamy in a socially useful way" and is the tried and true way for men to reinstate innate gender norms. As Devlin writes, "Men are supposed to have authority over women; that is part of what a marriage is."[74] In essence, these alt-right thinkers envisage the glorious return of the imperious paterfamilias, with men overseeing mating and matrimonial decisions for the benefit and propagation of the white race. Greg Johnson, for example, has suggested that it is imperative to "roll back sexual liberation by reestablishing social shaming for female promiscuity and, most importantly, involving the family—particularly fathers and brothers—in the process by which women choose suitors and husbands."[75]

If the yin of restoring order focuses on women, the yang is all about men. The alt-right drinks at a deep well of male narcissism, and thus it is not surprising that its men devote extensive energy to proposals for rebuilding manhood. Jack Donovan, author of *The Way of Men* and three other books on masculinity, carries the flag on this issue. His profile is similar to McInnes's; Donovan has been at the forefront of the men's rights movement, an early adapter in the manosphere, and a dependable amplifier of anti-feminism and anti-womanism.[76] Espousing male primitivism, he calls himself not a white nationalist but a "Wolves nationalist," referring to the Wolves of Vinland, a neo-Volkisch, neo-pagan survivalist group founded in Virginia that is listed on the Southern Poverty Law Center's hate map.[77] Donovan runs a Wolves chapter in Oregon. This band of brothers trains, strengthens, and perfects its outdoor skills in the rugged terrain of the Pacific Northwest.[78] Donovan espouses an exclusive homosociality that privileges bonds, including intimate and erotic ones, between men, as the quintessence of human communion. Donovan is open about his same-sex orientation, though, in his eyes, that does not make him part of the LGBTQ community, which he loathes for its political and moral relativism. Rather, he sees himself as a man's man who prioritizes rough-and-tumble maleness.

For Donovan, "above all things, masculinity is about what men want from each other."[79] Like other alt-right and alt-light thinkers, he views gender differences as "basic and biological." For Donovan, bodies naturally sort us into categories, and women's bodies are not hard-wired to complete the same tasks as men. Biology makes men "more daring, probably more mechanically inclined, and generally better at navigating. Men are hard wired for aggressive play." *The Way of Men* is both a manifesto for crystallizing gender differences and a manual for how to reorganize masculine society into small units of men called "gangs." According to Donovan, the gang is the most basic unit of survival and male bonding; it is the "kernel" of society and of "ethnic, tribal, and national identity." If modern men are going to survive in a hostile, hazardous world, they must group into tribes to gain physical and mental prowess, and build endurance and stamina. Donovan's gangs operate according to a zero-sum logic, where there is heavy competition for limited resources and a constant threat of attack and deprivation.

Like other alt-righters, Donovan blames feminism, globalism, and liberal values of diversity and equality for bludgeoning men into simpering weaklings, slaves of a system over which they have diminishing control. Men are trapped in "caged manhood" and feminism has taken the key. The unfulfilling options left for men are to simulate masculinity through video games, pornography, and over-managed activities. This can only produce incels and betas, and dreary lives of clerkdom and masturbation. Masculinity will be squelched; there will be no opportunities for risk-taking and masculine prowess. Donovan has no shortage of examples of what cramps male style; the astonishingly long list he recites in *The Way of Men* includes "more examinations, more certifications, mandatory prerequisites, screening processes, background checks, personality tests, and politicized diagnoses" and "more helmets and goggles and harnesses and bright orange vests with reflective tape," as well as "more counseling and sensitivity training." In sum, men are being bled dry of their masculine vitality by "more micro-managed living, pettier regulations, heavier fines, and harsher penalties."

Hypermasculinity is idealized by the alt-right, and its popularity can help to explain the alt-right's equivocal relationship to homosexuality, which, being male-centric, focuses almost entirely on gay men, not on lesbians. Some alt-righters countenance if not celebrate male homosexuality as the pinnacle of the twenty-first-century *Männerbund*. For example, author James O'Meara, in *Homo and Negro*, published by Counter-Currents, juxtaposes white American men's deficit of masculinity with excessive "Negrofication." For O'Meara, the country needs a heavy jolt of masculinization, even if it verges on homoeroticism, and an attenuation of black cultural influence, which, he claims, engenders decadence and submission. O'Meara asserts that it is time for white men to become "possessed of a heathen morality and thus certainly open to homosexuals," which would bring forth a "culture of excellence, creativity and active participation in all aspects of life."[80] This glorification of male bonding, as well as the fact that several of the alt-right literati purportedly are gay men, provides clues to why, in some formulations, gay people would be admitted to the white ethnostate, although without the option of same-sex marriage, since unions in the homogenous homeland exist for the purposes of procreation.[81]

Yet many other alt-righters wear unchecked homophobia on their sleeves, as witnessed by gazillions of bytes of rampant online gay-bashing. Fiery exchanges about the place of homosexuality in the movement erupt online periodically, often exposing cleavages between alt-right intellectuals, who are more likely to accept homosexuality, and rank-and-file

advocates, who express venomous homophobia. These countervailing
sentiments have simmered under the surface since the movement emerged
but have become more intense since the Charlottesville debacle, as white
nationalists are consumed with policing the boundaries of alt-right belonging. In late 2018, the webzine *Occidental Dissent*, founded in 2008 by a
neo-Confederate nationalist based in Alabama, published the post "A Call
for Unity," which directly attacked, among others, Greg Johnson, who has
all but come out as gay; Jared Taylor, for American Renaissance's refusal
to condemn Jews; and Andrew Anglin, for being a "Nazi-sociopath."[82]
This shrill if convoluted blog post demanded more support for neo-Nazi
groups like the anti-Semitic Traditionalist Worker Party and the secessionist League of the South, and less for white nationalist wannabes and
"cucks" weakening the movement.

More revealing than this harangue itself were the nearly 150 comments it received, which mocked Richard Spencer for blowing up the
alt-right with his recklessness, upbraided Taylor for being soft on the JQ,
and both applauded and slammed Anglin and the Daily Stormer for their
unabashed indulgence of neo-Nazi symbols and slogans. Nevertheless,
the most pointed comments focused on homosexuality. Greg Johnson
defended himself with this hypothetical scenario: "Let's say that a white
homosexual becomes convinced that what is happening to white people
today is the greatest crime in world history. Let's say he is intelligent,
educated, possesses useful skills, and has money and social connections.
He wants to contribute these to the movement."[83] Despite his attempt at
logical reasoning to demonstrate his necessary inclusion in the alt-right,
Johnson bore the brunt of homophobic remarks in the comments section. For example, Daniel Friberg, founder of Arktos media, with whom
Johnson has been engaged in a protracted feud, wrote, "Greg Johnson is a
perfect example of why tolerance of open homosexuals within the movement must come to an end." He accused Johnson of "nasty, petty, catty
behaviour that is unbecoming of any man" and of being the ringleader
of a "homosexual clique" whose membership was an open secret.[84] If this
litany of comments is taken as a barometer of the alt-right's position, then,
despite a few shrugs of indifference, Friberg's position prevailed, rein-
forced with expressions of disgust, hatred, and absolute intolerance; as
one commenter wrote, "Faggots forcing association with us makes us look
bad and deters serious people from taking us seriously."[85]

Indubitably this rancorous discussion about the fate of homosexuality in the alt-right will continue to play out, reflecting profound agitation about the limits of masculine identity in a hypermale movement. These concerns are less pronounced among the alt-light, which either evinces little interest in gay issues or, in the case of the revamped Proud Boys, invites all races, all religions, and gay or straight men to join a chapter today.[86] What is resoundingly clear is that transphobia sits at the embroiled crux of the alt-right and the alt-light, a reflection of near pathological uneasiness with gender nonbinariness. The alt-verse wants nothing more than containment and order. Within a cisgendered system, at least gay identities and bodies are stable. The alt-verse can tolerate a person who is born with XY sex chromosomes and unambiguous male genitalia who can be considered 100 percent male, even if he prefers the company of other men. What most unsettles the alt-right and the alt-light are gender nonbinariness, gender fluidity, and transgender bodies.

The IQ and DNA of Racial Essentialism

Just as sexism and transphobia serve as a conduit between the alt-light and the alt-right, so too does racism, propelled largely by the discredited tenets of biological determinism. Stefan Molyneux is one of the most popular alt-lighters on social media, and he produces a lot of content propagating theories of innate racial difference. He is fond of interviewing psychologists and scientists who do research on the relationship between heredity and social groups. Two of his highly watched YouTube interviews are with Charles Murray and Linda Gottfredson, both of whom have had long academic careers dedicated to demonstrating the putative heritability of intelligence and its uneven distribution across racial and ethnic groups.[87] In prefacing his conversation with Gottfredson (which, typical of his posts, has over 200,000 views and 2,500 comments), Molyneux advises viewers that "once you really start to understand intelligence and its bell curve distribution across the populations," it is hard not to reassess society, seeing problems with greater accuracy and compassion.[88] Molyneux has described waking up to the reality that genetics drives intelligence, a truth he finds sobering and liberating, insofar as it suggests that social interventions cannot be premised on universal equality but rather are informed by the undeniability of a natural hierarchy. In an interview on the Rubin Report, Molyneux describes this revelation as "heartbreaking."[89] It is the truth, he says, that no one wants to accept: "The most recent data I've seen is that by the time you're eighteen, 80% of your IQ is genetic."[90] For Molyneux, absorbing the findings of researchers such as Murray, Gottfredson, and the Danish psychologist Helmuth Nyborg prompts a mental paradigm shift: "A mind once stretched by a new idea, never regains its original shape."[91]

Jordan Peterson shares Molyneux's interest in pontificating on the fixity of intelligence, which he usually refers to as IQ or the G Factor, which stands for "general intelligence." In Peterson's view, omnipresent political correctness makes it impossible to acknowledge this plain truth.[92] Peterson's assumptions about genetics and intelligence are integral to his assertions about dominance hierarchies and humans. Unraveling the distinction between the seemingly generic phrases "equality of opportunity" and "equality of outcome" is telling in this regard. For Peterson, "equality of opportunity" is acceptable and allows all members of a society to pursue careers and life paths commensurate with their inherent abilities. This means that someone destined to be a janitor will be the world's best janitor and that someone wired to be a consummate business leader will become wealthy and successful. "Equality of opportunity" thus represents an organicist vision of social stratification in which people are ascribed functions they are capable of performing—nothing less and certainly nothing more. Conversely, "equality of outcome"—"equity" in shorthand—involves nonsensical overreach and inevitably will create scenarios in which egalitarianism is imposed through affirmative action, diversity training, and special programs for immigrants and other freeloaders who will be placed in roles that they, as limited human organisms, are unable to perform.[93] Wife with a Purpose sums up this idea succinctly in one of her vlogs: "People are different. We're not going to have equality of outcome for everyone because we are different."[94]

The alt-right and alt-light rely on the same baseline of ideas about human capacity and heredity, often extended to ideas about gender, race, and intelligence. Unlike Molyneux and Peterson, white nationalists do not employ these ideas to convey smug compassion about individual and group limitations but to vilify blacks, immigrants, and multiracialism. The network of bloggers and speakers affiliated with American Renaissance, for instance, are well versed in cherry-picking scientific studies in an effort to show that human beings organize themselves into racial groups, that cross-racial mixing produces disharmony in social interaction and offspring, and that diversity can produce nothing but conflict. In *White Identity: Racial Consciousness in the 21st Century*, Jared Taylor asserts that since 1965 America has endeavored to build a cohesive country out of disparate groups, an experiment he believes has floundered miserably. Taylor sees the wreckage all around him, of an Orwellian society in which Americans are being force-fed diversity, on television, in political rhetoric, and especially in universities and other educational institutions.[95] This path is not just leading to social strife; it portends white extinction. As Taylor recently told the audience at the ethnonationalist Scandza Forum, held in Copenhagen in fall 2018, "You must fight these ideas absolutely tooth and nail," because "we really are fighting for our lives."[96]

In this alt-right equation, "diversity" is a euphemism for white genocide and is catalyzing the transformation of whites in America from an empowered majority to a spurned minority vulnerable to persecution and marginalization: "The demographic forces we have set in motion have created conditions that are inherently unstable and potentially violent."[97] George Shaw, who edited an anthology by and for the alt-right, reiterates these concerns, writing that "'diversity' and 'multiculturalism' do not ultimately enrich white lives, but rather, tend to make white societies poorer, more dangerous, and finally unlivable for whites."[98] With their backs against a demographic wall, in the alt-right mind-set, the only viable option is for whites to reclaim their own tribal identity and struggle to form themselves into a homogenous community ordered by the biological truths of racial difference and gender essentialism.

Viewing race as primarily biological has been a mainstay of white nationalism for decades. In the first half of the twentieth century, scientific racism was elaborated and expounded by Madison Grant, Lothrop Stoddard, and the standard-bearer of American eugenics, Charles Davenport. Eugenics theories of race and intelligence affected education, health, immigration, and social policies with far-reaching consequences. Yet biases related to human differences and intelligence did not disappear even when the eugenics movement lost credibility in the mid-twentieth century. They became baked into certain, and increasingly controversial, subfields of psychology and sociobiology, and emergent areas in behavioral genetics.[99] Although many academic and clinical researchers rejected biological reductionism, and the racism and sexism that often accompanied it, the flame of eugenically motivated work was kept alit financially by organizations like the Pioneer Fund. This foundation supported the work of psychologist Arthur Jensen, who published a lengthy landmark essay in the *Harvard Educational Review* in 1969 assessing the effects of educational programs designed to improve the performance of disadvantaged and minority children.[100] The takeaway from this synthetic review was that "compensatory and enrichment programs" had failed because intelligence, which he measured as the "g factor," was hereditary and could not be modified by educational interventions. Moreover, this unchangeable trait was distributed unevenly among racial groups, such that "the intelligence of blacks was congenitally inferior to that of whites."[101]

Jensen was one of over a dozen scientists funded by the Pioneer Fund. Others included Philippe Rushton, a longtime professor at the University of Western Ontario who developed the genetic similarity theory, or the concept that people are attracted to people like them, phenotypically and genetically, and that healthy partnerships, especially procreative ones, are rooted in biological similarity. In his quest to prove the existence of racial differences, Rushton employed an array of methods, including MRI, to measure brain size; he found that "Orientals have the largest brains (on average), Blacks the smallest, and Whites in between," and surmised that "these differences in brain size probably explain the racial differences in IQ and cultural achievement."[102] Though Rushton's work is both passé and discredited, white nationalists like Greg Johnson and Jared Taylor cling to his work, including his crude "R/k" theory of reproduction, which Rushton extrapolated from research on plants and animals. He applied the theory to humans, divided into racial groups, to contend that African Americans have more children and are worse parents (high R/low k), whereas Asians and whites have fewer children and are superior caregivers (low R/high k).[103] From its inception to today, the Pioneer Fund has bankrolled research projects big and small conducted by academics intent on demonstrating correlations between race, intelligence, and behavior. About twenty of the authors cited in Murray and Herrnstein's *The Bell Curve*, received funding from the Pioneer Fund, including Gottfredson.[104] Tracing the money of the Pioneer Fund over the past eighty years reveals an enduring thread from the eugenics movement of the previous century to the alt-right today.

An interest in genetics extends to everyday online white nationalists, who are attracted to ancestry and DNA testing because they want to corroborate their white and European heritage.[105] They are pleased when they receive results that confirm this, but even if their ancestry is more complex, they have developed workarounds to ensure they remain in the tribe. Sometimes they question the validity of the tests, and the tests' reference population sets, acquiring enough genetic literacy to push back against percentages that might identify them as less than 100 percent white. As Aaron Panofsky and Joan Donovan show in their study of Genetic Ancestry Testing discussions on Stormfront, unsatisfactory results can have the effect of expanding the boundaries of white belonging through references to shared culture and ideology, or the assertion of a primeval sense of identity. As a Stormfront commenter said, grappling with received genetic ancestry results, "I am white in body soul and spirit through and through."[106] There are serious limitations to the kind of information that can be provided by commercialized ancestry testing, which is only as robust as the reference populations in the dataset, and, moreover, do not test long-history ancestry but rather one's genetic proximity to individuals living today.[107] Alarmed by white nationalists' use of ancestry testing to try to prove their racial purity, the American Society of Human Genetics recently denounced this trend and affirmed its commitment to "debunk genetics-based arguments promoting racial supremacy."[108]

White nationalists aren't the only ones interested in biological essentialism. Millions of Americans of all political persuasions have sent their swabs to 23andme and Ancestry.com, hoping to learn about their racial and ethnic ancestry. Even Democratic senator Elizabeth Warren thought a DNA test could prove finally she is partly Cherokee in an effort to combat charges from President Trump that she has lied about her ancestry. Recent studies have shown that mere exposure to the idea of genetic ancestry tests increases "one's belief in the essential differences between racial groups," even if they don't actually exist.[109] When it comes to recreational genetic testing, the alt-right is not inventing something new but rather augmenting and distorting more popular understandings of heredity and human difference that circulate in mainstream society. In a moment of excitement and trepidation about new gene editing techniques like Crispr, which one Chinese scientist allegedly used to create genetically modified babies, and the growing currency of the field of sociogenomics, which offers up genetic determinism as an explanation for challenging social problems, a revamped brand of white nationalist eugenics can find multiple points of scientific inspiration.[110]

In *The Nature of Race*, her fascinating and sobering book on racial conceptions in American academia and public discourse, sociologist Ann Morning suggests that while phenotypical understandings of race are no longer popular, racial essentialism "is perfectly consistent with the claim that societal discrimination no longer exists, it is a helpful tool for explaining why race differentials still obtain in income, education, and just about any other measure of social status. In fact, it would be much harder to maintain that the U.S. is post racial if we did not have inherent biological difference to fall back on as an explanation for inequality."[111] Disturbingly, this liberal line of reasoning is not that far afield from the precepts of "human biodiversity," a pseudo-academic area popular among some alt-righters positing that if racial and population differences among humans are written in DNA, then it's nature's hand at work.[112] Moreover, if organisms are unique, they should be protected from endangerment, a policy that alt-righters think should be extended to whites. Racial and gender essentialism is more accepted than anathema in American society, potentially making it easier for alt-lighters, and alt-righters, to dispense red pills.

CHAPTER 5

LIVING THE TRADLIFE

Babies, Butter, and the Vanishing of Bre Faucheux

For about one year the pseudonymous Bre Faucheux was one of the most active and visible alt-right social media personalities. She ran her own channel, 27Crows Radio, cohosted the YouTube show *This Week on the Alt-Right*, and appeared on episodes of Red Ice TV and other white nationalist programs. She interviewed the biggest names in the movement—Richard Spencer, Greg Johnson, and Lana Lokteff—and regularly collaborated with British nationalist Mark Collett. Yet in early April 2018, she fled the scene, abandoning these projects and her Twitter account, which had five thousand followers. Then, in a dramatic turn, Faucheux, her hairstyle changed and her appearance slightly altered, posted a grainy YouTube video from an undisclosed location announcing that she "had some personal things" to deal with and "wasn't going to be home."[1] Given these unforeseen circumstances, Faucheux said she would no longer host *This Week on the Alt-Right*. Several comments across alt-right social media indicated that she had been doxed—her real name and home address divulged—in a news story and then hounded, most likely by the malicious misogynists associated with MGTOW (Men Going Their Own Way), who insist that women have no place in the alt-right.[2] A similar fate befell Tara McCarthy, who cohosted *This Week on the Alt-Right* before Faucheux. McCarthy's Twitter and YouTube feeds ended abruptly in spring 2018, ostensibly due to both leftist trolling and "well-known 'Nazi,' anti-woman, alt-right Trump cheerleaders."[3]

Faucheux's farewell video has received over twenty-three thousand views and nearly six hundred comments, testament to the large fanbase she established in just one year online. YouTuber and sister traditionalist Lacey Lynn commented on this video, extolling Faucheux and Collett because they had "red pilled me and I owe yall so much. I hope the alt right will stick together, we are a family." Another regretted Faucheux's departure: "Noooooo, you're supposed to be the gateway drug for other women!" One listener intuited that something unpleasant had happened: "Hmm, this concerns me a lot because whatever the reason Bre is discontinuing her show it's obviously a big negative from her expressions and attitude." And finally, including a reference to Tara McCarthy, Faucheux's predecessor on *This Week on the Alt-Right*, one commenter exclaimed, "Oh no, two great AR women have now departed. All the best to you for red pilling the masses. The bangs look good."[4]

In December 2018, Faucheux announced via Twitter and Gab that she would be returning to social media after the New Year with an original podcast and website.[5] In her first appearance since the spring, Faucheux showed off her wedding ring on Red Ice's Yule Live Stream and gleamingly stated that in a year of many black pills, the biggest white pill for her was getting married. She also waxed about seeing the white nationalist tribe expand as alt-right couples in her real-life networks bred many babies. Although Faucheux reiterated that "serious family stuff" had compelled her offline, Lokteff initiated the conversation by reminding viewers that "there were some attacks of some single women in our circle" last year, referring to what had transpired with Faucheux. Clearly, for alt-right women, putting a ring on it can serve as a shield against doxing and MGTOW harassment.[6]

Faucheux's fleeting stardom, subsequent exile, and promised return reveals the complexities and ugliness of alt-right gender politics. Being an alt-right leader is next to impossible in a movement grounded in ultra-essentialist conceptions of women as breeders and helpmates, and populated in good measure by vitriolic and unrelenting misogynists who police women and do whatever they can to exclude them. Yet this incident also illustrates that the alt-right's stage is the internet—where the drama unfolds, and social connections are forged and shredded. By alt-right estimates, about 90 percent of the movement happens online, mediated through a cyberscape of interlinking programs and platforms like You-Tube, Twitter, Facebook, and, increasingly, the shadow sites of Gab and BitChute. These digital spaces are more than springboards for the dissemination of alt-right propaganda; they constitute what one scholar calls a "networked public," a porous yet cohesive online community whose connectivity is enabled by posting, re-posting, sharing, and commenting.[7] Some of the most trenchant analysis of the alt-right has tracked how it has capitalized giddily and strategically on the internet, to meme, troll, and confound.

There is no denying that the frenzy of snarky re-tweeting and meme-ing dished out by alt-righters and fellow travelers in 2015 and 2016 helped pave the way for Trump's ascension to the White House. However, there is another salient, less-explored dimension of alt-right social media, namely how, in the words of communications scholar Zizi Papacharissi, it can "enable expression and information sharing that liberate the individual and collective imagination."[8] Among networked publics, interactive social media facilitates a genre of affective and open-ended storytelling, and creates the conditions for the composition of personal and collective narratives. Thus, a red-pilling journey narrated on someone's vlog can be disseminated, spliced, repurposed, and textured as it moves through nodes and platforms in embedded and hyperlinked forms. These stories might at once live on their original platforms and travel far and wide, becoming interwoven into metanarratives with the potential to reshape discourse and what is knowable and expressible. Almost twenty years ago, when the World Wide Web was more rudimentary, Tara McPherson observed such networked publics at play in what she called Confederate cyberspace, where Southern secessionists and rebels found each other online in websites and chat rooms replete with "a desire for origin and place."[9] Alt-righters are using the same formula today, now with many more digital tools at their disposal.

Because the alt-right is marginal and "stalks the great taboos," it sticks principally to the internet, where anonymity and plausible deniability are built-in features.[10] After Charlottesville, which demonstrated that alt-righters had vastly overestimated both their sway and ability to handle themselves offline, the internet has become even more of a refuge. It is also the frontline for pitched battles over the alleged biases of algorithms and search engine protocols that alt-righters decry as controlled by liberals. Indeed, 2018 was the year of the alt-right's incessant moaning about deplatforming. Yet digital studies scholarship shows that, if anything, the architecture of the internet has enabled, not limited, the reach of the purveyors of white nationalism.[11] As Jessie Daniels has pointed out, white nationalists were early adopters of these technologies, utilizing them in ways that were "innovative, sophisticated, and cunning."[12]

In this digital jungle, alt-right women have staked out a niche where they maintain an uneasy foothold. A cursory perusal of prominent alt-right websites and blogs like the Daily Stormer, *Counter-Currents*, American Renaissance, and VDARE reveals barely any female contributors. Almost to a person, the alt-right is a world for men, by men, and of men—and straight white men. Women do not lead organizations or speak at nationalist gatherings. For instance, there were no female presenters and scant female attendance at the recent conferences held by Identity Evropa, American Renaissance, and the Scandza Forum in 2018.[13] They do not write the books or signature essays that constitute the canon of the alt-right, and with few exceptions, no female authors are distributed by nationalist presses. Alt-right intellectual production is the bailiwick of white men writing from a decidedly masculinist perspective, no matter the topic at hand. This void reflects the alt-right's essentialist and retrograde division of labor and of gender possibilities, which presumes that only men possess rationality and creativity for true erudition and the "Faustian spirit" that can spearhead meaningful social transformation. Jared Taylor and Paul Kersey, in one of their weekly conversations on the American Renaissance podcast, responded to a question posed by a listener about the dearth of women in the alt-right. To them, this absence is a natural outcome of the fact that "men are always society's revolutionaries" above all in dissident movements. According to them, it's men, and seldom women, who can "build a new vision."[14] Even though women have minimal representation in the alt-right, they are symbolically omnipresent. They are showcased in nostalgic ideas about an ethnonationalist future, since, after all, they will produce the babies, and become targets of belittlement and hostility when the depravities of feminism are under discussion.

The boys' club of the alt-right engages with the Woman Question (WQ) from varying and shifting perspectives. Media coverage has probed the manosphere, with its ricocheting cacophony of brutalizing hatred, and scholars have dubbed this environment a "toxic technoculture." This online realm is sustained by Pick Up Artists (PUA) like Roosh V (whose chosen tag is "super toxic masculinity") and unfolds 24/7 in a frenzy of comments on Reddit, 4chan, and 8chan.[15] These online forums are spaces where men can post sexual-assault and rape fantasies, where "badass" women are eviscerated, and where sarcasm bludgeons feminism.[16] Gamergate encapsulates this misogynistic dynamic. It unfolded in 2014, when a female video-game producer became the target of nasty, relentless attacks that exposed and animated anti-woman activism on the internet. Gamergate occurred not just because men were behaving badly but because the design and functionalities of 4chan and Reddit, including the ease of creating anonymous user accounts and the rewarding of upvoted individual content (no matter how offensive), enabled hateful messages and memes to explode. The "extremely hands-off" moderation policies of these platforms means that only after enormous pressure from critics willing to register complaints about heinous content will a chat room be regulated or removed, often with negligible results, since users can migrate to another forum.[17]

Yet some of the most high-profile men in the alt-right are dismayed by the manosphere's hostility, worried that it has become rife with young men who have been black pilled, turned into angry nihilists who might become homicidal or suicidal incels. Algorithms and chat rooms have served as the fueling stations for flesh-and-blood violence, as in the case of Elliott Rodger, an incel who uploaded his "Retribution" salvo onto YouTube before going on a shooting rampage at the University of California at Santa Barbara in 2014, targeting sorority girls who symbolized taunting rejection. There is a realpolitik subset of alt-right men who realize that if white nationalism wants to sustain a viable patriarchy, and build up their people, they need to change their tune around women and turn down the hate. Without white women on board as breeders to turn the tide of the "Great Replacement," there will be no White Republic, ethnostate, or supermajority.

After Trump's election, the expansion of the metapolitical realm of online social media brought in women like Tara McCarthy and Bre Faucheux.[18] Their presence buoyed the alt-right by lending it telegenic charm and helping to normalize anti-egalitarian beliefs such as diversity equals racism and white extinction is underway. Inhabiting a virtual space that is simultaneously public and homebound, alt-right female social media personalities are educated and forthright, and embody traditionalism and revere patriarchy. They echo their male counterparts as they unabashedly espouse white identitarianism, anti-feminism, heterosexual monogamy, the imperative to procreate, and the sanctity of wife and mother.[19] Alt-right women can be more stridently anti-LGBTQ than their male counterparts, whose hypermasculinism sometimes allows a space for homosocial solidarity and a don't ask, don't tell attitude toward gay people. Alt-right women esteem TradLife, but they are not passive playthings. These media-savvy women debunk caricatures of alt-right women as servants who spend all day cleaning, cooking, and changing diapers. Instead, they see themselves as purveyors of a distinct feminine message and as superb managers of a patriarchal subculture. They are cogent narrators of the epic tale of white men's victimization and champion white self-determination.

Male and female alt-righters alike reinscribe rigid gender roles, contending that the sexes are biologically and spiritually unequal by design.[20] They concur that feminism is the fulcrum of contemporary social chaos and impending societal collapse. Of course, patriarchal norms are not new to right-leaning political ideologies and movements; they have been ideologically central from the John Birch Society of the 1960s to the neoconservatives and Christian Right of the 1990s.[21] And white women have been instrumental in conservative causes, from the anti-abortion crusade to the full-throated contestation of civil rights gains. For instance, the "massive resistance" waged by white Southerners against desegregation and to uphold white supremacy, which used slogans of states' rights and anti-busing, had a sizable female flank.[22] Southern women associated with the White Citizens' Council organized bake sales to raise funds for their efforts and galvanized political support through their networks. Similarly, the emergence of modern political conservatism in Southern California in the 1960s was inextricably tied to female "suburban warriors" who linked patriotism, motherhood, and family in a vision of a traditionalist white America opposed to communism and liberalism.[23] As author Kathleen Belew shows, for white power militants in the 1970s and 1980s, women often served as the glue that held the extended family together and fortified networks behind the scenes.[24]

"WHITE BABY CHALLENGE"

If the alt-right is galvanized by one overarching narrative, it is that demographic change will reduce whites to a hated minority and eventually lead to white extinction. The alt-right frequently expounds on and alludes to the declining white birth rate and refers to concerning numbers of suicide among middle-aged white men, as well as the devastating opioid epidemic and its impact on white families.[25] Recent surveys do show that American women of all backgrounds are having fewer babies, less than the replacement level of 2.1, mainly due to deep economic concerns like the high costs of child care.[26] Depending on how race and ethnicity data in the US Census is interpreted, non-Hispanic whites will constitute less than 50 percent of the population around 2050. Alt-righters weaponize census projections relying on the narrowest percentages to count whites (as non-Hispanic whites with no mixed race identity), and thereby hype their claims of impending white genocide. These problematic projections serve the alt-right well in whipping up demographic fear, which is propagated by mainstream right-wing pundits like Laura Ingraham, Ann Coulter, and Tucker Carlson. The alt-right twists these fertility and mortality statistics away from questions of health disparities and income equality to prima facie evidence of a nearly conspiratorial campaign of white extinction.

One response to looming "white extinction anxiety" is to produce white babies—many more white babies—principally of Northern and Western European ancestry.[27] Unlike immigration or refugee bans, forced deportations, or the reintroduction of racial segregation, which require heavy-handed policies, white nationalism can grow through procreative means, boosted by pronatalist programs. As one contributor to *Counter-Currents* proposes: "Having three—or five or eight—White children is probably the most 'pro-White' thing a person can do—and the most resistant to any charge of 'racism.' How about that?"[28] Propagating wildly does mean that alt-right men will need to convince themselves that procreation and coupling—and a likely future of vanilla sex with a wife—are enticing. This tamed path of husband and father is far afield from the erotic conquests and hook-ups prioritized in the manosphere. Greg Johnson of Counter-Currents broaches the difficulties of convincing horny and entitled twenty- and thirtysomethings to bite the bullet and breed. The smackdown he gives this audience focuses on the urgency of perpetuating ancestral white bloodlines: "If you are worried about having kids, or you're not sure if it's a good idea, or you're not sure if you're up to it, or you're afraid that you're bringing them into a terrible world, just think about all of the ancestors that you had going back to the very beginning of our race. Every one of these people probably had it harder than you." He asks them the berating question: "Are you going to be the whiny little maggot who brings all of their striving and struggles to oblivion because you just can't get your act together and decide to go off the goddamn pill or stop using condoms or whatever and just take the plunge and carry the race forward one more generation?"[29]

Appeals to ancestry abound in the alt-right, and nationalist women express some of the loudest calls for white-baby making. In 2017, Wife with a Purpose, the alt-right social media activist who chronicles her life as a proud nationalist and Mormon mother, was taken with a tweet posted by Iowa representative Steve King. Itself riffing off a tweet from the acerbic right-wing Dutch politician Geert Wilders about the threat of Muslims to the Netherlands and the foreseen demographic disappearance of whites, King aped, "We can't restore our civilization with somebody else's babies."[30] This resulted in swift condemnation and ridicule in many quarters of the mainstream media, and King himself received bemused and angry tweets from congressional colleagues, some posting photos of their smiling multiracial children. Wife with a Purpose, who asserts that "her primary duty is having children and supporting her husband," issued a "white baby challenge," throwing down the breeding gauntlet: "As a mother of 6, I challenge families to have as many white babies as I have contributed."[31] Once her challenge went viral on social media, Wife with a Purpose received much censure. Telling, however, were the thousands of comments praising and defending her on her YouTube channel: "I stand in solidarity with Ayla," "Love This Woman!," "She is 100% right," and "Make White Babies Great Again!"[32]

Red Ice's *Radio 3Fourteen*, hosted by Lana Lokteff, is the most visible online arena for discussions of nationalism from a female alt-right perspective. Lokteff's interviews and vlogs receive ten thousand to two hundred thousand views, depending on the topics, which range from the benefits of New Age herbs to the wonders of being a traditional wife, and from criticisms of the positive depictions of interracial couples on the mainstream media to the hazards of "migrant invasions." Lokteff and Red Ice TV provide the online base camp for a networked public of alt-right women, who act as a chorus to demand preservation of the exalted Western civilization that their white men built.[33] In her vlog *They Want You Dead White Man!* Lokteff delivers an impassioned commentary as a cascade of sensationalistic headlines flash across the screen and paint a frenzied picture of relentless attacks on white men in Europe and the United States. Lokteff reminds her viewers that straight white men are the world's great inventors and creators and, moreover, that these tolerant and kind souls always are the ones to come to rescue the less fortunate. What would the world be like without these saviors? It would be "hell on earth," she proclaims, behind a backdrop of film clips of brown and black people rioting and rickety boats of North African refugees. In a not-so-veiled threat, Lokteff warns that SJWs are taking political correctness and diversity campaigns "way too far, too fast," and are "waking a sleeping giant."[34] Once roused, this mighty force of white saviors will take control, restore order, and reclaim Western civilization. The video weaves white male victimhood with racism through scaremongering and foregrounding the themes of imminent white genocide, the bias of the liberal media, and the fortification of the tribe. Lana praises alt-right men as "fighting for a future for women and children." In her words, they are not "fags" but want to have sex and procreate with women.[35]

As a home for the small but active alt-right sisterhood, *Radio 3Fourteen* brings together female alt-righters with their followers on social media. Regulars include Wife with a Purpose (Ayla Stewart), Bre Faucheux (before and after her online departure), Canadian white nationalists Lauren Southern and Faith Goldy, Lacey Lynn, and Blonde in the Belly of the Beast, who shares her experiences as a red-pilled anti-feminist living in the liberal bastion of Seattle.[36] Also in the mix is TheBlondeButterMaker, who vlogs about organic recipes designed to nourish her family, including butter with pesto and bone broth, while endorsing a brand of white European paganism.[37] The power of these alt-right women to push the Overton window and move alt-right discourse into the mainstream should not be underestimated. These are not just amicable Google chats with women with conservative leanings but virtual salons that make scorching and simplistic critiques of feminism, globalism, diversity, and multiculturalism sound urgent, sexy, and like plain old common sense to some ears. These women position themselves as the new counterculture, pitting themselves against a more backward Left. According to Lokteff, "A lot of these liberal women, they're not risk-takers, even though they have piercings or blue hair. . . . What we do, the things we talk about, I don't think it can get any more high-risk."[38] They fancy themselves alt-right handmaidens of a reinvigorated white culture and spokeswomen for their ostensibly beleaguered male defenders.

"CHECK YOUR GENDER EQUALITY AT THE DOOR"

Alt-right women with a visible media presence are the tip of the white nationalist iceberg. Lurking below them is a much vaster anonymous online space where anti-feminism and gender essentialism reign supreme. While the most toxic varieties of anti-feminism exist in the manosphere, women mirror these digital domains with a seemingly more sensible style. Foremost among these mirrors is Reddit's Red Pill Women, with its hot-pink banner, where women aligned with the gender politics of the alt-right can find their kind.[39] RPW appears to have started in 2013, founded by women who felt that the "venting" and "locker room atmosphere" of the male-controlled Reddit forum Red Pill was off-putting and vulgar.[40] Although RPW's core moderators agreed with the basic gender tenets of the original Red Pill, they wanted to make these meaningful to women. RPW is not organized primarily around white nationalism, or questions of race or immigration, but rather around sexual strategy, gender roles, and relationships. It is based on a set of axioms, including "women are gatekeepers of sex, while men are gatekeepers of commitment," and "relationships generally work better if the man is in charge" due "to the inherent dominant nature of men and submissive nature of women."[41] Goals include self-improvement and awareness of one's own desires and the biological realities of gender and sexual differences.

RPW includes threads that would be quite at home in magazines like *Cosmopolitan* or *Woman's Day*, such as how to maintain a long-term relationship or be a winning party hostess. But other RPW threads lunge toward the alt-right and act as forums where women can share their stories of conversion, told as blue-to-red-pill metamorphoses. Common are accounts of women red pilled after watching Jordan Peterson videos explaining why feminism doesn't make women happy or why leftism is the great scourge of modern society. For others, red pilling occurred while reading books like *The Surrendered Wife*, which tout the virtues of traditional women's roles; others stumbled onto RPW after searching for like-minded communities on Tumblr.[42]

RPW foregrounds the "reality" of hard-wired differences and the distinct evolutionary sexual strategies of women and men. The site prioritizes long-term commitments with men that result in matrimony, children, and the realization of gender-complementary unions. New arrivals are reminded that "strategies for securing no-commitment sex from men will not be discussed. This is not only incongruent with the desires of the vast majority of women, it is also so easy to do that no 'strategy' is required."[43] Perhaps the most important principle of "Red Pill 101" is female hypergamy, or the idea that women marry up because they are more discriminating than men when it comes to choosing a mate; women want good genes and a protector. Men, conversely, are driven by sexual desires and urges to "spread seed far and wide," and will tend toward polygamy.[44] Rebuttals to these and any other guiding RPW maxims have included "this is an anti-feminist community, and as such, we are not interested in being 'saved' by feminism," and users are counseled to "check your gender equality at the door."[45]

The RPW forum is typical of chat rooms, where people post questions or experiences, looking for advice or insights. One contributor, for example, went on a mountain hike with her husband but was unable to keep up with his faster pace. Soon after this outing he chastised her for being the "slowest person on the mountain," a criticism that left her crestfallen because she cherishes hiking with him. Instead of trying to come to a compromise with her husband to accommodate each other's different paces, she stated that her plan was to "eat far less so that I will be thinner and lighter (and maybe faster)" and "train every day to walk and hike faster."[46] Someone offered her three tips to enjoy "sports with your man": "admire his manly sports abilities," "don't try to excel him at the sport and rub it in his face," and, lastly, "be sure to mention frequently how much fun it is to be active/do sports with him."[47]

The particular alt-right dimensions of RPW are apparent in conversations that explore outright rejections or retreats from feminism and liberalism; these are key elements of stories about brainwashed SJWs who finally see the light. One young woman, for instance, after being led astray by lefty and liberal values at a small high school was introduced to RPW by her parents. She reminded the group that "r/RedPillWomen doesn't just help us get an Alpha man. It allows us to be our feminine selves without hesitation."[48] Her insights are applauded, as commenters identify with her experience, offer more examples of how Jordan Peterson convinced them of the evils of feminist consumer culture, of how trans people should learn to take gender pronoun jokes in stride, and of the hypocrisy of political correctness, which falsely purports to be open-minded. Stories of indoctrination at liberal universities abound. The usual scenario involves the inculcation of college women by leftist professors, who turn them into deluded diversity proponents programmed to uphold the status quo: "You're just one more cog in the feminist/Marxist/socialist machine that is modern US liberal progressivism."[49] Once exposed to RPW, members have been primed at the alt-light pump; ultra-traditionalism might be the springboard from which to leap to the alt-right.

ANCESTRY, HERITAGE, PEOPLE

On *Radio 3Fourteen*, red pilling is overtly linked to white nationalism through discussions presided over by a clique of fetching white women who are forcefully racist and xenophobic. Beyond celebrations of "red pilled love and friendships" and TradLife, guests discuss how they awoke to the "sham we call post-modern society," deplore the menace of immigration, and ridicule notions of diversity and multiculturalism.[50] Like men, these women found the alt-right along different pathways. Lacey Lynn, for example, was unwittingly red pilled while watching *Leave It to Beaver*: it dawned on her that the white-bread image of 1950s America was her utopia. Notably, in her first vlog on YouTube, "In Defense of June Cleaver," Lynn cheerily justifies doing housework in pearls and high heels and narrates her transformation. After watching McCarthy, Faucheux, Collett, and Molyneux, Lynn, who was raised to worship God, country, and family in rural Texas, felt assured in her conviction that "biological differences dictate different roles" for men and women and for racial groups. These ideas were the stepping-stones that led her to a firm stance in favor of white nationalism. Notably, Lynn emphatically concludes her "Red Pill 1965" video with the declaration that she is "not a civic nationalist."[51] Another guest on *Radio 3Fourteen* found the alt-right during the lead-up to the 2016 presidential election, as she started to listen to Richard Spencer and Millennial Woes and read Kevin MacDonald and

Jared Taylor, soon grasping that she shared their convictions.[52] Faucheux explains on her (now defunct) website that she launched 27Crows Radio, named after an Irish legend, after realizing that feminism and liberalism were lies and that the mantra of diversity and equality was a bankrupt "excuse for dispossessing the white race of their history, heritage, culture, and countries." She began to call herself an identitarian and started her podcast in an effort to "red pill many people on these issues."[53]

Reading the comments suggests that shows like *Radio 3Fourteen* allow for the construction and reinforcement of narratives of self- and collective discovery, of red pilling, which are directly connected to gender norms, to endorsing biological essentialism and embodying traditional gender roles. This alt-right brand of feminization, moreover, is tinged with the emotional pull of white tribalism and calls to preserve Western civilization. As Lynn tells her home-schooled children, the "West was built, and . . . the white men did it, and there is nothing to be ashamed about that."[54] Through this gendered networked public, alt-right women build an affective community—a virtual family—held together by reinforcing bonds and beliefs of nationalism and traditionalism. Such sentiments of belonging and connection are captured in the comments on Lynn's "1965 Red Pill" vlog, which include "Come join your family the Alt-Right!" and "A beautiful white woman who will make beautiful white babies. Loving it!!!!"[55]

In a *Radio 3Fourteen* roundtable with the host and four nationalist women, the group sets out to debunk a *Harper's* article contending "that nationalism is hostile towards women."[56] They begin by clarifying that those who hate women exist only on the fringes of the movement: "you are not going to gain any ground as a nationalist by promoting hatred of half your race." Moreover, they claim that obnoxious fringe has never caused them any headaches; they have never been doxed by MGTOW folks, only by leftist journalists, although Faucheux's experience several months after the roundtable broadcast certainly indicates otherwise. For these women, the alt-right movement is "what's most in line with reality. It's a movement that's willing to discuss things like demographics, and human biodiversity, and gender roles, and traditionalism . . . because it's about going after things that are in balance with the world." For women, egalitarianism is a lie because advanced societies would not exist if their white men had not built them in the first place. Like their men, these nationalist women want to see the "restoration and preservation of tra-ditional values" and of their bloodlines, and, by extension, the closure of national borders; they don't want their homelands invaded or to pay high taxes for welfare programs for undesirables. For these alt-right women, their idealized world is one defined by nationalism, safety, order, peace, family, beauty, spirituality, and the pursuit of truth, where "white men are the protectors and providers [sic] of women." Furthermore, this rigid gen-der arrangement carries a heavy dose of Islamophobia, as white nation-alist women stereotype Muslim and African men as the bona fide brutal misogynists.[57]

One episode of *Radio 3Fourteen* underscores the trans-Atlantic aspects of the alt-right and the power of stories of racial roots and communion to alt-right women. The woman on this episode shares her red-pilling experience—which took her full circle from North Dakota, to Boston, to Heidelberg, and then back home to the Plains, peopled with hard-working Scandinavian and German stock. "How the Migrant Invasion Made Me Become a Trad Wife" features a native North Dakotan from a fourth-generation Norwegian farming family. She recounts her move from rural America to study voice at a Boston conservatory, where she felt completely alienated. She tried to fit in with the "lefties," even pro-testing US wars in the Middle East and dating a "mixed race" guy who talked about being an "illegal alien"—all part of what she now refers to as "Marxist indoctrination."[58] In the early 2000s, she moved to Heidel-berg, Germany, to study and perform classical music. There she witnessed firsthand the ravages of liberalism, globalism, and multiculturalism. She recalls that the city she initially moved to was a safe place where she could bike carefreely at 3 a.m. But it morphed, seemingly overnight, into a dan-ger zone teeming with North African and Muslim migrants. She started fearing for her safety as a "blond, blue-eyed, Scandinavian woman." How-ever, it was verboten to talk about the "invasion" among her music cir-cles, as most were devout "lefties." These factors prompted her to return to her North Dakota homeland, where she got married and is raising a white family. Reflecting on her time in Germany, she recollects being an assistant at an integrative health clinic for a doctor who identified himself as a proud descendent of a physician active in the Third Reich. Her boss did not hesitate to air his views about foreigners and changes afoot in German society. At the time she silently branded him a Nazi, but she later remembered their conversations and decided he was right all along about the imperative to preserve white European racial purity against black and brown migrants. In retrospect, this right-wing physician handed her the red pill, which she later swallowed, enabling her to envision, in her words, a "brave new world" of white nationalist possibilities.

Once back in North Dakota, this singer embraced the white settler colonialist tradition of the American West. From her perspective, her ancestors fought, struggled, and tamed the Plains West, triumphs that should prompt celebration, not induce white guilt. According to her, the multicultural agenda makes white people rootless, with no knowledge of their family history or ancestral lines. She closed the conversation by fretting about the increasing number of Somalis and North Africans being placed in Fargo by Lutheran Social Services and touting the aesthetic superiority of her blue-eyed Scandinavian husband and similarly "gorgeous" son. She and Lokteff both assert that "ideal beauty" is Northern European; since the majority of the world has brown eyes, blond hair and blue eyes are rare and exceptional—even more reason to fight against white genocide.[59]

As observers have noted, *Radio 3Fourteen* offers a combination of "fervent racial nationalism, anti-political correctness, and opposition to feminism."[60] Relying on the foundational ideas of the alt-right, Lokteff and her female ensemble are doing metapolitical work. Though the alt-right professes dislike of globalism, the ladies who make the rounds on Red Ice TV have formed their worldviews through cosmopolitan lifestyles and inhabit transnational media circuits, through which they exchange jubilance over Brexit and thoughts on strict border enforcement against refugees and "illegals." Asking her viewers for financial support at the close of one show, Lokteff exclaims, "Every day I receive moving messages from people sharing their story of how they found Red Ice and the alt-right, even from housewives in North Dakota who grasp the current reality better than anyone on mainstream media. We are a rapidly growing demographic, and no amount of anti-white propaganda is going to stop it. We may not get that border wall, but in our hearts and minds, it exists. Protecting what we hold dear: our ancestry, our heritage, and our people."[61]

A broader historical lens shows that narratives of red pill awakening are characteristic of right-wing movements and tend to be expressed in particular ways by women. In her research on women in American neo-Nazi organizations, Kathleen Blee found that women's membership often was "the outgrowth of dramatic personal transformation."[62] Frequently these involved a major bodily event, where women felt threatened by invasion, attack, or trauma; such incidents acquired a racial dimension. In her prescient early 2000s scholarship on the surge of white nationalism in America, Carol Swain interviewed Lisa Turner, the coordinator of Women's Information at the World Church of the Creator. A self-labeled Nazi who believed that "whites have both a right and a moral imperative to preserve themselves and to expand their influence around the globe," Turner transformed her liberal perspective into racial animus when she was living in Southern California in the 1990s. As she describes it, an influx of "Mexican aliens" came into the neighborhood and destroyed it almost overnight.[63] Eventually Turner's anti-Mexican sentiment was augmented by a more extreme anti-Semitism.

Before her 2018 online exit, Bre Faucheux wrote one of two essays by women in the alt-right anthology *A Fair Hearing*, seeking to disabuse readers of the implication "that women who do join the alt-right or hold alt-right ideas are psychologically defective, and worse still, they enjoy being abused and dominated by men who are also psychologically defective."[64] The actual problem, she said, is that white women have been deceived by feminism; they are slaving away at futile careers during their childbearing years, ultimately becoming barren and bitter. This not only deprives women of their essential womanhood; it presages white genocide: "The additional and more ominous problem, is that these women are accelerating a demographic shift that will eventually cancel out many of the liberties Western women *have* traditionally enjoyed." The solution, she claims, is a return to gender complementarity, of men as protectors and women as homemakers, that has existed since time immemorial. According to Faucheux, the alt-right bottom line is that "women desire to be cherished, men desire to be respected." Faucheux, Lokteff, and their white nationalist sorority convey at full volume that now is the time for a course correction, before it's too late.

As adept media personalities, they assure listeners, many of them men, that many white women are committed to traditional life, gender essentialism, and the restoration of primordial patriarchy. Some even go so far as to suggest that women should relinquish voting rights. Lokteff, for example, has alluded to an arrangement where households, led by patriarchs, vote as a unit.[65] Adulated is the woman who embodies the "nationalist housewife extraordinaire" and devotes herself to being a full-time mother. These alt-right pioneers implement anti-liberalism and anti-feminism through quotidian life: they homeschool their kids; incorporate "heritage, race, culture," and nation into learning plans; and spend time sewing, cleaning, and canning. TheBlondeButterMaker, for example, combines white nationalism with organic food preparation techniques. Her YouTube channel features DIY videos on lacto-fermentation and how to make nut milk and beef jerky.[66] Their picturesque domestic life might replicate the 1950s' *Leave It to Beaver* or it might harken back to a fantasy medieval past. Whichever the imagined reference, the house runs smoothly and is well managed—an ordered, self-sufficient nuclear family that can serve as a building block for the White Republic.

The alt-right is replete with male egos trying to upstage one another and a tendency to devour their own. It remains to be seen if the misogynists will be kept at bay. Alt-right women have staked a shaky claim rooted largely in their loyalty to patriarchy and tradition, and have the potential to grow the movement through teaching their female kin that homeschooling and butter churning are exciting and fun. Alt-right women with the largest followings, such as Lokteff and Goldy, seem to have found a way to walk that fine line between provocative and informed, and outgoing and demure. Goldy, in an interview with Mark Collett, said she recognizes that the "dissident right is a boys' club" and believes that "a woman's role in the public space is a bit more nuanced." In that conversation Goldy says she would like "nationalist, traditionalist women" to "read books that will help make us more serious in our debates."[67] It looks like she took her own advice to heart, having run a failed bid for mayor of Toronto on a nationalist, anti-immigrant, and pro-safety platform. Although Goldy was ignored by mainstream news outlets and not invited to join the other candidates in debates, she maintained a lively social media presence and ultimately finished third, winning 3.4% of the vote (25,667).[68] She received a tweeted endorsement from US Republican congressman Steve King, who called her "an excellent candidate for Toronto mayor," who is "pro Rule of Law, pro Make Canada Safe Again, pro balanced budget, & . . . BEST of all, Pro Western Civilization and a fighter for our values."[69] As with his previous tweets pushing white nationalism, King was criticized, but that is unlikely to stop him from posting another message about white extinction and the superiority of white babies sometime soon.[70]

Alt-right women are traversing a tightrope, and they seem to believe it's a sturdy one gripped firmly by their white male heroes. Yet the experiences of women like Faucheux, who unwittingly left social media under clouded circumstances and now, only with the protection of a wedding ring, can plot her return, reveals the precariousness of this balancing act. Nevertheless, any examination of the alt-right must explore the networked and affective domains of white nationalist women. As wobbly as their position may be, they inarguably are one of the movement's greatest assets.

CHAPTER 6

NORMALIZING NATIONALISM

Alt-Right Creep

In the late 2010s, the alt-right's mantra is normalization. The movement strives to earn a badge of respectability, an effort that has been redoubled by the perceived need to carve out distance from the "bad optics" associated with Charlottesville.[1] The more restrained alt-righters know that they cannot grow the movement without an image makeover. These days the alt-right fathers try with exasperation to rein in their hormonally driven angry sons, who breathe energy into the movement but also end up setting things ablaze and shitposting with such exaggeration that they threaten to sink the entire ship. The benevolent patriarchs would prefer that less airtime was granted to race baiters like Christopher Cantwell, who was arrested for three felony assaults at the 2017 Unite the Right rally and hosts the rabid *Radical Agenda*, and more attention paid to suit-and-tie spokesmen and well-groomed foot soldiers. Such upstanding white nationalists carry a big alt-right stick, but they do not shout, salute, or scuffle.[2] Yet it is nearly impossible to enforce the boundaries between neo-Nazism and the alt-right when they coexist in a Venn diagram of overlapping individuals and groups that are hyperlinked online, and when white power references brim under the surface.

This concerted push to rebrand brings to mind white nationalists in the early 2000s who realized that hoods and swastikas were alienating rather than attracting potential followers. Stormfront, for instance, the oldest white supremacist website and message board, was founded in 1995 by former Ku Klux Klan leader Don Black, who foresaw the potential of the internet as a vehicle to disseminate racism.[3] Cognizant of the Right's major image problem, due in part to the insights of his son, Derek, who later disavowed white nationalism, in 2008 Black prohibited the swastika and Klan symbols from the website. His mentor and collaborator David Duke endorsed this removal as "a no brainer to me. Avatars that promote or satirize lynchings or mass murder, or that promote NS [National Socialist] or Klan symbology, only get in the way of our most fundamental task: the task of awakening, educating, motivating and organizing our people around the world."[4] Duke, once a KKK Grand Wizard and an unwavering hardline presence in white nationalism since the 1970s, recognized, if only for public relations reasons, the strategic importance of redesigning the face and symbols of the movement in the twenty-first century.

This defanging helped propel the migration of white power icons to multiplying online spaces such as 4chan (/pol/), 8chan, Reddit (r/_The Donald), and, most recently, Gab and BitChute, where they have proliferated with abandon.[5] Five minutes of lurking in these virtual communities yields a panoply of symbols and references, to iron crosses, black suns, ancient runes, numerals such as eighty-eight for "Heil Hitler" (H is the eighth letter of alphabet) and fourteen for the adage coined by the Order's David Lane ("we must secure the existence of our people and a future for white children"), as well as invocations of the Kali Yuga and the Golden Age. These anonymous realms are inhabited by racist agitators, avatars, and aliases, and contain digital chasms drenched in blood-curdling ripostes and depraved cartoon depictions of the death and dismemberment of Jews, blacks, immigrants, and women.

Today the alt-right is a movement with one foot planted in recalcitrant white supremacy and neo-Nazism, and the other foot walking in step with ethnonationalism, identitarianism, and "white identity politics." Although the former incarnation is far from defunct and carries a transgressive charge that some alt-righters find irresistible, many of the new disciples of white nationalism consider it a relic of the twentieth century. Gone are the days of insular organizations like the KKK or Aryan Nations, the latter of which holed up in compounds in remote regions of the West with big caches of guns and ammunition, waiting for raids and rapture.[6] As the Southern Poverty Law Center commented in its review of hate and extremism in 2017, "It's clear that the new generation of white supremacists is rejecting the hooded movement that was founded after the Civil War."[7]

The alt-right is more international, suited-up, and image conscious than its predecessors. It strives to fine-tune its skills of dissimulation and its techniques for winning over "normies" and infiltrating mainstream institutions. Contemporary admonitions are "Don't carry a Nazi flag" and "Care about how you look."[8] Selling the brand is at the top of the agenda. At the second Scandza Forum in Stockholm, Sweden, in spring 2018, white nationalist torchbearers Jared Taylor, Greg Johnson, and Patrick Casey all addressed in some way how the movement should employ advertising techniques for the purposes of product persuasion and marketing.[9] Many alt-righters sneer, if hypocritically, at the tattooed rabble-rousers who take to the streets to confront protestors or carry out acts of carnage like the massacre of eleven Jewish parishioners at the Temple of Life synagogue in Pittsburgh in fall 2018. These kinds of actors are lampooned as cosplayers, LARPers, and trigger-ready maniacs who defame the movement and do "nothing to advance our cause and much to set us back."[10]

One comment posted to a July 2018 Identity Evropa podcast taking stock of the alt-right captured this attitude: "We need to, with our actions, show the people around us that we are not 'Nazis' running around with baseball bats and being thugs. We are not thugs, we are gentlemen and honorable people."[11] As James Allsup, a leader in Students for Trump during the 2016 election who affiliates with the alt-right, explains, it is a serious detriment if "the public face of identitarianism is a slack-jawed obese guy, you know, throwing up Roman salutes in a stahlhelm." More than ever, alt-righters want to prove that they "are not the caricature the media puts out there" but rather "are normal young men and women who want to raise our kids in a nation that looks more like the nation our parents and grandparents grew up in."[12]

The push to normalize nationalism is plainly visible at in-person alt-right gatherings. In Tennessee in spring 2018, tucked away from media intrusion by the likes of *Huffington Post*, which requested but was denied access, American Renaissance held its sixteenth annual meeting with the theme "Courage and Perseverance." The program included eight speakers and reports from the leaders of Identity Evropa, Counter-Currents' publishing arm, the anti-immigrant VDARE, and *Occidental Quarterly*, run by the anti-Semite Kevin MacDonald.[13] About two hundred fifty people listened to a standard fare of talks on the menace of Muslim immigration in Europe, the ostensible plight of Boers/whites in South Africa, and the biological basis for racial differences in IQ and other human traits. In addition, much due was paid to rising identitarian movements in Europe. There was consensus that the alt-right is at a crossroads of countervailing forces, disseminating a message that they believe will resonate with an increasing number of white people, while fighting against the headwinds of media censure and deplatforming: "More people than ever are joining our cause, and science reveals new findings that support us almost every week. Across the West, there is a palpable sense of white people awakening to their identity and destiny. At the same time, we face unprecedented repression."[14]

The trend of "normalizing nationalism" is exemplified by Identity Evropa (recently rebranded the American Identity Movement), an explicitly identitarian group whose mission as an expressed "non-violent organization" is "to create a better world for people of European heritage—particularly in America—by peacefully effecting cultural change."[15] Sporting a scrubbed, well-dressed image that favors preppy clothing, Identity Evropa appeals to millennials and Generation Z, who hit the ground for guerrilla theater and flash mobs, although it claims a generational range extending to middle-aged members. Its recruits are expected to join community action projects like cleaning up debris at local parks and donation drives for the Purple Heart Foundation. Identity Evropa is the cutting edge of the alt-right, refashioning European-style ethnonationalism for the American context. This group has seen significant growth, from a single founding chapter in 2017 to fifteen chapters and counting as of fall 2018.[16]

More specifically, Identity Evropa embodies the transition from the twentieth-century white power movement to the twenty-first-century alt-right. In order to keep out the LARPers and ruffians, its application requires verification that, in addition to being of European descent, its members have no felonies and bear no tattoos.[17] IE spokesmen like to describe their organization as packed with "high agency men" and "carefully selected high quality people." On a segment of the *Identitarian Action* podcast focused on anti-immigration activism on the San Diego-Tijuana border, the conversation veered several times into the centrality of fitness and bodybuilding. Participants agreed that IE members must stay in tip-top shape by exercising—preferably weight training and martial arts—because in their organization, "there shouldn't be anyone who is obese. There shouldn't be anyone who is out of shape."[18]

Reflecting the alt-right's fixation on fitness, the Golden One (aka Marcus Follin), a Swedish bodybuilder who maintains a popular YouTube site, was an invited speaker at the American Renaissance meeting. Cultivating an image of himself as a blond-haired and blue-eyed Thor ready for a World Wide Wrestling match, the Golden One flexed his biceps and stressed physique and self-care. His YouTube channel, started in 2012, features workout routines, often performed in natural settings and against backdrops that evoke Nordic mythology.[19] The Golden One implored men to adhere to a regimented lifestyle and shared his eight rules for self-regulation, the first two of which are "We should always dress well, appropriately to the occasion," and "We should be fit and pursue the ideal of a 'healthy mind in a healthy body.'" Following these regimens will help mainstream "the radical notion that it's OK to be white, the radical notion that we don't want to be replaced in our own nations."[20]

All the speakers at the flagship alt-right meetings in 2018 were men. Despite homage paid to wholesome white families and communities, the drive toward normalization is utterly male-centric. The number of female attendees at alt-right meetings is exceedingly low. A photograph taken at the Identity Evropa conference, for instance shows only two women among the seventy attendees.[21] If the alt-right is consistently anything, it is a white fraternity in which men perform for other men, and the expectation is that women will stay on the margins, serve as helpmates, or, if they are vocal, remain on script online endorsing traditionalism and patriarchal arrangements.

Recent developments have rearranged the cast of the alt-right, particularly with regard to figurehead Richard Spencer. Media coverage gives the impression that Spencer remains the de facto leader of the alt-right. However, his star has faded among alt-righters considerably. Spencer is dismissed, even considered radioactive, viewed as a blowhard who has sidled up to déclassé agitators and made tactical errors. For example, Greg Johnson (who, according to the Southern Poverty Law Center, is known for cantankerous squabbling) criticized Spencer in 2014 for stubbornly holding a conference in Budapest, even after the government stated it would cancel the event and arrest participants. Johnson did not participate, and Spencer was imprisoned for a short while in Hungary.[22] RamZPaul, who hosts the weekly YouTube show *Happy Homelands*, rebuked Spencer for Hailgate and for aligning with the Daily Stormer, the website run by Andrew Anglin, one of the most active purveyors of neo-Nazism online: "I warned Richard about the dangers of associating with these Hollywood Nazis privately and in a video response to him. But he insisted on doing a podcast with Anglin the week after Heilgate."[23] Spencer has taken the most heat for co-organizing the 2017 Charlottesville rally, which Paul Kersey, the Yogi Berra of white nationalists, knew was doomed from the beginning. The event was premature and badly planned, said Kersey: "The great travesty of Charlottesville was the iconography that was used to promote the event, and a lot of the flyers that came out. There was no coherent message."[24]

Spencer's ventures, such as Altright.com, *Radix Journal*, and the National Policy Institute, have seen little activity since 2017. From breakout status as the alt-right emperor in the early 2010s, Spencer has become something of a pariah on the sidelines, banned from twenty-six European countries. In summer 2018 he was remanded from Iceland back to the United States en route to a conference in Poland.[25] Although Spencer counts a respectable 78,000 followers on Twitter and occasionally appears on alt-right YouTube livestreams, he is more character actor than leading man. There are figures, like the Americans RamZPaul (Paul Ramsey) and Nick Fuentes, the British Mark Collett, the Scottish Millennial Woes (Colin Robertson), the Swedish Henrik Palmgren, and the French Canadian J. P. Gariépy, who are more involved in blogging, vlogging, hosting shows, and speaking at alt-right gatherings. Spencer is given his due as a foundational figure and continues to be admired by some but is repeatedly criticized as narcissistic or off point in online comments on Twitter, Facebook, Gab, and other fora.

The void left by the sunsetting of Spencer, against the backdrop of continued post-Charlottesville regrouping, has prompted some critics to suggest that the alt-right has peaked.[26] It would be more accurate to say that the alt-right has gone full circle, back to where it was in 2015, before the boom of 2016, the bust of 2017, and the triage of 2018. Nevertheless, over this period, the alt-right has expanded horizontally, shored up publicly by social media networking and behind the scenes by private chat platforms such as Discord and secret Facebook groups.

Paradoxically, shock-and-awe news reporting that conflates neo-Nazis, white supremacists, and the alt-right has worked to infuse alt-right messages and vocabulary into the mainstream.[27] Many alt-righters are more optimistic than ever. Kersey thinks their "nameless movement" can capitalize on current political "disharmony," and Casey asserts that "things are moving in the right direction."[28] Taylor, who traveled to Poland, France, and the Netherlands after the Scandza Forum in fall 2018 to give a series of lectures, reported that his trip was "hugely invigorating" because he was met by adulating crowds of "young, attractive, accomplished, well-informed people who see the world identically." He claims that twenty years earlier a similar trip would have involved giving speeches to rooms of listless "geezers." Now Taylor finds in these European countries young people who are "fully racially wide awake."[29] Johnson was giddy about Unite the Right 2, declaring it "*good* for white identity politics." In part he was relieved that the "marchers were peaceful and mostly presentable," conferring respectability to the movement. On *This Week on The Alt-Right* in early 2019, Mike Enoch, who runs the white nationalist website The Right Stuff, which is home to the podcast *The Daily Shoah*, enthusiastically described 2018 as a great year because "so many babies were born" and alt-right in-person communities grew by leaps and bounds.[30] Even if Alt-Right 1.0 is dead, there is great hope for Alt-Right 2.0, as long as it doesn't jump the neo-Nazi shark.[31]

CONDITIONS OF POSSIBILITY

As the alt-right continues to strive toward normalization with the end goal of conducting a "mass seduction of society," there are several political and demographic trends in American society that suggest the future is conducive to alt-right creep.[32] It is reassuring to learn that the portion of the American population estimated as alt-right is very small. According to researcher George Hawley, who wrote the book *Making Sense of the Alt-Right* and has mined survey data to produce some of the only demographic analysis of the alt-right, 6 percent, or eleven million, of the two hundred million whites in America have beliefs that would classify them as white nationalists.[33] Extracting data from 3,083 non-Hispanic whites sampled in the 2016 American National Election Survey (ANES), Hawley identified three questions that could be correlated with alt-right sympathy: 1) a strong sense of white identity, 2) a belief in white solidarity, and 3) a feeling of white victimization. To be placed in the alt-right camp, respondents needed to indicate that these three beliefs were "very" or "extremely" important to them, criteria that produced a convergence of 6 percent.

Although it is prudent to set a stringent bar to qualify as alt-right or white nationalist, it is eye-opening that significantly higher percentages of the sample agreed with at least one of the three statements, with 27 percent expressing feelings of white victimization, 28 percent of white identity, and 38 percent of white solidarity. The strongest correlations with alt-right sentiments were among people with low-income levels ($29,000 or less annually), no college degree, and who were divorced. Respondents over sixty-five years of age were the most likely to take alt-right ideas to heart. White women were slightly more likely than white men to identify with these beliefs, underscoring the appeal of conceptions of heritage, ancestry, and racial preservation to white women and the prospect of more female converts.[34]

A 2017 Reuters/Ipsos poll conducted in conjunction with the University of Virginia Center for Politics found similar patterns.[35] This survey included a sample of 5,360 adults of all racial and ethnic backgrounds, including 2,255 Democrats, 1,915 Republicans, and 689 independents. Only 6 percent said they supported the alt-right, and even fewer, 4 percent, endorsed neo-Nazis, compared with 32 percent support for Black Lives Matter. Nevertheless, 31 percent agreed with the statement that "America must protect and preserve its White European heritage." A larger percentage, 59 percent, concurred that "political correctness" jeopardizes Americans' freedom to "speak our minds." Survey results reveal awareness of persistent racism and solid backing for racial equality, with 82 percent believing that all races are equal and 55 percent that racial minorities are under attack in the United States. However, a noticeable 39 percent believe that "white people are currently under attack in this country," with 21 percent of Democrats in agreement compared to 63 percent of Republicans.[36]

Beyond looking at beliefs about white victimization or threatened European heritage that might resonate with the alt-right, there are overarching attitudinal trends that indicate openness to authoritarian and populist politics. Recent political opinion surveys in the United States and several European countries have found that younger people are not sanguine about or even particularly invested in democracy as a political system. They are more likely to gravitate toward either the left or right side of the political spectrum than the center, and, troublingly, "almost half of millennials [have] expressed approval for a 'strong leader.'"[37] Memories of World War II and the Holocaust, which set the stage for the post-war global order of human rights, are fading as the "greatest generation" dies.[38] Countries such as Hungary and Poland have enshrined ethnona-tionalism as the foremost principle for nationhood, forging more space in Europe for the acceptance of anti-immigration policies and xenophobic political parties.

In a related vein, political scientists have analyzed data tracking as-sociations between perceived normative threats and authoritarianism in Europe, and conclude that the seeds of illiberalism and anti-democratic populism are encased in "advanced liberal democracies." In short, democ-racy is not a bulwark against authoritarianism, which can manifest when circumstances allow: "there is remarkably little evidence that living in a liberal democracy generally makes people more democratic and toler-ant."[39] Political psychologist Karen Stenner suggests that authoritarianism is driven less by an "aversion to change but by an aversion to complex-ity," a disposition that raises formidable questions about how American democracy will weather growing multiculturalism in the coming decades.[40] Geopolitically, developments around the world, including the rise of au-tocratic leaders and support among younger generations for military-style governments, suggest that "the long century during which Western liberal democracies dominated the globe has ended for good."[41] Populism does not intrinsically lean to the right, nor precipitate fascism, but the vari-ants of national populism taking hold in the United States and Europe are animated by a toxic combination of xenophobia and a potent sense of dispossession among whites. This solidifying wave of national populism, characterized by a deep distrust of liberalism and political insiders and by existential concerns about demographic change, reflects, according to scholars Roger Eatwell and Matthew Goodwin, not the "'last howl of rage' from old white men soon to be replaced by tolerant Millennials" but rather a "new era of political fragmentation, volatility, and disruption."[42]

Compounding these unnerving trends is intensifying partisan polarization in the United States, which is linked first and foremost to divergence between Republican and Democratic voters when it comes to racial make-up and racial attitudes. This trend, which started in the 1970s, reached an all-time high in the 2016 election and shows no sign of abating. Over the past fifty years, the Republican electorate has become whiter and more conservative; its Democratic counterpart has become multiracial. For instance, from 1976 to 2012, as America's diversity increased, nonwhite Republican voters participating in presidential elections rose slightly from 4 percent to 10 percent. In comparison, nonwhite Democratic voters shot up from 15 percent to 45 percent over the same period.[43]

Conventional wisdom has suggested that economic resentment breeds racial discrimination, and that can explain voters who opposed Obama in the 2008 and 2012 elections, and backed Trump in the last presidential election. However, Alan Abramowitz, author of *The Great Realignment: Race, Party Transformation, and the Rise of Donald Trump*, concludes that the reverse is true. Racial division is the principal explanation for the widening ideological, regional, and demographic crevasse between Democrats and Republicans, propelled by ratcheting racial resentment among Republican voters. According to Abramowitz, "The key to Trump's success in the 2016 Republican primaries was the dramatic increase in racial resentment among GOP voters between the 1980s and 2010s that created a receptive audience for his racist appeals."[44] The sociologist Arlie Hochschild witnessed these sentiments firsthand when conducting her ethnographic study of the everyday experiences, emotional outlooks, and political affiliations of poor whites in rural Louisiana, who were attracted to Trump as the "identity politics candidate for white men."[45]

An integral and troublesome dimension of this racism is the animus of whites against Latina/os, the country's largest ethnic group. Indeed, the noticeable shift of whites from the Democratic to the Republican Party over the past several decades is correlated with proliferating negative stereotypes of Latina/os: "There is an ongoing and often-repeated threat narrative that links the United States' immigrant and Latino populations to a host of pernicious fiscal, social, and cultural consequences."[46] Trump has taken this anti-Latina/o sentiment to unprecedented heights, enacting a "zero tolerance" policy on the US-Mexico border that has separated parents and children and circumscribed criteria for asylum, and called for an end to due process for border crossers, a right secured by the Fourteenth Amendment.[47] In the 2016 election, Republican voters, the vast majority of whom are white, were particularly swayed by Trump's "calls for deportation of undocumented immigrants and a ban on Muslim immigration, along with his proposal to build a wall along the Mexican border."[48] This dynamic is illustrated by a Pew Research poll that found that though Democrats opposed the border wall by an 84 percent margin, Republicans supported it by 63 percent.[49] Anti-Latina/o and anti-immigrant racism is transposed to Muslims, and has analogues throughout Europe, where right-wing parties have surged in the past decade, driven by concerns about "migrant invasions" and the abasement of European culture.[50] Xenophobic parties are winnings seats in Sweden, France, and the Netherlands, and ethnonationalist leaders have been elected in Poland and Italy; this advancing right-wing flank is exerting pressure on Germany and the European Union to shut the gates to migrants and refugees.[51]

The alt-right wants to take advantage of these partisan and racial divides, to locate whites and Republicans who might be receptive to its message and to use political mechanisms, where possible, to expand its reach. Allsup, for example, is less interested in the metapolitical than in crafting political messaging that will get white nationalist results.[52] On one hand, alt-righters want to stealthily detect their brethren by testing the waters among friends and family. One tactic is to dog-whistle issues and drop the names of "our guys" like Ann Coulter, Tucker Carlson, and Steve Sailer in casual conversation and assess reactions. On the other, the alt-right strategy is to build capacity through local politics, joining the PTA or the transportation board, and infusing alt-right values one local institution at a time. As one alt-righter said in an *Identitarian Action* podcast, it is "only a matter of time until the next Flint water crisis," and when it arrives, white nationalists need to be prepared to capitalize on the moment and attain greater visibility and legitimacy.[53]

In the meantime, the alt-right devotes a great deal of its airtime to loudly conveying data drawn from the US Census, which projects that by 2050, if not earlier, the population will transform from majority white to a racial plurality, a realignment already consolidated in California and Texas. Americans who identify as white only (with no Hispanic or multiracial heritage) are having fewer children, and white men, in particular, are dying at higher rates than previously, a phenomenon that has raised public-health concerns.[54] Armed with this information and relying on the most constricted interpretation of the category "white"—as exclusively non-Hispanic whites—alt-righters view the mid-twenty-first century as the point of no return. Their claims actually have been facilitated by changes to the US Census, which, starting in 2000, adjusted how it counts populations and racial groups and designs its projection series. According to political scientists who have studied political attitudes around census information, "These changes have generated an unintended exaggeration of the pace of future white decline."[55] Indeed, how census projections have been presented and disseminated in recent years has given the impression that "demographic change was accelerating toward the threshold of a majority-minority society." Notably, if Hispanic, an ethnic category, were conflated with white in racial demographic projections, then whites would remain the majority until 2060. And if whites with any multiracial heritage were included (i.e., white mother and black father), then whites would remain the majority for the foreseeable future.

Based on the most reductionist of demographic projections, alt-righters clang the bell of white extinction: "If present trends are not reversed, whites will disappear as a distinct race."[56] It is significant that white nationalists are not a minuscule minority when it comes to negative assessments of America's unfolding demographic transition. A poll conducted by the nonpartisan Public Religion Research Institute found that when asked the broad question "Do you think the likely impact of this coming demographic change will be mostly negative or mostly positive," the majority of Americans, 64 percent, responded that it would be positive. Yet nearly one-third, 31 percent, indicated they thought it would be deleterious. More striking, while 85 percent of Democrats responded affirmatively to this question, half of Republicans (50 percent) believe that diversity is detrimental.[57] How information about census projections is worded in surveys has an impact on whether whites evince apprehension about demographic changes, including the terminology "majority-minority," which imparts the idea that whites will fall from demographic grace and become outnumbered by minorities. One study, for example, found that "information about the 'majority-minority' racial demographic shift increases whites' sense that their racial group's societal status is in jeopardy, which, in turn, leads to greater support for politically conservative parties, policies and candidates."[58] Thus, the language of demographic transition—how such projections are phrased—is critical to political discourse, and terms like "majority-minority" are more conducive to the alt-right than ones accentuating ethnoracial plurality.

ASSAULTING CIVIC NATIONALISM

One of the most disconcerting facets of the alt-right is how it seeks to undermine civic nationalism in the United States. The line between civic nationalism and ethno- or racial nationalism is being abraded to the point of erasure. Although Democrats and Republicans often take differing positions on a wide range of issues, these frequently are articulated through the frameworks of civic nationalism, which is "premised on an ideological commitment to a common destiny and government through shared civic institutions."[59] After all, the "Southern strategy" shrewdly employed by politicians such as Richard Nixon repackaged white racism against blacks into a set of coded phrases like "states' rights" and "law and order" in order to stay grudgingly within, not exceed, the bounds of civic nationalism. The racial meanings of these euphemisms might have been an open secret, but blatant racial nationalism as the primary motor of politics was frowned upon.[60] These days, racial nationalism, which "derives its force from a sense of kinship and a myth of shared ancestry that is thought to predate statehood" has gained substantial traction in America and across the world.[61]

America has always been a racial state, a nation founded on slavery and white supremacy, that only recognized African Americans as citizens in 1868 ("all persons born or naturalized in the United States") and kept the tenets of the Naturalization Act of 1790, which reserved full-fledged citizenship for "free white persons," on the books until 1952. Civic principles—as embodied in the US Constitution and milestone legal precedents—have offered tools for people marginalized and relegated to second-class citizenship to fight for their rights and for a more inclusive society, no matter how partial those victories might have been.[62] The boundaries of civic nationalism have been transgressed again and again in American history when racism or xenophobia erupted, for example, with the passage of the 1882 Chinese Exclusion Act or during the internment of Japanese Americans during World War II. Nikhil Pan Singh suggests that America has oscillated rumbustiously between its noble universalizing abstractions and a "persistent regression" to exclusionary white nationalism.[63]

In the current moment, the forces of regression are bracingly strong, and intensifying. According to Steven Levitsky and Daniel Ziblatt, authors of *How Democracies Die*, Trump, like authoritarian leaders past and present who came to power not through a coup d'état but legally, through the ballot box, is implementing policies and behaving in ways that severely undercut American democracy. Specifically, Trump has met in spades the four warning signs formulated by these two scholars to identify incipient authoritarianism. He has rejected "the democratic rules of the game," denied "the legitimacy of his opponents," countenanced or promoted violence, and shown a "willingness to curtail the civil liberties of opponents, including the media."[64] In the current context, cherished principles of rights and liberal subjecthood, codified in the Constitution and in law, are under grave assault.[65] As this ground buckles, the alt-right eagerly eyes and eggs on the eclipse of civic nationalism and its replacement, whether through abrupt or gradual means, with ethnonationalism, culminating in a white "homeland of our own."[66]

Terminating birthright citizenship, which Trump has proposed doing by fiat in the form of an executive order, epitomizes these trends, as does the policy of "extreme vetting" for potential immigrants and citizens.[67] Yet such exacting scrutiny wins support from both self-identified civic and racial nationalists. In a recent YouTube debate hosted by Allsup, civic nationalists were represented by a member of the fraternal group the Proud Boys and racial nationalists by a host of *The Daily Shoah*. Yet rather than displaying disagreement, this debate quickly lapsed into a consensus that "every single person should be vetted to the most extreme standard" and that "mass immigration of any group" should never be permitted.[68] Similarly, British white nationalist Mark Collett was very pleased with Trump's comments in summer 2018 about immigration changing Europe's culture for the worse; in a YouTube video montage with voice-over Collett told subscribers, referring to the right-wing British National Party, that Trump's jeremiad "sounds like a headline from a Nationalist leaflet."[69] Increasingly, white nationalist anti-immigrant positions are becoming mainstream. Our country has become home to dehumanizing policies and practices that involve the open-ended detention of more than fourteen thousand children in camps at the US-Mexico border, emulating strategies of racial containment in the proposed white ethnostate, which specifically targets nonwhite children for expulsion.[70] Nastily caricatured as "anchor babies," children born in the United States to undocumented parents, who received right-wing scrutiny in the past, have become "suspect citizens" seen as diminished and unworthy.[71]

Ethnonationalism is built on "blood and soil" antipathy to the Enlightenment and the worship of an imagined prelapsarian time of tribal solidarity, before the existence of social contracts, citizen subjects, and human rights. As Casey of Identity Evropa told the audience at his organization's inaugural meeting in 2018, identitarianism's objective is to supplant equality with hierarchy, individualism with duty and responsibility, and progress with what benefits white people.[72] More succinctly, American Thinker, an alt-right avatar, tweeted, "Defeating egalitarianism is the total victory."[73] Such a transformation entails a repudiation of the foundational tenets of equality, liberty, and justice for all. The alt-right's screeds against globalism, often grossly anti-Semitic, capture this thirst for archaism, as does its gender politics, which foregrounds patriarchal roles in which men are warriors, protectors, and providers and women are wives, breeders, and nurturers. Nevertheless, the alt-right is not simply on a nostalgia trip about the halcyon days. It expresses great interest in adapting modern technologies, scientific and informatic, into Faye's "archeofuturism," a term fetishized by many on the alt-right, including Casey, whose blog *Reactionary Futurism* clarifies his view: "I value the past, but I have no desire to try to return to it."[74]

It should not be forgotten that the alt-right has subcultural appeal because it can tell a tidy and compelling story, in which racial groups are collective actors and the social strife and complexity generated by multiculturalism, feminism, and demographic change can be overwhelmed by *Volk* cohesion and closeness. Some alt-right fantasies about the white ethnostate, for example, disclose a sentimental thirst for connection and community: "There is an intense, uncontrollable longing that marks our daily lives. We know there is something out of place. From the moment we are born, it is there."[75] This itching for belonging resembles what Michael Ignatieff described in his peregrinations to six regions of the world in the early 1990s after the fall of the Berlin Wall and the thawing of the Cold War. In places as distinct as Croatia and Serbia, Quebec and Kurdistan, he chronicled the stirrings of a new brand of ethnic nationalism, realized most profoundly when it tapped into "full belonging" or "the warm sensation that people understand not merely what you say but what you mean," which is possible "only when you are among your own people in your native land."[76] For now the ethnostate is only accessible virtually, through the web and on platforms like Twitter and YouTube. *Counter-Currents* thus likes to talk about developing an expandable and resilient "electronic ethnostate" that can act as a fortress and digital arena from which white nationalists can lob their "missives, arrows, and ravens" as they prepare for an actual homogenous homeland.[77]

As these cravings illustrate, virtual domains allow for mediated, interactive, and shared modalities of connection and identity formation. As is the case with online communities, the alt-right benefits from the "soft, networked structures of feeling" that draw users to internet spaces.[78] The alt-right enjoys and exploits the affective dimensions of the online platforms, which enable the enactment of everyday practices of meaning making, through speech, image, and meme utterances, and through the habituation and repetition that reinforces underlying ideologies and assumptions.[79]

Alongside the alt-right's noisy vitriol, anger, and mordancy, then, is a complementary if contradictory quest for authenticity, wholeness, and boundedness, which is narrated individualistically through tales of red pilling and expressed collectively through parables of metapolitical awakening. Alt-righters want to come home, to the safety and sameness of their tribe. Yet for all its sentimentality, alt-right storytelling is buttressed by a harsh dualistic worldview: order over chaos. Dominance hierarchies rigidly tied to male and female, and all racial groups, imagined as discrete populations, in their separate places. Neatness, order, and control are fascist hallmarks of the alt-right mindset.

In closing, I'd like to bring this analysis back home to Ann Arbor, Michigan, where this project started. Recently Austin, an African American colleague who has been active in antiracist struggles at the University of Michigan campus and nationwide, shared with me a letter, with no return address, that had been surreptitiously left at his apartment complex by someone who managed to enter the locked entry door. Written by "Iron Mitten" (an avatar that combines a neo-Nazi nod to iron's relevance in Third Reich iconography with a visual representation of Michigan's geographic mitten shape), a tweeter who trolled Austin and other colleagues in 2016 when we spoke out against the plastering of racist flyers on our campus, this three-page letter is a testament to the influence of alt-right thinking on a Michigander. Iron Mitten offered Austin the alt-right version of a backhanded compliment for his antiracist work—"you sincerely care about your people, and that is something I respect"—followed by a litany of white nationalist talking points about the impending demise of white people and the inherent violence of blacks.

Iron Mitten, like other alt-righters discussed in this chapter, is optimistic about the future, stating, "We have slaughtered the sacred cows of the left with memes made of humor and facts," and emphasizing that more and more "normies" are grasping the truth about biological racial differences and the ramifications of the 1965 Hart-Celler Immigration Act. He warns Austin, writing, "My views will be normalized and almost mainstream [in] a few short years if Tucker Carlson is any indication, and I suspect you will miss the days when White people had been distracted with individualism."[80] Iron Mitten states that he wants to write a book about the alt-right, assuring Austin he will have "a spot in the acknowledgments." A good portion of the letter focuses on the need, due to racial disharmony and differences, to create a black ethnostate: "The most simple and peaceful solution is to choose a couple Southern states with the largest Black populations and make them into the Federated Black States of America or something to that effect." Although one lone letter, stalkingly delivered to a single person, is not evidence of extensive alt-right creep, this communication captures the ripple effects, and interlocking noxious beliefs, of an avatar with real-life ambitions. This letter contains many of the concepts, ideas, and keywords explored in this book and can serve as an admonition of the pernicious mind-set and emotional valences of white nationalism in the twenty-first century.

DECODING AND DERAILING WHITE NATIONALIST DISCOURSE

The alt-right is nowhere and everywhere. Nowhere, because its core believers constitute a tiny fraction of the white nationalist faithful in a bigger multicultural and multiracial sea. Its brand is dismissed and derided, and ongoing deplatforming has compelled its leaders and acolytes to play a perpetual game of online whack-a-mole. Everywhere, because alt-right ideas have set down sinewy roots in American discourse, culture, and politics. Terms such as "cuck," "identitarian," and "red pill" are recognized by many and Google-able by all. Worse, Trumpian rhetoric and policies have opened the door to an unwanted visitor peddling ideas that are antithetical to cherished values of social equality, racial inclusion, human rights, and collective dignity. It is not the first time that this intimate stranger has come calling. It has long lurked ominously just outside the door, and it has traumatized, handcuffed, shot, whipped, punished, restrained, maimed, murdered, and condescended in the name of patriarchal white America in the past. Yet right now the contemporary conditions are hospitable for an extended stay. Alt-right ideas might be held tightly by a few, but in the current climate their potential reach is perilously large.

This book has sought to provide tools for mapping and understanding the magnifying presence, ideas, and outgrowth of the alt-right, right here, right now. This exercise involves teasing out manifestations of fascism in white nationalist narratives and unpacking tropes of individual and collective rebirth, cyclical time, gender essentialism, and racial difference. It also requires discernment of the profound affective dimensions of digital worlds and platforms, which have mediated and modulated alt-right identities and networks, granting them a wider berth and multiple points of access. My hope is that by dismantling and disassembling alt-right ideas, and scrutinizing their flawed logics and bigoted assumptions, we will be better able to defuse and short-circuit them.

It is challenging, when living through a time of passage to a darker, scarier place, to find the respite and footing to analyze how things as amorphous as ideas and concepts can insinuate themselves into, and shape, politics and discourse.[1] Even though such tracking will, by virtue of being amidst the swirling mess of the moment, be confounding and imprecise, it is imperative to try with the tools at our disposal. With that motivation in mind, we can unpack a handful of examples of alt-right messaging, illuminating the mercurial back-and-forth movement between the margins of the internet and the zenith of presidential power. I have chosen three vignettes that bear out the extent to which alt-right terminology and concepts are setting the parameters of possibility and have become legible ways of seeing and knowing. This discursive realignment is exactly what the alt-right means when they talk about metapolitical change, and it's why there is reason for optimism among white nationalists, even as they are suspended on Twitter and blocked on YouTube. This also is why hastily labeling them as neo-Nazis and white supremacists, while an understandable impulse, can be counterproductive. Rather than rushing to see them as outliers, today's white nationalists might be more aptly recognized as intimate strangers underhandedly outstretching to reach America's alt-right "tipping point."[2] As one alt-righter explained to a *New York Times* reporter in a recent article on the shocking indifference of law enforcement to rising white nationalism: "This idea that the alt-right is falling apart and is going to go away, it's not true." Referring to the tropes of white genocide and migrant caravans, he crowed, "The alt-right formulates all these ideas," adding, "What Tucker Carlson talks about, we talked about a year ago."[3]

"White genocide" is one of these nefarious ideas, conjured into being by alt-right media warriors, right-wing pundits, and the POTUS himself.

In August 2018, on his Fox News show, Tucker Carlson criticized the US State Department for failing to protect white South African farmers from land seizures, putatively being carried out en masse by the black African–led government.[4] Although the reference for this specific claim was not clear, it is an open secret that white nationalists are the primary group making the most noise about the ostensibly out-of-control killing of white South African farmers. Most notably, Lauren Southern, a Canadian nationalist, who has been banned from the UK for strident Islamophobia but managed to tour Australia with Stefan Molyneux in summer 2018, released the movie *Farmlands*.[5] In this agitprop, Southern wears the cloak of objectivity, assuring viewers that she is on the hunt for the "real story," but the one she tells is decidedly about white eradication, dramatizing the made-up travesty of the seizure of centuries-held Afrikaner homesteads. Carlson's reference of the plight of white South African farmers, thus, was practically a plug for *Farmlands* and an endorsement of the platform of AfriForum, an Afrikaner rights organization, which the Council on Foreign Relations cautions is "raising the specter of the murder of white farmers and stoking fears of 'white genocide' among American, European, and Australian leaders and media outlets."[6]

Within two hours of Carlson's broadcast, Trump issued a tweet, tagging Carlson, indicating that he had asked Secretary of State Mike Pompeo to "closely study the South Africa land and farm seizures and expropriations and the large scale killing of farmers."[7] Not surprisingly, Trump's tweet elicited praise from the alt-right and from Southern, who glowed, "To have Donald Trump tweet about the seizure of white [owned] land in South Africa, as well as the farm murders, is finally going to put this on the global issues that we're talking about."[8] For its part, the South African government condemned Trump's tweet as a mistruth, and major news outlets reported at some length on the issue, finding that extant information contradicts allegations that Afrikaner farmers are being killed at exorbitant rates. For instance, a recent report by a "consortium of agricultural associations said that the number of farmers killed from 2017 to 2018—47—was actually at a 20-year low."[9] The BBC reports, "There is no reliable data to suggest farmers are at greater risk of being murdered than the average South African."[10] For its part, the Anti-Defamation League lambasted POTUS' tweet as "one of the most startling examples of this president indulging in racist thinking."[11]

The power of this confabulation—of white farmers being ethnically cleansed and murdered by marauding vengeful blacks—could have been pulled directly out of *The Turner Diaries* or Harold Covington's *Brigade*. In these scenarios, the survival of dispossessed whites, who have been reduced to a pathetic and persecuted smattering, is on the line, and the only response to racial annihilation is white vigilante resistance and insurrection. The specter of "white genocide" pervades *Farmlands*, making South Africa the screen onto which alt-righters project their smoldering rage because America is mutating into a country where whites will be nothing more than a despised minority, subject to untold oppression and left to fend for themselves.[12]

Alt-righters brazenly appropriate the word "genocide," which acquired its contemporary meaning in the immediate aftermath of World War II, when the United Nations defined it as acts carried out with the "intent to destroy, in whole or in part, a national, ethnical, racial or religious group," including "killing members of the group; causing serious bodily or mental harm to members of the group"; or "deliberately inflicting on the group conditions of life calculated to bring about its physical destruction."[13] Even though as of 2018 whites constitute 61 percent of the US population, and 77 percent if white Hispanics are included in the count, and white families possess a median worth ten times that of black families, in the alt-right dystopia "whites are an endangered race" whose extinction is being expedited by the bulldozing combination of "habitat loss, invasive species, hybridization, and predation."[14] "White" plus "genocide" is a match invented by alt-righters, one we must question at every step and utterance, and not accept with complacency.

We must exert similar pushback against alt-right renditions of demographic change, which raise fears about an accelerated timescape of white extinction and the browning of America. This alt-right standard was played by another Fox News host, Laura Ingraham, on her show *The Ingraham Angle* in August 2018. In the context of the unpredicted victory of Democratic Socialist Alexandria Ocasio-Cortez, Ingraham reflected on political transformations afoot in America. Ingraham quipped, "In some parts of the country, it does seem like the America we know and love doesn't exist anymore. Massive demographic changes have been foisted upon the American people. And they're changes that none of us ever voted for and most of us don't like. From Virginia to California, we see stark examples of how radically, in some ways, the country has changed. How much of this is related to both illegal and, in some cases, legal immigration that, of course, progressives love."[15]

Ingraham's requiem was for a bygone white conservative America. In her telling, this idyllic homeland has been swamped by interlopers and undergone an irrevocable demographic make-over. Scratch the surface and you find ideas of white displacement and dreams of the resurrection of the white ethnostate. Unpack the implicit chronology of her monologue and it's evident the "massive" changes that she complains did not occur at the ballot box can be attributed in large part to the 1965 Hart-Celler Act, the alt-right's demographic watershed.

This was not the first time Ingraham has indulged in alt-right rhetoric, but this statement became a political lightning rod.[16] She was rebuked by progressives and liberals and lauded by white nationalists. David Duke, for example, posted in a later-deleted tweet that her commentary was "one of the most important (truthful) monologues in the history of MSM."[17] In response, Ingraham contended that her monologue did not concern race but rather immigration, emphasizing that Democrats recklessly have supported open border policies. She insisted that her remarks were misconstrued, and aware that Duke had repeated them, she pivoted away from any perceived affiliation with white nationalism, asserting that her "commentary had nothing to do with race or ethnicity." She ran for cover under the canopy of civic nationalism, insisting that her main concern was the "shared goal of keeping America safe and her citizens safe and prosperous."[18] But her backtracking was inconsequential; Ingraham's white dispossession dirge had gone viral on social media. The foreboding, loss, and nostalgia evinced by alt-righters for 90 percent white 1965 America was skipping into the mainstream, chided by some, welcomed by others, but widely understood. What was unspeakable had become speakable and decamped to the center of political discourse and debate. As a reporter for the *Observer* writing about the Ingraham incident recapped, "White nationalism, xenophobia, racism and a fear of so-called 'white genocide' have increasingly moved out of the sketchier corners of the far-right and disreputable online forums, and become entrenched in establishment discourse."[19]

These examples illustrate how alt-right unease about extinction and dispossession revolves around race and immigration. However, this unease also is profoundly linked to insecurities about gender and sexuality, more specifically, the perception that cisgendered male identity is being dethroned by feminism and multiculturalism. That trans people and gender nonbinariness do not and should not exist is an essential belief shared by Trump, the alt-right, and the alt-light. From the outset of his presidency, Trump has assailed trans folks. In short order, he rolled out transgender military bans that have been stymied in the courts but stoked perpetual uncertainty. In October 2018 the Trump administration intensified this animus, announcing sweeping changes to the definition of "transgender," in a move that would erase trans folks from existence by mandating that "sex means a person's status as male or female based on immutable biological traits identifiable by or before birth."[20] Clearly this policy is an attempt to reverse the LGBTQ gains made during the Obama administration. But it is not just another conservative manifestation of sexism and homophobia but rather malignant and punishing transphobia. In his astute analysis of coalescing fascism in the United States, Jason Stanley, author of *How Fascism Works: The Politics of Us and Them*, connects transphobia to fears of white male victimhood, identifying gender nonbinariness as the ultimate menace: "attacking trans women and representing the feared other as a threat to the manhood of the nation are ways of placing the very idea of manhood at the center of political attention."[21] In short, obliterating the possibility of gender fluidity is integral to the restoration of patriarchal white America.

Transphobia is the butter on the bread of much alt-right and alt-light vlogging. For example, in one of his videos, social media personality RamZPaul aims for a thorough take-down of the GenderBread Person, a model created in 2011 by Sam Killermann, a self-described social justice comedian and activist, to promote "understanding the complexity of gender."[22] This infographic often is used in classroom settings, and is akin to the Gender Unicorn, which also stresses gender fluidity and is preferred by some trans activists.[23] From RamZPaul's perspective, the GenderBread Person has tarnished his innocent childhood memories of his grandmother baking gingerbread cookies during Christmas. But, according to RamZPaul, this is par for the course for leftists, who "like to take every childhood symbol and turn it into this rainbow perversion" and "describe to little children their fucked-up views" of "sexuality, and genderness, and gender fluidity."[24] RamZPaul strives to dismember this "gingerbread frankenstein" by ridiculing its four components: gender identity, gender expression, biological sex, and romantic attraction. To RamZPaul, these distinctions are immaterial and bogus, and contradict the proven fact that sex is biological. According to him, each human is either male or female, and, moreover, the gender thing is "bullshit"—people have a sex, not a gender. Being categorically male or female is in our DNA, is genetic, and can't be altered. Gender is sex is biological destiny. This video garnered almost 5,000 views and about 150 comments, many of which are brief, sarcastic, and cruel. One avatar, Generation Zyklon (referring to the euthanizing gas used in Nazi concentration camps), writes, "Everyone grab a rope and go to town," invoking the "day of the rope" incitation in *The Turner Diaries*, when white renegades round up race traitors and hang them in public. In response, another avatar writes, "Synthetic rope for wiggers and trannys is the rule." Alt-right venom against trans folks is expressed with the language of race wars and violence, highlighting the close proximity of white nationalism and transphobia in the alt-right imagination.

Although alt-lighters purposefully abstain from "day of the rope" racism, they do not hesitate to dehumanize trans folks and gender non-binariness on a regular basis. For example, Jordan Peterson voices an almost identical dislike of the GenderBread Person in one of his podcasts. Speaking with Claire Lehmann, the editor of the politically incorrect online webzine *Quillette*, Peterson, in a wide-ranging conversation about the excesses of leftism and feminism, singles out the GenderBread Person as a "ridiculous animation" that is "being pushed forward very hard in institutions all across Canada: elementary schools, junior high schools, the military, police."[25] For him, this infographic is a simplistic crutch that "social constructionists" employ to "enforce what they cannot prove scientifically." Peterson gripes, "The idea that gender identity is independent of biological sex is insane. It's wrong. It's wrong. The scientific data are not only clear; they're clear beyond dispute. It's as bad as claiming that the world is flat, by my estimation." Never mind that the contemporary scientific consensus about sex and gender holds that "there is no single biological measure that unassailably places each and every human into one of two categories—male or female."[26]

Through a multiplicity of channels, alt-right ideas have slipped and seeped into discourse and culture; they are reshaping and warping the

American imagination. Facets of these ideas are not new; racism and sexism often have been repackaged in the reliable American tradition of white domination and privilege. But the alt-right has gained a foothold at a time of tumult and restlessness, of worries about the fate of the planet, of refugees and migrants with nowhere to live and nowhere to land. A virulent brand of national populism is gaining ground, bolstered by xenophobia and contempt for democratic political institutions. European and American demographics are changing, and where some whites, like me and millions of others, see multicultural promise, others see near-guaranteed extinction. The alt-right's younger generations can command social media and have learned from the Left and popular culture how to market an idea encapsulated in a meme. Those of us who cherish civic nationalism, which yes has disappointed as often as it has delivered, must be on alert. White nationalists are sore losers, and they are upset that they no longer dictate the rules of the game.

The alt-right emerged in earnest alongside the Obama administration, gaining traction and solidifying its online counter-presence during those eight years; in the Trump era white nationalism has been unleashed with fury, both incurring intense opprobrium and attracting loyal followers in a compressed period of time. So, you might ask, what are concrete ways to counteract the alt-right? From my perspective as a scholar-activist, I know that we can interrogate and disassemble its metaphors and language, and remain mindful of the perfidious implications of concepts such as the ethnostate and white genocide. We can work tirelessly to keep the alt-right perpetually in a reduced realm of the metapolitical, where "white advocates" can plot but never realize their political schemes. We can impugn the unapologetic rhetoric of white nationalist congressman Steve King, and of other politicians and pundits who speak with less audacious, but dangerously insidious, alt-right forked tongues. We can support watchdog groups like the Southern Poverty Law Center and listen closely to journalists like *Vice*'s Elspeth Reeve, who does bold exposés on Richard Spencer and other white nationalists.[27] We can be vigilant and insist on the human rights of the vulnerable, like undocumented people, families and children of color, and trans folks, who the alt-right wants to banish from the white kingdom. We can expect that white people of good conscience call out sexist and racist narratives of white victimhood and dispposession. Finally, we need to become attuned to the tentacular reach of white identity media, tracking alt-right platforms and modes of dissemination and distribution, and demanding accountability and action from digital services and providers who, despite some pushback, remain hospitable to the perpetuation of alt-right messages and networking.[28] But even if we do all these things and more, we should refrain from hubris and not make the mistake of feeling secure in the current moment.

ACKNOWLEDGMENTS

The idea for this book originated at a conference organized by Osagie, Terence, and Khiara; the forum they provided to begin to assess the political dimensions of racism and bigotry in the Trump era was formative. The manuscript has benefited from the insights of colleagues and friends, and I thank Lisa, Anne, Laura, Johannes, Verena, Andrew, Isabel, Jeff, Josh, Ben, Katie, and Austin for their comments. I also thank my family for their ongoing support. Most of all I am grateful to my editor, Amy, for sticking with me as this book evolved and for being such an engaged and smart editor.

NOTES

INTRODUCTION: THE NEW AND OLD OF WHITE NATIONALISM

1. Katie Reilly, "Here Are All the Times Donald Trump Insulted Mexico," *Time*, August 31, 2016, http://time.com/4473972/donald-trump-mexico-meeting-insult.

2. Arthur Kemp, *March of the Titans: The Complete History of the White Race* (Burlington, IA: Ostara Publications, 2012), Kindle ed., 401.

3. Madison Grant, *The Passing of the Great Race or the Racial Basis of European History* (1916), centenary ed. (Burlington, IA: Ostara Publications, 2016).

4. On the genealogy of the term "alt-right," which was proposed as "alternative right" by both Richard Spencer and Paul Gottfried in summer 2008 and became popularized by 2010, see https://www.spreaker.com/user/bre_faucheux/27cr-richard-spencer-ep-1-mp3_1; site now discontinued. See also Mike Wendling, *Alt-Right: From 4chan to the White House* (London: Pluto Press, 2018).

5. Richard Spencer, "Madison Grant and the American Nation," *Radix Journal*, October 8, 2016, https://radixjournal.com/2016/10/2016-10-6-madison-grant-and-the-american-nation.

6. Nell Irvin Painter, *The History of White People* (New York: W. W. Norton, 2010), 308.

7. "The Passing of the Great Race," *Counter-Currents Publishing*, https://www.counter-currents.com/the-passing-of-the-great-race, accessed December 31, 2018.

8. Greg Johnson, "Remembering Madison Grant: November 19, 1865 to May 30, 1937," *Counter-Currents Publishing*, November 19, 2017, https://www.counter-currents.com/2017/11/remembering-madison-grant.

9. A. Graham, "Profiles of Early Conservationists," *Counter-Currents Publishing*, August 17, 2018, https://www.counter-currents.com/2018/08/profiles-of-early-conservationists/#more-84778.

10. Margot Metroland, "Lothrop Stoddard in Geopolitics," *Counter-Currents Publishing*, June 29, 2016, https://www.counter-currents.com/2016/06/lothrop-stoddard-in-geopolitics.

11. Carol Anderson, *White Rage: The Unspoken Truth of Our Racial Divide* (New York: Bloomsbury, 2016).

12. "About the Internet Archive," Archive.org, https://archive.org/about, accessed October 1, 2018.

13. Quoted in Wendling, *Alt-Right*, 18.

14. Wendling, *Alt-Right*, 17-20; also see David Neiwert, *Alt-America: The Rise of the Radical Right in the Age of Trump* (New York: Verso, 2017).

15. Paul Ramsey (RamZPaul), "The Alt Right—What Went Wrong?," RamZ Paul.com, August 17, 2017, http://www.ramzpaul.com/2017/08the-alt-right-what -went-wrong.html; also see Paul Ramsey, "What Is the Alternative Right?," *Return of Kings*, January 5, 2016, http://www.returnofkings.com/76454/what-is-the -alternative-right.

16. Some of the most insightful are Angela Nagle, *Kill All Normies: Online Culture Wars from 4Chan and Tumblr to Trump and the Alt-Right* (Washington, DC: Zero Books, 2017); Matthew Lyons, Bromma, and It's Going Down, *Ctrl-Alt-Delete* (Montreal: Kersplebedeb Publishing, 2017); Wendling, *Alt-Right*; George Hawley, *Making Sense of the Alt-Right* (New York: Columbia University Press, 2017).

17. Jessica Roy, "How 'Pepe the Frog' Went from Harmless to Hate Symbol," *Los Angeles Times*, October 11, 2016, http://www.latimes.com/politics/la-na-pol-pepe -the-frog-hate-symbol-20161011-snap-htmlstory.html.

18. Team Fix, Abby Ohlheiser, and Caitlin Dewey, "Hillary Clinton's Alt-Right Speech, Annotated," *Washington Post*, August 25, 2016, https://www.washington post.com/news/the-fix/wp/2016/08/25/hillary-clintons-alt-right-speech-annotated /?noredirect=on&utm_term=.454d55c75ac4.

19. Jeff Rindskopf, "20 of Trump's Worst Tweets (So Far)," *Cheat Sheet*, June 15, 2018, https://www.cheatsheet.com/entertainment/trumps-worst-tweets-so-far .html; on the public square, see Henry Jenkins, Mizuko Ito, and danah boyd, *Participatory Culture in a Networked Era: A Conversation on Youth, Learning, Commerce, and Politics* (Cambridge, UK: Polity Press, 2015).

20. Richard Spencer, "Long Live the Emperor!," *Radix Journal*, November 21, 2016, https://www.radixjournal.com/2016/11/2016-11-21-long-live-the-emperor.

21. Andrew Joyce, "Why Trump?," *Radix Journal*, November 11, 2016, https:// www.radixjournal.com/2016/11/2016-11-10-why-trump.

22. Richard Spencer, "We Are the Vanguard Now," *Radix Journal*, November 9, 2016, https://www.radixjournal.com/2016/11/2016-11-9-we-are-the-vanguard -now; site now discontinued.

23. Daniel Lombroso and Yoni Appelbaum, "'Hail Trump!' White Nationalists Salute the President-Elect," *Atlantic*, November 21, 2016, https://www.theatlantic .com/politics/archive/2016/11/richard-spencer-speech-npi/508379.

24. Patrick Casey, "Red Ice Radio: Paul Kersey—Civil Unrest: America Is Coming Undone," Daily Stormer, July 2, 2018, https://dailystormer.name/red-ice -radio-paul-kersey-civil-unrest-america-is-coming-undone.

25. "Happy Homelands—Paul Gottfried," YouTube video, posted by RamZ-Paul, September 8, 2018, https://www.youtube.com/watch?v=Lbr_G5GGiWc& feature=youtu.be.

26. See, for example, patrickcaseyie, "A Tropical Dispatch," *Reactionary Futurism*, October 3, 2018, https://reactionaryfuturism.com/2018/10/03/a -tropical-dispatch. After the exposure of private conversations on the online platforms Discord and Slack, obtained by journalists affiliated with the organization Unicorn Riot and published on the Unicorn Riot site in March 2019, Patrick Casey decided to discontinue Identity Evropa and founded the American Identity Movement, announced with logos brandishing American symbols. Freddy Martinez, Caroline Sinders, and Chris Schiano, "Identity Evropa's Neo-Nazi Organizing Plans Revealed In New Leaks," Unicorn Riot, March 8, 2019, https://unicornriot.ninja/2019/identity-evropas-neo -nazi-organizing-plans-revealed-in-new-leaks.

27. "The End of the Alt-Right: Colin Liddell Interviewed by Quebec Nationalist Magazine 'Harfang,'" *Affirmative Right Blog*, August 15, 2018, https://affirmativeright.blogspot.com/2018/08/the-end-of-alt-right-colin-liddell.html.

28. "The Scandza Forum: Copenhagen 15.9.2018 part 1/2," YouTube video, posted by Vihapuhe FM, September 15, 2018, https://www.youtube.com/watch?v=U9_hohglTYo&feature=youtu.be.

29. "Yule 2018 Live Stream," Red Ice TV, 36:00, December 22, 2018, https://redice.tv/red-ice-tv/yule-2018-live-stream.

30. Madeline Peltz, "What Happens When the No. 1 Cable News Channel Is Steeped in White Nationalist Rhetoric?," *MediaMatters*, December 18, 2018, https://www.mediamatters.org/blog/2018/12/18/tucker-carlsons-advertisers-are-sponsoring-fascism/222348.

31. Jared Holt, "Conservative Media Sure Sound a Whole Lot Like an Alt-Right Podcast Right Now," Right Wing Watch, June 19, 2018, http://www.rightwingwatch.org/post.conservative-media-sure-sound-a-whole-lot-like-an-alt-right-podcast-right-now; site now discontinued. Also see Whitney Philips, "The Oxygen of Amplification: Better Practices for Reporting on Extremists, Antagonists, and Manipulators Online," *Data & Society*, May 23, 2018, https://datasociety.net/wp-content/uploads/2018/05/FULLREPORT_Oxygen_of_Amplification_DS.pdf.

32. Eli Saslow, *Rising Out of Hatred: The Awakening of a Former White Nationalist* (New York: Doubleday, 2018), Kindle ed.

33. Ramsey (RamZPaul), "The Alt Right—What Went Wrong?"

34. For ideas of fascism, I draw on Roger Griffin, *Fascism: An Introduction to Comparative Fascist Studies* (Cambridge, UK: Polity Press, 2018); Shane Burley, *Fascism Today: What It Is and How to End It* (Chico, CA: AK Press, 2017); and Jason Stanley, *How Fascism Works: The Politics of Us and Them* (New York: Random House, 2018).

35. Donna Zuckerburg, *Not All Dead White Men: Classics and Misogyny in the Digital Age* (Cambridge, MA: Harvard University Press, 2018).

36. Stanley, *How Fascism Works*.

37. See Adam Serwer, "The White Nationalists Are Winning," *Atlantic*, August 10, 2018, https://www.theatlantic.com/ideas/archive/2018/08/the-battle-that-erupted-in-charlottesville-is-far-from-over/567167; Leo R. Chavez, *Anchor Babies and the Challenges of Birthright Citizenship* (Palo Alto, CA: Stanford University Press, 2017); Ediberto Román and Ernesto Sagás, "Birthright Citizenship Under Attack: How Dominican Nationality Laws May Be the Future of U.S. Exclusion," *American University Law Review* 66:1383 (2017), https://ecollections.law.fiu.edu/faculty_publications/353.

38. Vann R. Newkirk II, "Trump's White-Nationalist Pipeline," *Atlantic*, August 23, 2018, https://www.theatlantic.com/politics/archive/2018/08/trump-white-nationalism/568393.

39. Timothy Snyder, *On Tyranny: Twenty Lessons from the Twentieth Century* (New York: Tim Duggan Books, 2017); Henry A. Giroux, *American Nightmare: Facing the Challenge of Fascism* (San Francisco: City Lights Books, 2018).

40. Hannah Arendt, *Eichmann in Jerusalem: A Report on the Banality of Evil* (New York: Viking Press, 1963), 273.

CHAPTER I: RED PILLS FOR THE MASSES

1. "Millennial Woes and the Alt Right," YouTube video, 1:28, posted by Europe Is Falling, August 7, 2018, https://www.youtube.com/watch?v=zZQyE5ucfao.

2. "Millennial Woes and the Alt Right."

3. *The Matrix*, Warner Home Video, 1999.

4. Zizi Papacharissi, *Affective Publics: Sentiment, Technology, and Politics* (New York: Oxford University Press, 2015), Kindle ed.

5. As quoted in Mike Pearl, "How to Tell If Your Alt-Right Relative Is Trying to Redpill You at Thanksgiving," *Vice*, November 22, 2016, https://www.vice.com/en_us/article/nnk3bm/how-to-tell-if-your-alt-right-relative-is-trying-to-redpill-you-at-thanksgiving.

6. Alice Marwick and Becca Lewis, "The Online Radicalization We're Not Talking About," *New York Magazine*, May 18, 2017, http://nymag.com/selectall/2017/05/the-online-radicalization-were-not-talking-about.html.

7. "Alt-Right Is All About the Future of White People," *Radio 3Fourteen with Lana*, 25:57, September 15, 2016, https://redice.tv/radio-3fourteen/alt-right-is-all-about-the-future-of-white-people.

8. "The Black Pill (Kingmaker Podcast)," YouTube video, posted by Roosh V, November 9, 2017, https://www.youtube.com/watch?v=ebJ1nXu1LV4.

9. Michelle Dione, "A Normies Guide to the Alt-Right, the New Right & Their Tactics for Recruitment," *Medium*, August 24, 2017, https://medium.com/@michelledione/a-normies-guide-to-the-alt-right-the-new-right-their-tactics-for-recruitment-55410a3dfe24.

10. Zuckerberg, *Not All Dead White Men*; Stephen Marche, "Swallowing the Red Pill: A Journey to the Heart of Modern Misogyny," *Guardian*, April 14, 2016, https://www.theguardian.com/technology/2016/apr/14/the-red-pill-reddit-modern-misogyny-manosphere-men; Aja Romano, "Reddit's TheRedPill, Notorious for Its Misogyny, Was Founded by a New Hampshire State Legislator," *Vox*, April 28, 2017, https://www.vox.com/culture/2017/4/28/15434770/red-pill-founded-by-robert-fisher-new-hampshire.

11. "Return of Kings: About," *Return of Kings*, http://www.returnofkings.com/about, accessed September 5, 2018.

12. "Château Heartiste," *Chateau Heartiste*, https://heartiste.wordpress.com accessed September 5, 2018.

13. "Return of Kings: About."

14. "A Message to Men, Take the Red Pill—MGTOW," YouTube video, posted by Howard Dare, May 29, 2017, https://www.youtube.com/watch?v=ak3r9bpGoFg.

15. See comments by theGid and TW3223 on "A Message to Men, Take the Red Pill—MGTOW," https://www.youtube.com/watch?v=ak3r9bpGoFg.

16. "Almost a Hundred Subscribers! Welcome Newcomers," *TheRedPill*, November 8, 2012, accessed through Archive.today, September 6, 2018, http://archive.is/20150610190226/www.reddit.com/r/TheRedPill/comments/12v1hf/almost_a_hundred_subscribers_welcome_newcomers.

17. Marche, "Swallowing the Red Pill."

18. Figures based on late October 2018 rechecking of subscribers and users.

19. As quoted in Marche, "Swallowing the Red Pill."

20. "Rules for TheRedPill," Reddit, https://www.reddit.com/r/TheRedPill/about/rules/, accessed September 6, 2018.

21. Comments by u/ashurrutia, u/AlexanderWolff1989, and u/needsomehelp3211 on "The Red Pill," https://www.reddit.com/r/TheRedPill/, accessed September 6, 2018.

22. Comments by u/KeffirLime on "The Red Pill," https://www.reddit.com/r/TheRedPill/, accessed September 6, 2018.

23. "Administration Reply to Appeal #1," Reddit r/TheRedPill, posted by u/redpillschool, October 15, 2018, https://www.reddit.com/r/TheRedPill/comments/9odos2/administration_reply_to_appeal_1.

24. Aja Romano, "How the Alt-Right's Sexism Lure Men into White Supremacy," *Vox*, April 26, 2018, https://www.vox.com/culture/2016/12/14/13576192/alt-right-sexism-recruitment.

25. "Freedomain Radio," YouTube channel, https://www.youtube.com/channel/UCFHyoiRW5Ya5HJc9laaoUfA/featured, accessed September 6, 2018.

26. "My Biggest Red Pill," YouTube video, posted by Stefan Molyneux, August 4, 2017, https://www.youtube.com/watch?v=c2MoZRIB29k.

27. Comments by Bre Faucheux, Racial Love, and other users on "My Biggest Red Pill," YouTube video, posted by Stefan Molyneux, August 4, 2017, https://www.youtube.com/watch?v=c2MoZRIB29k.

28. Robert Evans, "From Memes to Infowars: How 75 Fascist Activists Were 'Red-Pilled,'" *Bellingcat*, October 11, 2018, https://www.bellingcat.com/news/americas/2018/10/11/memes-infowars-75-fascist-activists-red-pilled/.

29. Pearl, "How to Tell If Your Alt-Right Relative Is Trying to Redpill You at Thanksgiving."

30. William Pierce, "Rudyard Kipling: The White Man's Poet," *Counter-Currents Publishing* (blog), August 27, 2010, https://www.counter-currents.com/2010/08/rudyard-kipling-the-white-mans-poet.

31. Austin Allen, "Iffy: Behind the Mask of Rudyard Kipling's Confidence," *Poetry Foundation*, December 15, 2015, https://www.poetryfoundation.org/articles/70303/iffy.

32. https://www.youtube.com/watch?v=S3T7mAbXu4; video no longer available.

33. For a glossary of alt-right terms, see Wendling, *Alt-Right*, 73–103.

34. On metaphors as concepts, see George Lakoff and Mark Johnson, *Metaphors We Live By* (Chicago: University of Chicago Press, 1980).

35. Roland Barthes, *Mythologies*, trans. Richard Howard and Annette Lavers (New York: Hill & Wang, 1957).

36. *Fash the Nation*, FashtheNation.com; site now discontinued; http://fashthenation.com/category/articles/redpill101/page/2/, accessed July 20, 2018.

37. Alba_Rising (@Alba_Risen), Twitter, July 11, 2018 (8:33 a.m.); account now suspended.

38. "The State of the Alt-Right Movement," Altright.com, March 2, 2018, https://altright.com/2018/03/02/the-state-of-the-alt-right-movement/.

39. Leonard Zeskind, *Blood and Politics: The History of the White Nationalist Movement from the Margins into the Mainstream* (New York: Farrar, Straus & Giroux, 2009).

40. A conversation between Richard Spencer and the late Jonathan Bowden about the Frankfurt School can be found here: "Jonathan Bowden Conversation on the Frankfurt School," YouTube video, posted by Gaelic Neoreactionary, January 9, 2015, https://www.youtube.com/watch?v=-G_eLMkJkNw. For a canonical history of the Frankfurt School, see Martin Jay, *The Dialectical Imagination: A History of the Frankfurt School and the Institute of Social Research, 1923-1950* (Berkeley: University of California Press, 1996). For an analysis of the alt-right's relationship to "cultural

Marxism," see Johannes von Moltke, "The Meme Is the Message: Down the Click-hole of 'Cultural Marxism' with the Alt-Right," unpublished manuscript, June 2018.

41. Richard Spencer as quoted in Marin Cogan, "The Alt-Right Gives a Press Conference," *New York Magazine*, September 11, 2016, http://nymag.com/daily /intelligencer/2016/09/the-alt-right-gives-a-press-conference.html.

42. José Pedro Zúquete, *The Identitarians: The Movement Against Globalism and Islam in Europe* (Notre Dame, IN: University of Notre Dame Press, 2018).

43. "The Evolution of a Metapolitical Warrior," YouTube video, 15:00, posted by Altright.com, April 4, 2018, https://www.youtube.com/watch?v=Ijj-Paqa_vU.

44. "The Evolution of a Metapolitical Warrior," 18:48.

45. "Recent Developments in Charlottesville with Gregory Conte," *Interregnum*, December 14, 2018, https://arktos.com/2018/12/14/recent-developments-in -charlottesville-with-gregory-conte/.

46. Bruno Bosteels, "Metapolitics," in *Encyclopedia of Political Theory*, ed. Mark Bevir (Thousand Oaks, CA: Sage Publications, 2010), 2, http://dx.doi.org/10 .4135/9781412958660.n282.

47. Leif Weatherby, "Politics Is Downstream from Culture, Part 1: Right Turn to Narrative," *The Hedgehog Review* (blog), February 22, 2017, http://iasc-culture .org/THR/channels/Infernal_Machine/2017/02/politics-is-downstream-from -culture-part-1-right-turn-to-narrative/; site now discontinued.

48. The most sophisticated alt-right analysis of this can be found in Michael O'Meara, *New Culture, New Right: Anti-Liberalism in Post-Modern Europe* (London: Arktos, 2013).

49. Jay, *The Dialectical Imagination*.

50. John Hellman, *The Communitarian Third Way: Alexandre Marc's Ordre Nouveau, 1930-2000* (Montreal: McGill-Queens University Press, 2002).

51. Massimiliano Capra Casadio, "The New Right and Metapolitics in France and Italy," trans. Melina Masteron, *Journal for the Study of Radicalism* 8, no. 1 (2014): 50.

52. O'Meara, *New Culture, New Right*, 65.

53. Casadio, "The New Right and Metapolitics in France and Italy," 51.

54. Roger Griffin as quoted in J. Lester Feder and Pierre Buet, "They Wanted to Be a Better Class of White Nationalists. They Claimed This Man as Their Father," *BuzzFeed News*, December 26, 2017, https://www.buzzfeed.com/lesterfeder /the-man-who-gave-white-nationalism-a-new-life?utm_term=.kn66AVDyyZ# .xyvpoZQYYk.

55. O'Meara, *New Culture, New Right*, 26.

56. Hellman, *The Communitarian Third Way*, 198.

57. Bosteels, "Metapolitics," 3.

58. Zúquete, *The Identitarians*, 13; Guillaume Faye, *Why We Fight: Manifesto of the European Resistance*, trans. Michael O'Meara (London: Arktos, 2011), Kindle ed.

59. Carol M. Swain and Russ Nieli, ed., *Contemporary Voices of White Nationalism in America* (Cambridge, UK: Cambridge University Press, 2003).

60. The American Renaissance think tank, founded by Jared Taylor in 1990, came the closest to its European counterparts, and indeed Taylor and American Renaissance have served as a between the neo-Nazi era of the 1980s and 1990s and the alt-right rise starting in the 2000s. For podcasts and publications, see the American Renaissance website at https://www.amren.com.

61. Thomas Chatterton Williams, "The French Origins of 'You Will Not Replace Us': The European Thinkers Behind the White-Nationalist Rallying Cry," *New Yorker*, December 4, 2017, https://www.newyorker.com/magazine/2017/12/04/the-french-origins-of-you-will-not-replace-us.

62. Vincent Law, "Marcuse's Blue Pill," *Radix Journal*, November 26, 2014, https://www.radixjournal.com/2014/11/2014-11-26-marcuses-blue-pill.

63. Herbert Marcuse, *One-Dimensional Man: Studies in the Ideology of Advanced Industrial Society* (Boston: Beacon Press, 1964).

64. Vincent Law, "Marcuse's Blue Pill," *Radix Journal*, November 26, 2014, https://www.radixjournal.com/2014/11/2014-11-26-marcuses-blue-pill.

65. Alex Kurtagic, "Interview with Greg Johnson," *Counter-Currents Publishing*, November 27, 2010, https://www.counter-currents.com/2010/11/interview-with-greg-johnson/.

66. Greg Johnson, "Politics, Metapolitics, [*sic*] & Hegemony," *Counter-Currents Publishing*, February 1, 2018, https://www.counter-currents.com/2018/02/politics-metapolitics-and-hegemony/.

67. White Republican, "On Metapolitics," *Counter-Currents Publishing*, November 16, 2010, https://www.counter-currents.com/2010/11/on-metapolitics.

68. Greg Johnson, foreword by Kevin MacDonald, *New Right Versus Old Right* (San Francisco: Counter-Currents Publishing, 2014).

69. Johnson, "Politics, Metapolitics, & Hegemony."

70. White Republican, "On Metapolitics."

71. Gregory Hood, *Waking Up from the American Dream* (San Francisco: Counter-Currents Publishing, 2016), Kindle ed.

72. Johnson, "Politics, Metapolitics, & Hegemony."

73. Margot Metroland, "The Metapolitics of Taylor Swift," *Counter-Currents Publishing*, December 11, 2015, https://www.counter-currents.com/2015/12/the-metapolitics-of-taylor-swift/.

74. Shannon Connellan, "Taylor Swift Breaks Political Silence to Support Senate Candidate Phil Bredesen," *Mashable*, October 7, 2018, https://mashable.com/article/taylor-swift-breaks-political-silence/.

75. Charles Jansen, "The Metapolitics of Harry Potter," *Counter-Currents Publishing*, December 2, 2015, https://www.counter-currents.com/2015/12/the-metapolitics-of-harry-potter/.

76. "The Identitarian Aesthetic in Europe," *Radix Journal*, November 6, 2014, https://www.radixjournal.com/2014/11/2014-11-5-the-identitarian-aesthetic-in-europe/; site now discontinued.

77. Buttercup Dew, "Skateboarding & White Identity," *Counter-Currents Publishing*, August 14, 2018, https://www.counter-currents.com/2018/08/skateboarding-and-white-identity/.

78. "Why Metal Is Right-Wing," *Radix Journal*, July 2, 2014, https://www.radixjournal.com/2014/07/2014-7-2-why-metal-is-right-wing/.

79. "Creating a Counter Culture," *Radix Journal*, February 18, 2015, https://www.radixjournal.com/2015/02/2015-02-18-creating-a-counter-culture; site now discontinued; "Why Metal Is Right-Wing."

80. Kirsten Dyck, *Reichsrock: The International Web of White-Power and Neo-Nazi Hate Music* (New Brunswick, NJ: Rutgers University Press, 2016), 4.

81. Dyck, 109.

82. Dyck, 115.

83. Zúquete, "Intellectual Foundations, Practices, and Networks," in *The Identitarians*.

84. Shane Burley, *Fascism Today: What It Is and How to End It* (Chico, CA: AK Press, 2017), 105.

85. "Arditi: Imposing Elitism," Arditi, www.arditi.tk, accessed November 3, 2018.

86. Kathleen Belew, *Bring the War Home: The White Power Movement and Paramilitary America* (Cambridge, MA: Harvard University Press, 2018); Chip Berlet and Carol Mason, "Swastikas in Cyberspace: How Hate Went Online," in *Digital Media Strategies of the Far-Right in Europe and the United States*, ed. Patricia Anne Simpson and Helga Druxes (Lanham, MD: Lexington Books, 2015), 21–36.

87. Greg Johnson, "Happy Birthday to Us!," *Counter-Currents Publishing*, June 11, 2018, https://www.counter-currents.com/2018/06/happy-birthday-to-us-8.

88. Jessie Daniels, "Twitter and White Supremacy: A Love Story," *DAME Magazine*, pre-publication version, October 19, 2017, https://www.damemagazine.com/2017/10/19/twitter-and-white-supremacy-love-story.

89. Keith Collins, "A Running List of Websites and Apps That Have Banned, Blocked, Deleted, and Otherwise Dropped White Supremacists," *Quartz*, August 16, 2017, https://qz.com/1055141/what-websites-and-apps-have-banned-neo-nazis-and-white-supremacists; "The Evolution of a Metapolitical Warrior," YouTube video, posted by Altright.com, April 4, 2018, https://www.youtube.com/watch?v=Ijj-Paqa_vU.

90. Jack Nicas, "Alex Jones and Infowars Content Is Removed from Apple, Facebook and YouTube," *New York Times*, August 6, 2018, https://www.nytimes.com/2018/08/06/technology/infowars-alex-jones-apple-facebook-spotify.html.

91. Janko Roettgers, "Twitter Shuts Down Accounts of Vice Co-Founder Gavin McInnes, Proud Boys Ahead of 'Unite the Right' Rally," *Variety*, August 10, 2018, https://variety.com/2018/digital/news/twitter-shuts-down-accounts-of-vice-co-founder-gavin-mcinnes-proud-boys-ahead-of-unite-the-right-rally-1202902397/.

92. Identity Evropa (@IdentityEvropa), "Payment processor deplatforming is one of the most pressing issues we face," Twitter, July 22, 2018 (12:15 p.m.), https://twitter.com/IdentityEvropa/status/1021111590857396224.

93. Kelly Weill, "Inside YouTube's Far-Right Radicalization Factory," *Daily Beast*, September 18, 2018, https://www.thedailybeast.com/inside-youtubes-far-right-radicalization-factory.

94. Johnson, "Politics, Metapolitics, & Hegemony."

CHAPTER 2: BACK TO THE FUTURE

1. "Patrick Casey: American Identitarianism/Leading Our People Forward 2018," YouTube video, posted by Identity Evropa, March 22, 2018, https://www.youtube.com/watch?v=QisDUMB6cIU.

2. "Who We Are," Identity Evropa, https://www.identityevropa.com/, accessed October 24, 2018.

3. Christine Murray, "Mexico Condemns Anti-Immigrant Chants Outside New York Consulate," Reuters, July 31, 2018, https://www.reuters.com/article/us-mexico-usa-racism/mexico-condemns-anti-immigrant-chants-outside-new-york-consulate-idUSKBN1KL2S3.

4. Samuel Argyle, "My Weekend with White Nationalists: I Wanted to Understand Identity Evropa. So I Became One of Them," *The Outline*, June 12, 2018, https://theoutline.com/post/4907/my-weekend-with-white-nationalists-convention-identity-evropa?zd=1&zi=ufek6bif.

5. "Patrick Casey: American Identitarianism," 9:13.

6. "Patrick Casey: American Identitarianism," 5:04. In the mission statement inaugurating *National Review*, William F. Buckley wrote that this new political magazine "stands athwart history, yelling Stop, at a time when no one is inclined to do so, or to have much patience with those who so urge it." See Buckley, "Our Mission Statement," *National Review*, November 19, 1955, https://www.nationalreview.com/1955/11/our-mission-statement-william-f-buckley-jr.

7. "Patrick Casey: American Identitarianism."

8. Snyder, *On Tyranny*.

9. National Policy Institute, "'2050' Is Coming Sooner Than We Thought," *National Policy Institute Blog*, August 17, 2018, https://nationalpolicy.institute/2018/08/17/2050-is-coming-sooner-than-we-thought.

10. "About," *Counter-Currents Publishing*, https://www.counter-currents.com, accessed October 25, 2018.

11. "About," Ostara Publications, https://ostarapublications.com/about, accessed October 25, 2018.

12. Red Ice TV, https://redice.tv, accessed October 25, 2018.

13. "Interregnum," Arktos, https://arktos.com/interregnum, accessed October 25, 2018; Daniel Friberg, *The Real Right Returns: A Handbook for the True Opposition* (London: Arktos, 2015), 93.

14. Ronald Beiner, *Dangerous Minds: Nietzsche, Heidegger, and the Return of the Far Right* (Philadelphia: University of Pennsylvania Press, 2018).

15. Guillaume Faye, *Sex and Deviance* (London: Arktos, 2014), Kindle ed.

16. "Author Archives: Savitri Devi," *Counter-Currents Publishing*, https://www.counter-currents.com/author/savitri/, accessed October 25, 2018.

17. Nicholas Goodrick-Clarke, *Hitler's Priestess: Savitri Devi, the Hindu-Aryan Myth, and Neo-Nazism* (New York: New York University Press, 1998), 4.

18. Savitri Devi, *The Lightning and the Sun*, 3rd ed., ed. R. G. Fowler (San Francisco: Counter-Currents Publishing, 2015), Kindle ed.

19. Devi, The Lightning and the Sun.

20. Goodrick-Clarke, *Hitler's Priestess*, 224.

21. Jonathan Bowden, *Extremists: Studies in Metapolitics*, ed. Greg Johnson (San Francisco: Counter-Currents Publishing, 2017), Kindle ed. Emphasis in the original.

22. Anna Green and Kathleen Troup, eds., *The Houses of History: A Critical Reader in Twentieth-Century History and Theory* (New York: Washington Square, 1999).

23. Roger Griffin, *The Nature of Fascism* (London: Routledge, 1991), 26.

24. Burley, *Fascism Today*.

25. "Neo-Nazi," Southern Poverty Law Center, https://www.splcenter.org/fighting-hate/extremist-files/ideology/neo-nazi, accessed October 26, 2018.

26. "About Counter-Currents Publishing & North American New Right," *Counter-Currents Publishing*, https://www.counter-currents.com/about, accessed October 26, 2018.

27. Joshua Green, "Inside the Secret, Strange Origins of Steve Bannon's Nationalist Fantasia," *Vanity Fair*, July 17, 2017, https://www.vanityfair.com/news/2017/07/the-strange-origins-of-steve-bannons-nationalist-fantasia.

28. Joshua Green, *Devil's Bargain: Steve Bannon, Donald Trump, and the Storming of the Presidency* (New York: Penguin Random House, 2017).

29. Robin Waterfield, *René Guénon and the Future of the West: The Life and Writings of a 20th-Century Metaphysician* (Great Britain: Crucible Books, 1987).

30. Rene Guénon, *The Reign of Quantity and the Signs of the Times*, trans. Lord Northbourne (Hillsdale, NY: Sophia Perennis, 2004), 41.

31. O'Meara, *New Culture, New Right*, 79.

32. O'Meara, *New Culture, New Right*.

33. Paul Furlong, *Social and Political Thought of Julius Evola* (New York: Routledge, 2011).

34. "Jonathan Bowden—Julius Evola: The World's Most Right Wing Thinker," YouTube video, posted by TheArmenianNation, June 11, 2013, https://www.youtube.com/watch?v=4YqKf3v2aPs.

35. Nicholas Goodrick-Clarke, *Black Sun: Aryan Cults, Esoteric Nazism and the Politics of Identity* (New York: New York University Press, 2002), 57. Also see Francesco Cassata, *Building the New Man: Eugenics, Racial Science and Genetics in Twentieth-Century Italy*, trans. Erin O'Loughlin (Budapest: Central European University Press, 2011).

36. Julius Evola, *Revolt Against the Modern World: Politics, Religion, and Social Order in the Kali Yuga* (1969), (Rochester, NY: Inner Traditions International, 1995).

37. Evola, *Revolt Against the Modern World*, 184. Further quotes in this section from pp. 143, 159, 164, 168, and 224.

38. It is worth noting here that Nietzsche's theories are often airlifted out of context and distorted by alt-right thinkers. See, for example, Sean Illing, "The Alt-Right Is Drunk on Bad Readings of Nietzsche. The Nazis Were Too," *Vox*, updated September 5, 2018, https://www.vox.com/2017/8/17/16140846/alt-right-nietzsche-richard-spencer-nazism.

39. O'Meara, *New Culture, New Right*, 154.

40. Roger Griffin, "Fascism's Modernist Revolution: A New Paradigm for the Study of Right-Wing Dictatorships," *Fascism* 5 (2016): 105–29.

41. Guillaume Faye, Archeofuturism: European Visions of the Post-Catastrophic Age (London: Arktos, 2010), Kindle ed.

42. Faye, *Archeofuturism*.

43. Faye, *Sex and Deviance*.

44. Zúquete, *The Identitarians*.

45. Greg Johnson, *You Asked for It: Selected Interviews, Vol. One* (San Francisco: Counter-Currents Publishing, 2017), 21–22.

46. Nick Land, *The Dark Enlightenment*, http://www.thedarkenlightenment.com/the-dark-enlightenment-by-nick-land/#part1, accessed October 26, 2018.

47. Rosie Gray, "Behind the Internet's Anti-Democracy Movement," *Atlantic*, February 10, 2017, https://www.theatlantic.com/politics/archive/2017/02/behind-the-internets-dark-anti-democracy-movement/516243/.

48. Hans-Hermann Hoppe, *Democracy—The God That Failed: The Economics and Politics of Monarchy, Democracy, and Natural Order* (New Brunswick, NJ: Transaction Publishers, 2001).

49. Julius Evola, *Ride the Tiger: A Survival Manual for the Aristocrats of the Soul*, trans. Joscelyn Godwin and Constance Fontana (Rochester, VT: Inner Traditions, 2003).

50. Alex Witoslawski's Twitter account, https://twitter.com/alexwitoslawski, accessed August 15, 2018; account now discontinued.

51. John Morgan, "What Would Evola Do?," *Counter-Currents Publishing*, May 19, 2018, https://www.counter-currents.com/2018/05/what-would-evola-do-2/.

52. Johnson, *You Asked for It*, 22.

53. Johnson, *You Asked for It*, 23.

54. Wendling, *Alt-Right*, 91.

55. Derek Robertson, "How an Obscure Conservative Theory Became the Trump Era's Go-to Nerd Phrase," *Politico Magazine*, February 25, 2018, https://www.politico.com/magazine/story/2018/02/25/overton-window-explained -definition-meaning-271010.

56. Jared Taylor, *White Identity: Racial Consciousness in the 21st Century* (Oakton, VA: New Century Books in conjunction with American Renaissance, 2011).

57. Hood, *Waking Up from the American Dream*.

58. Michael Kimmel, *Angry White Men: American Masculinity at the End of an Era* (New York: Nation Books, 2013).

59. See, for instance, Andrew Breitbart, *Righteous Indignation: Excuse Me While I Save the World!* (New York: Grand Central Publishing, 2011).

60. Bre Faucheux interview with Richard Spencer, 27Crows Radio, July 25, 2017, 27crowsradio.com/index.php/2017/07/25/richard-spen...; site now discontinued, accessed November 4, 2018, via the Wayback Machine, http//:27crowsradio .com:80/index.php/2017/07/25/richard-spencer-breaking-the-paradigm-27crows -radio-1.

61. Ward Kendall, *Beyond the Horizon: A White Nationalist Blueprint for Tomorrow* (United States: Alternate Future Publishing, 2016), 86.

62. Kevin MacDonald, "Foreword," in Greg Johnson, *New Right Versus Old Right* (San Francisco: Counter-Currents Publishing, 2013), Kindle ed.

63. Johnson, *New Right Versus Old Right*.

64. Johnson, *New Right Versus Old Right*.

65. "American Identity Showcase," *identitarianaction's podcast*, October 1, 2018, https://identitarianaction.libsyn.com/american-identity-showcase.

66. Ann Coulter, ¡Adios, America! The Left's Plan to Turn Our Country into a Third World Hellhole (Washington, DC: Regnery, 2015), Kindle ed.

67. Kevin MacDonald, *The Culture of Critique: An Evolutionary Analysis of Jewish Involvement in Twentieth-Century Intellectual and Political Movements* (Westport: Praeger, 1998), Kindle ed.

68. "The 1965 Red Pill," YouTube video, posted by Lacey Lynn, January 9, 2018, https://www.youtube.com/watch?v=EIDUHhMBYPg.

69. See extended discussion of diversity in Taylor, *White Identity*.

70. Patrick Casey, "Civil Unrest: America Is Coming Undone," Red Ice Radio, June 29, 2018, https://redice.tv/red-ice-radio/civil-unrest-america-is-coming -undone.

71. Patrick Casey (@PatrickCaseyIE), "If we're lucky, 2019 will be 2015 on steroids," Twitter, December 31, 2018, 8:24 p.m., https://twitter.com/patrickcaseyie ?lang=en.

CHAPTER 3: WHITOPIA

1. Griffin, *Fascism*; Griffin, "Fascism's Modernist Revolution," 105–29.

2. Foreign Policy Research Institute, "'Nationality Is Ethnicity': Estonia's Problematic Citizenship Policy—Analysis," *Eurasia Review* (March 15, 2017), https://www.eurasiareview.com/15032017-nationality-is-ethnicity-estonias-problematic-citizenship-policy-analysis; "Ethnostate-States Will Never Work," YouTube video, posted by Red Ice TV, August 17, 2018, https://www.youtube.com/watch?v=CFwckUOZBGE.

3. James Ciment, *Another America: The Story of Liberia and the Former Slaves Who Ruled It* (New York: Hill and Wang, 2013); Roberto Ramón Lint Sagarena, *Aztlán and Arcadia: Religion, Ethnicity, and the Creation of Place* (New York: New York University Press, 2014).

4. "Wakanda: The Perfect Ethnostate?," YouTube video, posted by American Renaissance, March 7, 2018, https://www.youtube.com/watch?v=JL6Zgw4FZVA.

5. John Derbyshire, "Will the United States Survive Until 2022?," *New English Review* (January 2007), https://www.newenglishreview.org/custpage.cfm?frm=5192&sec_id=5192.

6. Quotes taken from transcription of Greg Johnson interview by French Marxist journalist Laura Raim. See Greg Johnson, "Greg Johnson Interviewed," *Counter-Currents Publishing*, August 22, 2016, https://www.counter-currents.com/2017/09/greg-johnson-interviewed. Also see Greg Johnson, "White Nationalism Is Inevitable," *Counter-Currents Publishing*, June 28, 2018, https://www.counter-currents.com/2018/06/video-of-the-daywhite-nationalism-is-inevitable/.

7. For example, see Greg Johnson, *The White Nationalist Manifesto* (San Francisco: Counter-Currents Publishing, 2018).

8. Sasha Polakow-Suransky, *Go Back to Where You Came From: The Backlash Against Immigration and the Fate of Western Democracy* (New York: Nation Books, 2017); Williams, "The French Origins of 'You Will Not Replace Us.'"

9. Joseph Bem, "Establishing a White Ethnostate in North America," *Fash the Nation*, January 24, 2018, http://fashthenation.com/2018/01/establishing-a-white-ethnostate-in-north-america/.

10. Quote taken from comments on Facebook roundtable, "R*ce, Culture, White Genoc*de: Roundtable Discussion," YouTube video, posted by Lauren Chen, April 11, 2017, https://www.youtube.com/watch?v=ZfSTbUVimTg&feature=youtu.be.

11. Greg Johnson, "The Slow Cleanse," *Counter-Currents Publishing*, June 24, 2014, https://www.counter-currents.com/2014/06/the-slow-cleanse.

12. "The Butler Plan: Four Phases," *Northwest Front*, http://northwestfront.org/about/the-butler-plan/the-butler-plan-four-phases/, accessed October 26, 2018.

13. "14 Words," Hate Symbols Database, Anti-Defamation League, https://www.adl.org/education/references/hate-symbols/14-words, accessed January 8, 2019.

14. Quote from "Greg Johnson Interviewed."

15. Greg Johnson, "Whitopia," *Counter-Currents Publishing*, January 26, 2018, https://www.counter-currents.com/2018/01/whitopia. Johnson lists "Aspen, or Chappaqua, or Martha's Vineyard" as model towns or areas. On Hayden Lake, see Meagan Day, "Welcome to Hayden Lake, Where White Supremacists Tried to Build Their Homeland," *Timeline*, November 4, 2016, https://timeline.com/white-supremacist-rural-paradise-fb62b74b29e0.

16. Johnson, "The Slow Cleanse"; "R*ce, Culture, White Genoc*de."

17. Johnson, "White Nationalism Is Inevitable."

18. "Happy Homelands—Greg Johnson," YouTube video, posted by RamZ-Paul, October 7, 2018, https://www.youtube.com/watch?v=vNNhz9PgFto&feature=youtu.be.

19. For historical background on racism and birthright citizenship, see ch. 3 in Natalia Molina, *How Race Is Made in America: Immigration, Citizenship, and the Historical Power of Racial Scripts* (Berkeley: University of California Press, 2014), and Martha S. Jones, *Birthright Citizens: A History of Race and Rights in Antebellum America* (Cambridge, UK: Cambridge University Press, 2018).

20. John Ingram, "Why We Push for an Ethnostate," *American Renaissance*, November 17, 2017, https://www.amren.com/commentary/2017/11/why-we-push-for-an-ethnostate-racial-separation/.

21. Bem, "Establishing a White Ethnostate in North America."

22. "'Ethnostates Will Never Work,'" YouTube video, 9:32, posted by Red Ice TV, August 17, 2018, https://www.youtube.com/watch?v=CFwckUOZBGE.

23. Johnson, "The Slow Cleanse."

24. Ethan Edwards, "The Last Big Battle of the Civil War," in *A Fair Hearing: The Alt-Right in the Words of Its Members and Leaders*, ed. George T. Shaw (London: Arktos, 2018), Kindle ed. Also see Kevin Alfred Strom, "The Ethnostate: Some Problems Nobody Thinks About," *National Vanguard*, June 9, 2016, https://nationalvanguard.org/2016/06/the-ethnostate-some-problems-nobody-thinks-about/.

25. Greg Johnson, *Truth, Justice, and a Nice White Country* (San Francisco: Counter-Currents Publishing, 2015), Kindle ed.

26. Ingram, "Why We Push for an Ethnostate."

27. "Greg Johnson Interviewed."

28. "Globalisation vs. the Ethno-State [Speech to the Scandza Forum in Oslo]," YouTube video, 4:18, posted by Millennial Woes, July 5, 2017, https://www.youtube.com/watch?v=3tYqRp9-jww.

29. "R*ce, Culture, White Genoc*de."

30. "Finding Identity and a Home in Future White America," *Renegade Tribune*, February 16, 2018, http://www.renegadetribune.com/finding-identity-home-future-white-america/.

31. Greg Johnson, "What's Wrong with Diversity?," *Counter-Currents Publishing*, July 25, 2018, https://www.counter-currents.com/2018/07/whats-wrong-with-diversity/#more-84091.

32. Thomas Hobbes, *Victoria: A Novel of 4th Generation Warfare* (Kouvola: Castalia House, 2014), Kindle ed.

33. "R*ce, Culture, White Genoc*de."

34. Hood, *Waking Up from the American Dream.*

35. "This Week Tonight on the Alt-Right—with Greg Johnson," YouTube video, posted by Mark Collett, August 1, 2018, https://www.youtube.com/watch?v=km5zvv1fH6U.

36. Max Greenwood, "Trump: Europe Is 'Losing Its Culture' Because of Immigration," *Hill*, July 12, 2018, http://thehill.com/homenews/administration/396803-trump-europe-is-losing-its-culture-because-of-immigration; Larisa Epatko, "How the World Is Reacting to Trump's Use of S***hole," *NewsHour*, PBS, January 12, 2018, https://www.pbs.org/newshour/world/how-the-world-is-reacting-to-trumps-use-of-shole.

37. Wilmot Robertson, *The Ethnostate: An Unblinkered Prospectus for an Advanced Statecraft* (Cape Canaveral, FL: Howard Allen, 1992).

38. See David Duke, "My Awakening: A Path to Racial Understanding," https://archive.org/stream/MyAwakeningAPathToRacialUnderstandingByDavid Duke/my-awakening-david-duke_djvu.txt, accessed October 26, 2018; Wilmot Robertson, *The Dispossessed Majority* (Cape Canaveral, FL: Howard Allen, 1972).

39. William H. Tucker, "A Closer Look at the Pioneer Fund: Response to Rushton," *Albany Law Review* 66 (2003): 1149.

40. Tucker; also see Zeskind, *Blood and Politics*.

41. Note the banner page article on the *Radix Journal* is titled "The Dispossessed Majority."

42. Robertson, *The Ethnostate*, ix. Further quotes in this section from pp. 10, 223, 173, 191, 120, 173, 223, and 22.

43. Paul A. Lombardo, "The American Breed: Nazi Eugenics and the Origins of the Pioneer Fund," *Albany Law Review* 65 (2002): 747.

44. Robertson, *The Ethnostate*, 71.

45. Robertson, *The Ethnostate*, 180.

46. Joanne Woiak, "Designing a Brave New World: Eugenics, Politics, and Fiction," *Public History* 29 (2007): 105–29, doi: 10.1525/tph.2007.29.3.105.

47. Kirkpatrick Sale as quoted in Robertson, *The Ethnostate*, 28.

48. Robertson, *The Ethnostate*, 223.

49. Robertson, *The Ethnostate*, 226.

50. Miles A. Powell, *Vanishing America: Species Extinction, Racial Peril, and the Origins of Conservation* (Cambridge, MA: Harvard University Press, 2016).

51. Rajani Bhatia, "Green or Brown: White Nativist Environmental Movements," in *Home-Grown Hate: Gender and Organized Racism*, ed. Abby L. Ferber (New York: Routledge, 2004), 205–26.

52. Robert Wald Sussman, *The Myth of Race: The Troubling Persistence of an Unscientific Idea* (Cambridge, MA: Harvard University Press, 2016).

53. Chad Crowley, "Towards a New European Palingenesis," *Counter-Currents Publishing*, July 12, 2018, https://www.counter-currents.com/2018/07/towards-a -new-european-palingenesis/; also see Greg Johnson, "Robert Stark Interviews Greg Johnson on Eco-Fascism," *Counter-Currents Publishing*, April 22, 2018, https://www.counter-currents.com/2018/04/robert-stark-interviews-greg-johnson -on-eco-fascism-2.

54. "White Supremacist Town Manager Envisions 'Homeland' for Whites," *ADL Blog*, January 22, 2018, https://www.adl.org/blog/white-supremacist-town -manager-envisions-homeland-for-whites.

55. "White Supremacist Town Manager Envisions 'Homeland' for Whites."

56. "White Supremacist Town Manager Envisions 'Homeland' for Whites."

57. Hailey Branson-Potts, "In California's Rural, Conservative North, There Are Big Dreams for Cleaving the State," *Los Angeles Times*, March 17, 2018, http:// www.latimes.com/local/lanow/la-me-ln-state-of-jefferson-activists-20180317-html story.html.

58. Heidi Beirich, "Second Vermont Republic Pushes for Independence of Vermont," *Intelligence Report -SPLC*, May 20, 2008, https://www.splcenter.org/fighting -hate/intelligence-report/2008/second-vermont-republic-pushes-independence -vermont; Thomas H. Naylor, *Secession: How Vermont and All Other States Can Save Themselves from the Empire* (Port Townsend, WA: Feral House, 2008).

59. Britta Lokting, "Fear and Loathing in Cascadia," *Baffler*, February 27, 2018, https://thebaffler.com/latest/cascadia-lokting.

60. See Gary Snyder, "Things to Do Around Seattle," *Poetry Magazine*, December 1966, https://www.poetryfoundation.org/poetrymagazine/browse?contentId =30487; Paul E. Nelson, "20 Year Cascadia Bioregional Cultural Investigating," https://www.paulenelson.com/home/; Lokting, "Fear and Loathing in Cascadia."

61. "What We Do," Cascadia Independence Party, http://cascadiaindependence party.strikingly.com/#home, accessed October 26, 2018.

62. See Dean Gunderson, "Cooperative Commonwealth of Idaho and Other Fictions: Utopian Writers and the Creation of the American West," *Blue Review Blog*, November 29, 2013, https://thebluereview.org/utopian-writers-american-west.

63. Ernest Callenbach, *Ecotopia: The Notebooks and Reports of William Weston* (Berkeley, CA: Banyan Tree Books, 1975), 164.

64. Callenbach, *Ecotopia*, 98.

65. Callenbach, *Ecotopia*, 151.

66. Lokting, "Fear and Loathing in Cascadia." See also US Census Bureau, "Quick Facts: Oregon," https://www.census.gov/quickfacts/or, for latest percentages; estimates from July 2017.

67. As quoted in Casey Michel, "Want to Meet America's Worst Racists? Come to the Northwest," *Politico Magazine*, July 7, 2015, https://www.politico.com /magazine/story/2015/07/northwest-front-americas-worst-racists-119803.

68. "NR35: Live from Northwest Forum!," *Nationalist Review Podcast*, 22:58, March 26, 2018, http://natrev.libsyn.com/nr35-live-from-northwest-forum; Greg Johnson, "West-Coast White Nationalism," *Counter-Currents Publishing*, December 10, 2010, https://www.counter-currents.com/2010/12/west-coast-white-nationalism/.

69. Lokting, "Fear and Loathing in Cascadia."

70. "Cascadia—AltRight Territory in the Pacific Northwest," YouTube Radio, 2:00, posted by Red Ice TV, posted March 26, 2017, https://www.youtube.com /watch?v=LfJGQon27vc.

71. "Cascadia—AltRight Territory in the Pacific Northwest."

72. In July 2018, truecascadia.com had been claimed by antifa, but as of August 2018 it is offline completely.

73. Evelyn A. Schlatter, *Aryan Cowboys: White Supremacists and the Search for a New Frontier, 1970–2000* (Austin: University of Texas Press, 2006).

74. "About," *Northwest Front*, http://northwestfront.org/about, accessed October 26, 2018.

75. "Tricolor Flag," *Northwest Front*, http://northwestfront.org/about/tricolor -flag/, accessed October 26, 2018.

76. For example, see "Episode 1: An Introduction to Radio Free Northwest," *Homeland Blog—Northwest Front*, January 15, 2010, http://northwestfront.org/2010 /01/episode-1/.

77. "Author on the Novels," *Northwest Front*, http://northwestfront.org/north west-novels/author-on-the-nw-novels/, accessed October 26, 2018.

78. H. A. Covington, *The Brigade* (Xlibris, 2008), Kindle ed.

79. Covington, *The Brigade*.

80. "r/DebateAltRight," Reddit, https://www.reddit.com/r/DebateAltRight /search?q=ethnostate&restrict, accessed October 26, 2018.

81. Ward Kendall, *Beyond This Horizon: A White Nationalist Blueprint for Tomorrow* (Alternate Future Publishing, 2016.)

82. Spencer J. Quinn, August 31, 2017, response to comment, "On Vetting & Entry into a White Ethnostate, Part III," *Counter-Currents Publishing*, August 29, 2017, https://www.counter-currents.com/2017/08/on-vetting-entry-into-a-white -ethnostate-part-iii/.

83. Nsikan Akpan, "How White Supremacists Respond When Their DNA Says They're Not 'White,'" *NewsHour*, PBS, August 20, 2017, https://www.pbs.org /newshour/science/white-supremacists-respond-genetics-say-theyre-not-white; Sarah Zhang, "When White Nationalists Get DNA Tests That Reveal African Ancestry," *Atlantic*, August 17, 2017, https://www.theatlantic.com/science/archive /2017/08/white-nationalists-dna-ancestry/537108/; Sarah Zhang, "Will the Alt-Right Promote a New Kind of Racist Genetics?," *Atlantic*, December 29, 2016, https://www.theatlantic.com/science/archive/2016/12/genetics-race-ancestry-tests /510962/.

84. Greg Johnson, "Whiteness," *Counter-Currents Publishing*, July 17, 2018, https://www.counter-currents.com/2018/07/whiteness; also see Johnson, *The White Nationalist Manifesto*.

85. Johnson, "Whiteness."

86. Johnson, "Whiteness."

87. See Spencer J. Quinn, "On Vetting & Entry into a White Ethnostate, Part I," *Counter-Currents Publishing*, August 10, 2017, https://www.counter-currents.com /2017/08/on-vetting-and-entry-into-a-white-ethnostate-part-i/; Spencer J. Quinn, "On Vetting & Entry into a White Ethnostate, Part II," *Counter-Currents Publishing*, August 16, 2017, https://www.counter-currents.com/2017/08/on-vetting-and -entry-into-a-white-ethnostate-part-ii; Spencer J. Quinn, "On Vetting & Entry into a White Ethnostate, Part III," *Counter-Currents Publishing*, August 29, 2017, https:// www.counter-currents.com/2017/08/on-vetting-entry-into-a-white-ethnostate -part-iii.

88. Quinn, "On Vetting & Entry into a White Ethnostate, Part II."

89. Quinn, "On Vetting & Entry into a White Ethnostate, Part I."

90. Quinn, "On Vetting & Entry into a White Ethnostate, Part II."

91. Quinn, "On Vetting & Entry into a White Ethnostate, Part III."

92. Graham Tom, "The White Ethnostate: Putting the Cart Before the Horse," *Renegade Tribune Blog*, February 2, 2018, http://www.renegadetribune.com /white-ethnostate-putting-cart-horse/.

93. Samuel Argyle, "My Weekend with White Nationalists," The Outline, June 12, 2018, https://theoutline.com/post/4907/my-weekend-with-white -nationalists-convention-identity-evropa.

94. As quoted in Argyle, "My Weekend with White Nationalists."

CHAPTER 4: CAT LADIES, WOLVES, AND LOBSTERS

1. "Welcome to the World's Greatest Fraternal Organization," Proud Boys website, http://proudboysusa.com, accessed January 9, 2018.

2. "Welcome to the World's Greatest Fraternal Organization."

3. White Haze," *This American Life*, 6:16, September 22, 2017, https://www .thisamericanlife.org/626/white-haze.

4. Gavin McInnes, "Introducing the Proud Boys," *Taki's Magazine*, September 15, 2016, http://takimag.com/article/introducing_the_proud_boys_gavin_mcinnes /print#ixzz5Ne20FUlU.

5. McInnes, "Introducing the Proud Boys."

6. "Welcome to the World's Greatest Fraternal Organization."

7. McInnes, "Introducing the Proud Boys."

8. "White Haze," 12:49.

9. Kimmel, *Angry White Men*, xi–xii.

10. Annie Kelly, "The Alt-Right: Reactionary Rehabilitation for White Masculinity," *Soundings* 66 (August 2017): 68–78, muse.jhu.edu/article/668239.

11. Debbie Ging, "Alphas, Betas, and Incels: Theorizing the Masculinities of the Manosphere," *Men and Masculinities* (2017), https://doi.org/10.1177/1097184X17706401.

12. Alfred W. Clark, "Cuckservative: A Definition," *Radix Journal*, July 17, 2015, https://www.radixjournal.com/2015/07/2015-7-16-cuckservative-a-definition.

13. Wendling, *Alt-Right*, 146.

14. Wendling, *Alt-Right*, 147.

15. "White Haze," 28:28.

16. "White Haze," *This American Life*, https://www.thisamericanlife.org/626/white-haze; Luke Barnes, "Proud Boys Founder Disavows Violence at Charlottesville but One of Its Members Organized the Event," *ThinkProgress*, August 24, 2017, https://thinkprogress.org/proud-boys-founder-tries-and-fails-to-distance-itself-from-charlottesville-6862fb8b3ae9/; "Proud Boys," Southern Poverty Law Center, https://www.splcenter.org/fighting-hate/extremist-files/group/proud-boys, accessed October 24, 2018.

17. Lester Black, "Patriot Prayer and the Proud Boys Are Rallying in Seattle on August 18: How Should Seattle Respond?," *Slog—The Stranger*, August 6, 2018, https://www.thestranger.com/slog/2018/08/06/30302621/patriot-prayer-and-the-proud-boys-are-rallying-in-seattle-on-august-18.

18. "Proud Boys Oregon," Facebook, https://www.facebook.com/ProudBoys Oregon/; page now discontinued.

19. Arun Gupta, "Why Young Men of Color Are Joining White-Supremacist Groups," *Daily Beast*, September 4, 2018, https://www.thedailybeast.com/why-young-men-of-color-are-joining-white-supremacist-groups.

20. "Proud Boys," Southern Poverty Law Center.

21. Ryan Mac and Blake Montgomery, "Twitter Suspended Proud Boys' and Founder Gavin McInnes' Accounts Ahead of the 'Unite the Right' Rally," *BuzzFeed News*, August 10, 2018, https://www.buzzfeednews.com/article/ryanmac/twitter-suspends-proud-boys-and-founder-gavin-mcinnes; Keith Wagstaff, "Twitter Suspends Proud Boys Before White Supremacist Rally," *Mashable*, August 10, 2018, https://mashable.com/article/twitter-bans-proud-boys-unite-the-right/#SMedESVU2qqL.

22. Daniel Politi, "Members of Far-Right Men's Group 'Proud Boys' Beat Up Protesters in New York," *Slate*, October 13, 2018, https://slate.com/news-and-politics/2018/10/proud-boys-members-beat-up-protesters-in-new-york-after-event-with-gavin-mcinnes.html.

23. Alan Feuer, "Proud Boys Founder: How He Went From Brooklyn Hipster to Far-Right Provocateur," *New York Times*, October 16, 2018, https://www.nytimes.com/2018/10/16/nyregion/proud-boys-gavin-mcinnes.html; Amelia McDonell-Parry, "Arrests Coming After Proud Boys Caught on Video Beating Protesters in New York," *Rolling Stone*, October 15, 2018, https://www.rollingstone.com/culture/culture-news/proud-boys-nyc-antifa-fight-nypd-738092.

24. Victoria Bekiempis, "NYPD Arrests Three More Proud Boys for Manhattan Brawl with Antifa," *Daily Beast*, October 22, 2018, https://www.thedailybeast.com/nypd-arrests-three-more-proud-boys-for-manhattan-brawl-with-antifa.

25. Jason Wilson, "Proud Boys Founder Gavin McInnes Quits 'Extremist' Far-Right Group," *Guardian*, November 22, 2018, https://www.theguardian.com/world/2018/nov/22/proud-boys-founder-gavin-mcinnes-quits-far-right-group; Brendan Krisel, "9 Proud Boys Now Arrested for UES Street Fight, Police Say," *Patch*, December 4, 2018, https://patch.com/new-york/upper-east-side-nyc/9-proud-boys-now-arrested-ues-street-fight-police-say.

26. Gavin McInnes, "We Are Not Alt-Right," Official Proud Boys, August 21, 2017, http://officialproudboys.com/proud-boys/we-are-not-alt-right.

27. For more on alt-right "ironic" constructs, see "Is That an OK Sign? A White Power Symbol? Or Just a Right-Wing Troll?," *Southern Poverty Law Center Blog*, September 18, 2018, https://www.splcenter.org/hatewatch/2018/09/18/ok-sign-white-power-symbol-or-just-right-wing-troll.

28. These are laid out in detail in Guillaume Faye, *Convergence of Catastrophes* (London: Arktos, 2012).

29. Some ethnonationalists, like the British Mark Collett, have dropped "alt-right" for the vague "white well-being." See "This Week on the Alt Right—with Simon Harris," YouTube video, posted by Mark Collett, October 24, 2018, https://www.youtube.com/watch?v=NJnkA3cJyak.

30. Jonathan Goldsbie and Graeme Gordon, "Faith Goldy Fired from The Rebel," *CanadalandShow*, August 17, 2017, https://www.canadalandshow.com/faith-goldy-gone-rebel.

31. "Wife with a Purpose," https://wifewithapurpose.com, accessed August 12, 2018.

32. Available in digital archive form via https://archive.org/details/JonathanBowdenFeminismLilithBeforeEveLondonForum2011, site now discontinued; access date July 10, 2018; online transcript available on *Counter-Currents Publishing*. See Jonathan Bowden, "Lilith Before Eve: Jonathan Bowden on Feminism," *Counter-Currents Publishing*, January 15, 2015, https://www.counter-currents.com/2015/01/lilith-before-eve-transcript.

33. Abby L. Ferber, *White Man Falling: Race, Gender, and White Supremacy* (Lanham, MD: Rowman & Littlefield, 1998), 86.

34. Burley, *Fascism Today*, 80.

35. Edward Helmore, "Milo Yiannopoulos Resigns from Breitbart News over Pedophilia Remarks," *Guardian: US News*, February 22, 2017, https://www.theguardian.com/us-news/2017/feb/21/milo-yiannopoulos-resigns-breitbart-pedophilia-comments; see also Burley, *Fascism Today*, 78–79.

36. Luke O'Brien, "How Pizzagate Pusher Mike Cernovich Keeps Getting People Fired," *Huffington Post*, July 21, 2018, https://www.huffingtonpost.com/entry/mike-cernovich-james-gunn-fired_us_5b5265cce4b0fd5c73c570ac.

37. "This Week Tonight on the Alt-Right—with Greg Johnson," YouTube video, posted by Mark Collett, August 1, 2018, https://www.youtube.com/watch?v=km5zvv1fH6U.

38. Evans, "From Memes to Infowars."

39. See "Millennial Woes and the Alt-Right," YouTube video, posted by Europe Is Falling, published August 7, 2018, https://www.youtube.com/watch?v=zZQyE5ucfao.

40. Hatewatch Staff, "McInnes, Molyneux, and 4chan: Investigating Pathways to the Alt-Right," *Southern Poverty Law Center*, April 19, 2018, https://www.spl center.org/20180419/mcinnes-molyneux-and-4chan-investigating-pathways-alt-right.

41. This document is only viewable now as an archived PDF since its removal. See Gavin McInnes, "Transphobia Is Perfectly Natural," *Thought Catalog*, August 12, 2014. https://www.doc-developpement-durable.org/file/programmes-de -sensibilisations/transphobie/transphobia-is-perfectly-natural_Gender%20 Identity%20Watch.pdf.

42. McInnes, "Transphobia Is Perfectly Natural."

43. Johnson, *Truth, Justice, and a Nice White Country*; see also Greg Johnson, "Further Confessions of a 'Transphobic,'" *Counter-Currents Publishing*, January 19, 2015, https://www.counter-currents.com/2015/01/further-confessions-of-a -transphobic.

44. "This Week on the Alt-Right—with Greg Johnson," YouTube video, posted by Mark Collett, August 1, 2018, https://www.youtube.com/watch?v=km 5zvv1fH6U.

45. Johnson, *Truth, Justice, and a Nice White Country*, Kindle ed.

46. "AMA 2018 Week #30," YouTube video, 12:30, posted by MW Live, July 31, 2018, https://www.youtube.com/watch?t v=EgrGutsshWQ.

47. Johnson, *Truth, Justice, and a Nice White Country*.

48. Johnson, *Truth, Justice, and a Nice White Country*.

49. Jessica Murphy, "Toronto Professor Jordan Peterson Takes On Gender-Neutral Pronouns," *BBC News*, November 4, 2016, https://www.bbc.com /news/world-us-canada-37875695; also see Nellie Bowles, "Jordan Peterson, Custodian of the Patriarchy," *New York Times*, May 18, 2018, https://www.nytimes .com/2018/05/18/style/jordan-peterson-12-rules-for-life.html.

50. Jordan Peterson as quoted in John Stossel, "Jordan Peterson vs. the Left," *Reason*, June 13, 2018, https://reason.com/archives/2018/06/13/jordan-peterson -vs-the-left; Murphy, "Toronto Professor Jordan Peterson Takes On Gender-Neutral Pronouns."

51. "Joe Rogan—Jordan Peterson Clarifies His Incels Comment," YouTube video, posted by JRE Clips, July 2, 2018, https://www.youtube.com/watch?v=js MqSBB3ZTY; Bowles, "Jordan Peterson, Custodian of the Patriarchy."

52. "Jordan Peterson Debate on the Gender Pay Gap, Campus Protests and Postmodernism," YouTube video, 3:20, posted by Channel 4 News, January 16, 2018, https://www.youtube.com/watch?v=aMcjxSThD54.

53. "Jordan Peterson Debate on the Gender Pay Gap, Campus Protests and Postmodernism," 26:35.

54. Jordan B. Peterson, *12 Rules for Life: An Antidote to Chaos* (Toronto: Random House Canada, 2018), 12.

55. See Emma McClatchey, "Guns, Fascism, Infighting and Couch-Surfing: Researcher Serena Tarr Recounts a Year Studying the Alt-Right," *Little Village Magazine*, October 3, 2018, https://littlevillagemag.com/guns-fascism-infighting -and-couch-surfing-researcher-serena-tarr-recounts-a-year-studying-the-alt-right.

56. Identity Evropa, *IE Showcase* podcast, August 2018, https://www.identity evropa.com/identitarian-action.

57. "A Cat Lady Culture," *Radix Journal*, June 2, 2015, https://www.radixjournal .com/2015/06/2015-6-2-cat-lady-culture/.

58. MacDonald, *The Culture of Critique*.

59. Paul Blumenthal and J. M. Rieger, "This Stunningly Racist French Novel Is How Steve Bannon Explains the World," *Huffington Post*, March 6, 2017, https://www.huffingtonpost.com/entry/steve-bannon-camp-of-the-saints-immigration _us_58b75206e4b0284854b3dc03. On other European fascist influences on Bannon, see Green, *Devil's Bargain*.

60. Jean Raspail, *The Camp of the Saints* (New York: Scribner, 1975), 15, 34.

61. Raspail, *The Camp of the Saints*, 313.

62. Raspail, *The Camp of the Saints*, 7.

63. Paul Ramsey (@ramzpaul), "The novel Camp of the Saints was prophetic," Twitter, July 31, 2018, 2:27 p.m.

64. CH, "This Is What Foreign Invasion Looks Like," *Chateau Heartiste*, August 1, 2018, https://heartiste.wordpress.com/2018/08/01/this-is-what-foreign -invasion-looks-like.

65. Zúquete, *The Identitarians*, 145–62.

66. Faye, Sex and Deviance.

67. Christopher Donovan, "Deathways: Four Race-Ending Life Paths of Young Whites," *Counter-Currents Publishing*, December 30, 2010, https://www.counter -currents.com/2010/12/deathways-four-race-ending-life-paths-of-young-whites.

68. F. Roger Devlin, *Sexual Utopia in Power: The Feminist Revolt Against Civilization* (San Francisco: Counter-Currents Publishing, 2015), Kindle ed.

69. See "Feminism: A Cancer on the West," YouTube video, posted by Mark Collett, July 13, 2018, https://www.youtube.com/watch?v=lF-umOajGGQ.

70. For more on MGTOW, see "Bre Faucheux on MGTOW, Feminism, Male-Female Relationships, Generational Differences in Technology," DavidDuke .com, March 29, 2018, https://davidduke.com/bre-faucheux-on-mgtow-feminism -male-female-relationships-generational-differences-in-technology/.

71. The Twitter handle of Empress Wife has been suspended, https://twitter .com/empress_wife?lang=en, accessed August 25, 2018.

72. WhiteDate for European Singles, https://www.whitedate.net, accessed October 26, 2018.

73. "The Myth of Patriarchy: Peter Lloyd and Stefan Molyneux," YouTube Radio, 52:00, posted by Stefan Molyneux, July 8, 2018, https://www.youtube.com /watch?v=ds8GoY5auuQ.

74. Devlin, *Sexual Utopia in Power*.

75. Johnson, *Truth, Justice, and a Nice White Country*.

76. Hatewatch Staff, "Chorus of Violence: Jack Donovan and the Organizing Power of Male Supremacy," Southern Poverty Law Center, March 27, 2018, https://www.splcenter.org/hatewatch/2017/03/27/chorus-violence-jack-donovan -and-organizing-power-male-supremacy.

77. "Neo-Volkisch," Southern Poverty Law Center, https://www.splcenter.org /fighting-hate/extremist-files/ideology/neo-volkisch, accessed October 26, 2018.

78. See Jack Donovan's webpage dedicated to the Wolves of Vinland, https:// www.jack-donovan.com/axis/tag/wolves-of-vinland/, accessed October 26, 2018.

79. Jack Donovan, *The Way of Men* (Milwaukie, OR: Dissonant Hum, 2012), Kindle ed.

80. James J. O'Meara, *The Homo and the Negro: Masculinist Meditations on Politics & Popular Culture*, ed. Greg Johnson (San Francisco: Counter-Currents Publishing, 2012), Kindle ed.

81. Greg Johnson, "Gay Panic on the Alt Right," *Counter-Currents Publishing*, March 18, 2016, https://www.counter-currents.com/2016/03/gay-panic-on-the-alt-right/; Maureen O'Connor, "The Philosophical Fascists of the Gay Alt-Right," *The Cut*, April 30, 2017, https://www.thecut.com/2017/04/jack-donovan-philosophical-fascists-of-the-gay-alt-right.html; Clay Bodnar, "Gay Men and the Alternative Right: An Overview," HopeNotHate.com, April 8, 2018, https://hopenothate.com/2018/04/08/gay-men-alternative-right-overview/; Shane Burley, "White Nationalist Groups Are Splitting Up Over Gay Inclusion," *Truthout*, September 20, 2017, https://truthout.org/articles/white-nationalist-groups-are-splitting-over-gay-inclusion/.

82. Trey Knickerbocker, "A Call for Unity," *Occidental Dissent*, December 15, 2018, http://www.occidentaldissent.com/2018/12/15/a-call-for-unity/#comment-3482285.

83. Greg Johnson, December 17, 2018, comment on Trey Knickerbocker, "A Call For Unity," *Occidental Dissent*, December 15, 2018, http://www.occidentaldissent.com/2018/12/15/a-call-for-unity.

84. Daniel Friberg, December 28, 2018, comment on Knickerbocker, "A Call for Unity," http://www.occidentaldissent.com/2018/12/15/a-call-for-unity/#comment-3482285.

85. James Kelly, December 17, 2018, comment on Knickerbocker, "A Call for Unity," http://www.occidentaldissent.com/2018/12/15/a-call-for-unity/#comment-3482285.

86. Proud Boy[s] home page, http://proudboysusa.com, accessed January 8, 2019.

87. "The Bell Curve: IQ, Race and Gender—Charles Murray and Stefan Molyneux," YouTube video, posted by Stefan Molyneux, September 14, 2015, https://www.youtube.com/watch?v=6lsa_97KIlc; "Race, Evolution, and Intelligence—Linda Gottfredson and Stefan Molyneux," YouTube video, December 29, 2015, https://www.youtube.com/watch?v=CZPsXYo7gpc.

88. "Race, Evolution, and Intelligence," 1:22.

89. Molyneux as quoted in "Stefan Molyneux on Race and IQ (Pt. 2)," YouTube video, 5:52, posted by the Rubin Report, November 9, 2017, https://www.youtube.com/watch?v=ToKKc6GbeNo. See also "Race, Evolution, and Intelligence"; "The Bell Curve: IQ, Race and Gender."

90. "Wrong About IQ?—Russell Warne and Stefan Molyneux," YouTube video, 44:25, posted by Stefan Molyneux, April 16, 2018, https://www.youtube.com/watch?v=EQO8I-j3Eac.

91. "Race, Evolution, and Intelligence," 1:34.

92. "The Neuroscience of Intelligence: Dr. Richard Haier," YouTube video, posted by Jordan B. Peterson, September 4, 2017, https://www.youtube.com/watch?v=PY4sShDt9to.

93. "Jordan Peterson on Why Equality of Outcome Is an IMPOSSIBLE Goal & TERRIBLE Idea," YouTube video, posted by Gravitahn, April 9, 2017, https://www.youtube.com/watch?v=jQYFVw-s2to.

94. "Who Is Wife with a Purpose? Ayla Stewart Sets the Record Straight," YouTube video, 23:07, posted by Ayla Stewart, Wife with a Purpose, April 2, 2017, https://www.youtube.com/watch?v=bKhIv4rfbwo.

95. Taylor, *White Identity*.

96. "Scandza Forum: Copenhagen 15.9.2018 part 2/2," YouTube, 1:08:24, posted by Vihapuhe FM, September 15, 2018, https://www.youtube.com/watch?v =z5IyEsapC9A.

97. Taylor, *White Identity*, 295.

98. George T. Shaw, ed., *A Fair Hearing: Alt-Right in the Words of Its Members and Leaders* (London: Arktos, 2018).

99. Aaron Panofsky, *Misbehaving Science: Controversy and the Development of Behavior Genetics* (Chicago: University of Chicago Press, 2014); Jefferson M. Fish, ed., *Race and Intelligence: Separating Science from Myth* (Mahwah, NJ: Lawrence Erlbaum Associates, 2002).

100. William H. Tucker, *The Funding of Scientific Racism: Wickliffe Draper and the Pioneer Fund* (Champaign-Urbana: University of Illinois Press, 2002).

101. Sussman, *The Myth of Race*, 235.

102. J. Philippe Rushton, *Race, Evolution, and Behavior: A Life History Perspective*, 2nd. ed. (Port Huron, MI: Charles Darwin Research Institute, 2000), 57–58.

103. Rushton, *Race, Evolution, and Behavior*, 82.

104. Sussman, *The Myth of Race*.

105. Sarah Zhang, "Will the Alt-Right Promote a New Kind of Racist Genetics?," *Atlantic*, December 2016, https://www.theatlantic.com/science/archive/2016 /12/genetics-race-ancestry-tests/510962.

106. Aaron Panofsky and Joan Donovan, "Genetic Ancestry Testing Among White Nationalists," unpublished, submitted on August 17, 2017, available online at SocArXiv Papers, https://osf.io/preprints/socarxiv/7f9bc.

107. Troy Duster, "Ancestry Testing and DNA: Uses, Limits, and *Caveat Emptor*," in *Genetics as Social Practice: Transdisciplinary Views on Science and Culture*, ed. Barbara Prainsack, Silke Schicktanz, and Gabriele Werner-Felmayer (London: Routledge, 2014); Sheldon Krimsky and Kathleen Sloan, *Race and the Genetic Revolution: Science, Myth, and Culture* (New York: Columbia University Press, 2011), 99–116; also see Alondra Nelson, *The Social Life of DNA: Race, Reparations, and Reconciliation After the Genome* (Boston: Beacon Press, 2016).

108. "ASHG Denounces Attempts to Link Genetics and Racial Supremacy," *American Society of Human Genetics Perspective* 103, no. 5 (November 1, 2018): P636, https://doi.org/10.1016/j.ajhg.2018.10.011.

109. Zhang, "Will the Alt-Right Promote a New Kind of Racist Genetics?"

110. Nathaniel Comfort, "Sociogenomics Is Opening a New Door to Eugenics," *MIT Technology Review*, October 23, 2018, https://www.technologyreview.com /s/612275/sociogenomics-is-opening-a-new-door-to-eugenics. On genetically modified babies, see Gina Kolata, Sui-Lee Wee, and Pam Belluck, "Chinese Scientist Claims to Use Crispr to Make First Genetically Edited Babies," *New York Times*, November 26, 2018, https://www.nytimes.com/2018/11/26/health/gene-editing -babies-china.html; also see Osagie Obasagie, "Revisting *Gattaca* in the Era of Trump," *Scientific American*, November 1, 2017, https://blogs.scientificamerican .com/observations/revisiting-gattaca-in-the-era-of-trump.

111. Ann Morning, *The Nature of Race: How Scientists Teach and Think About Human Difference* (Berkeley: University of California Press, 2011).

112. Ari Feldman, "Human Biodiversity: The Pseudoscientific Racism of the Alt-Right," *Forward*, August 5, 2016, https://forward.com/opinion/national/346533 /human-biodiversity-the-psuedoscientific-racism-of-the-alt-right; Panofsky and Donovan, "Genetic Ancestry Testing Among White Nationalists."

CHAPTER 5: LIVING THE TRADLIFE

1. "I Will No Longer Host 'This Week on the Alt-Right,'" YouTube video, https://www.youtube.com/watch?v=b8XHvtdoCN8, accessed September 2018; post now removed.

2. Harry Shukman, "Exposed: This Racist Alt-Right Leader Used to Be a Pro LGBT Beauty Blogger," *babe*, March 26, 2018, https://babe.net/2018/03/26/who -is-bre-faucheux-alt-right-we-found-her-real-name-44539.

3. Kevin Alfred Strom, "Is Tara McCarthy White?," *National Vanguard*, December 20, 2017, https://nationalvanguard.org/2017/12/is-tara-mccarthy-white/. This publication, despite its helpful information on Tara McCarthy's sudden departure from the alt-right media landscape, is highly problematic. The majority of the article—pulled from a nationalist website—focuses on identifying McCarthy's ethnicity and race.

4. "I Will No Longer Host 'This Week on the Alt-Right.'"

5. Bre Faucheux (@Bre_Faucheux), "Guess who's backkkkkkk???!!!!," Twitter, December 19, 2018, 8:49 a.m., https://twitter.com/Bre_Faucheux.

6. "Yule 2018 Live Stream," Red Ice TV, 26:45, December 22, 2018, https:// redice.tv/red-ice-tv/yule-2018-live-stream.

7. danah boyd, "Social Networked Sites as Networked Publics: Affordances, Dynamics, and Implications," in *A Networked Self: Identity, Community, and Culture on Social Network Sites*, ed. Zizi Papacharissi (New York: Routledge, 2011).

8. Papacharissi, *Affective Publics*.

9. Tara McPherson, "I'll Take My Stand in Dixie-Net: White Guys, the South, and Cyberspace," in *Race in Cyberspace*, ed. Beth E. Kolko, Lisa Nakamura, and Gilbert B. Rodman (New York: Routledge, 2000), 128.

10. Bre Faucheux interview with Richard Spencer, 27Crows Radio, July 25, 2017, 27crowsradio.com/index.php/2017/07/25/richard-spen…, site now discontinued, accessed November 4, 2018, via the Wayback Machine.

11. Safiya Umoja Noble, *Algorithms of Oppression: How Search Engines Reinforce Racism* (New York: New York University Press, 2018); John Cheney-Lippold, *We Are Data: Algorithms and the Making of Our Digital Selves* (New York: New York University Press, 2017); Joshua New, "Pretending Algorithms Have an Anti-Conservative Bias Is Dangerous," Center for Data Innovation, September 7, 2018, https://www.datainnovation.org/2018/09/pretending-algorithms-have-an-anti -conservative-bias-is-dangerous.

12. Jessie Daniels, *Cyber Racism: White Supremacy Online and the New Attack on Civil Rights* (Lanham, MD: Rowman & Littlefield, 2009), 3.

13. Argyle, "My Weekend with White Nationalists."

14. "Dreaming of a White Christmas: Warm Wishes from Radio Renaissance," American Renaissance, 15:00, December 20, 2018, https://www.amren.com /podcasts/2018/12/dreaming-of-a-white-christmas/.

15. Ging, "Alphas, Betas, and Incels."

16. Adam Klein, *Fanaticism, Racism, and Rage Online: Corrupting the Digital Sphere* (Cham, Switzerland: Palgrave, 2017).

17. Adrienne Massanari, "Gamergate and the Fappening: How Reddit's Algorithm, Governance, and Culture Support Toxic Technocultures," *New Media & Society* 19, no. 3 (2017): 329–46.

18. Seyward Darby, "The Rise of the Valkyries: In the Alt-Right, Women Are the Future, and the Problem," *Harper's Magazine*, September 2017, https://harpers .org/archive/2017/09/the-rise-of-the-valkyries/5/.

19. Annie Kelly, "The Housewives of White Supremacy," *New York Times*, June 1, 2018, https://www.nytimes.com/2018/06/01/opinion/sunday/tradwives-women -alt-right.html.

20. For instance, in chronicling the rise of activist Lana Lokteff and her role in prescribing alt-right female behavior, Seyward Darby writes that even among alt-right women, "men are strong and rational, women yielding and emotional; men are good at navigating politics, women at nurturing family units; men make decisions, women provide counsel. The survival of the white race depends on both sexes embracing their roles." Darby, "The Rise of the Valkyries."

21. Kathryn Joyce, *Quiverfull: Inside the Christian Patriarchy Movement* (Boston: Beacon Press, 2009).

22. Elizabeth Gillespie McRae, *Mothers of Massive Resistance: White Women and the Politics of White Supremacy* (New York: Oxford University Press, 2018).

23. Lisa McGirr, *Suburban Warriors: The Origins of the New American Right* (Princeton, NJ: Princeton University Press, 2001).

24. Belew, *Bring the War Home*.

25. For commentary on the declining white birth rate, see "The Vanishing White American," *CNN Video*, June 30, 2018, https://www.cnn.com/videos/tv/2018 /06/30/the-vanishing-white-american.cnn.

26. Claire Cain Miller, "Americans Are Having Fewer Babies. They Told Us Why," *New York Times*, July 5, 2018, https://www.nytimes.com/2018/07/05/upshot /americans-are-having-fewer-babies-they-told-us-why.html; see also Ariana Eun-jung Cha, "As U.S. Fertility Rates Collapse, Finger-Pointing and Blame Follow," *Washington Post*, October 19, 2018, https://www.washingtonpost.com/health/2018 /10/19/us-fertility-rates-collapse-finger-pointing-blame-follow/?utm_term= .7c85b84ae9e5; Sabrina Tavernise, "U.S. Fertility Rate Fell to a Record Low, for a Second Straight Year," *New York Times*, May 16, 2018, https://www.nytimes.com /2018/05/17/us/fertility-rate-decline-united-states.html.

27. See Charles M. Blow, "White Extinction Anxiety," *New York Times*, June 24, 2018, https://www.nytimes.com/2018/06/24/opinion/america-white-extinction .html.

28. Christopher Donovan, "Deathways: Four Race-Ending Life Paths of Young Whites," *Counter-Currents Publishing*, December 30, 2010, https://www.counter -currents.com/2010/12/deathways-four-race-ending-life-paths-of-young-whites/.

29. Greg Johnson as quoted in "Forced to Be Free: Interview with Mike Enoch," *You Asked For It: Selected Interviews, Vol. One* (San Francisco: Counter-Currents Pub-lishing, 2017), 65.

30. See Theodore Schleifer, "King Doubles Down on Controversial 'Babies' Tweet," CNN, March 14, 2017, https://edition.cnn.com/2017/03/13/politics/steve -king-babies-tweet-cnntv/index.html. King now is recognized triumphantly by alt-righters—including Andrew Anglin of Stormfront and Richard Spencer—as an open white nationalist.

31. See "Who Is Wife with a Purpose? Ayla Stewart Sets the Record Straight," YouTube video, posted by Ayla Stewart (Wife With a Purpose), April 2, 2017, https://www.youtube.com/watch?time_continue=26&v=bKhIv4rfbwo; "Woman Who Issued White Baby Challenge Responds to Media Attacks," YouTube video, posted by Red Ice TV, April 2, 2017, https://www.youtube.com/watch?v=wRY2k _kgb3c. See also Burley, *Fascism Today*, 92.

32. See comments by HuhWhiteHorse, Govhater, and Moloch Oven on "Woman Who Issued White Baby Challenge Responds to Media Attacks," YouTube video, https://www.youtube.com/watch?v=wRY2k_kgb3c.

33. "Is a Traditional Housewife the Ideal Woman?," *Radio 3Fourteen with Lana*, February 27, 2018, https://redice.tv/radio-3fourteen/is-a-traditional-housewife-the-ideal-woman.

34. "They Want You Dead White Man!," YouTube video, 3:44, posted by Red Ice TV, June 30, 2018, https://www.youtube.com/watch?v=XZkumsoVrvk, accessed October 22, 2018.

35. Bre Faucheux interview with Lana Lokteff, "How Women Can Course Correct," 27Crows Radio, February 28, 2018, http://brefaucheux.com/index.php/2018/02/26/lana-lokteff-how-women-can-course-correct-27crows-radio, accessed October 24, 2018, via the Wayback Machine, https://web.archive.org/web/20180820215302.

36. See Blonde in the Belly of the Beast, YouTube channel, https://www.youtube.com/channel/UCpbyOgUSjTSPpvVUAT2OyHw, accessed October 22, 2018.

37. See TheBlondeButterMaker, YouTube channel, https://www.youtube.com/channel/UCW9mamBv3maRhnCOFXf9d4A/featured, accessed October 22, 2018.

38. Lana Lokteff as quoted in Darby, "The Rise of the Valkyries."

39. See "Red Pill Women," *Red Pill Women*, https://www.reddit.com/r/RedPillWomen, accessed October 23, 2018.

40. "Welcome to RedPill Women!" *Red Pill Women*, https://www.reddit.com/r/RedPillWomen/wiki/index, accessed October 23, 2018.

41. "Welcome to RedPill Women!"; "The Official Axioms of RPW," *Red Pill Women*, https://www.reddit.com/r/RedPillWomen/wiki/index/tableofcontents/axioms, accessed October 23, 2018.

42. Laura Doyle, *The Surrendered Wife: A Practical Guide to Finding Intimacy, Passion, and Peace with a Man* (New York: Fireside, 1999.)

43. "Red Pill Women: R/RedPillWomen Rules," *Red Pill Women*, https://www.reddit.com/r/RedPillWomen, accessed October 23, 2018.

44. See thread "I Just Realized How Different Men and Women Are" on *Red Pill Women*, May 29, 2018, https://www.reddit.com/r/RedPillWomen/comments/8mylsd/i_just_realized_how_different_men_and_women_are/.

45. "Red Pill Women: R/RedPillWomen Rules," https://www.reddit.com/r/RedPillWomen/. Note that this rule was since updated to "Anybody stopping in to weight-in [*sic*] with the feminist perspective will be shown the door, as it is off topic," accessed October 23, 2018.

46. u/Nessunolosa, "Very Specific Issue: How to Deal with Male/Female Differences When Hiking (or Exercising Together in General)?," *Red Pill Women*, June 25, 2018, https://www.reddit.com/r/RedPillWomen/comments/8tqn1s/very_specific_issue_how_to_deal_with_malefemale/.

47. Curious_kitty, June 25, 2018, comment on u/Nessunolosa, "Very Specific Issue: How to Deal with Male/Female Differences When Hiking (or Exercising Together in General)?," *Red Pill Women*, June 25, 2018, https://www.reddit.com/r/RedPillWomen/comments/8tqn1s/very_specific_issue_how_to_deal_with_malefemale/.

48. u/biohazardhoe, "I Used to Be an SJW," *Red Pill Women*, June 14, 2018, https://www.reddit.com/r/RedPillWomen/comments/8r2ww2/i_used_to_be_an_sjw/.

49. LateralThinker13, June 21, 2018, comment on u/biohazardhoe, "I Used to Be an SJW," *Red Pill Women*, June 14, 2018, https://www.reddit.com/r/RedPill Women/comments/8r2ww2/i_used_to_be_an_sjw/.

50. "Melissa—Modern Women Need to Be Lied To—Radio 3Fourteen," YouTube video, posted by Red Ice TV, October 31, 2016, https://www.youtube .com/watch?v=Tb24YQN7COI.

51. "The 1965 Red Pill," YouTube video, posted by Lacey Lynn, January 9, 2018, https://www.youtube.com/watch?v=EIDUHhMBYPg.

52. "Erica—What Is White Identity? —Radio 3Fourteen," YouTube video, posted by Red Ice TV, December 14, 2016, https://www.youtube.com/watch?v =Nki9wWafteM.

53. Bre Faucheux, "About," *27Crows Radio*, Revive Our People, accessed October 28, 2018, via the Wayback Machine, https://web.archive.org/web /20170913180619/http://27crowsradio.com:80/index.php/about/.

54. "The 1965 Red Pill," YouTube video, 9:59, https://www.youtube.com /watch?v=EIDUHhMBYPg.

55. James Edward and Smufter16 comments on "The 1965 Red Pill," YouTube video, 9:59, posted by Lacey Lynn, January 9, 2018, https://www.youtube.com /watch?v=EIDUHhMBYPg.

56. "Debunking the Claim That Nationalism Is Hostile Towards Women," *Radio 3Fourteen*, November 30, 2017, https://redice.tv/radio-3fourteen/debunking -the-claim-that-nationalism-is-hostile-towards-women.

57. "Debunking the Claim That Nationalism Is Hostile Towards Women," 8:15.

58. "How the Migrant Invasion Made Me Become a Trad Wife," *Radio 3Fourteen*, April 19, 2017, https://redice.tv/radio-3fourteen/how-the-migrant -invasion-made-me-become-a-trad-wife.

59. "How the Migrant Invasion Made Me Become a Trad Wife."

60. Burley, *Fascism Today*, 92.

61. "How the Migrant Invasion Made Me Become a Trad Wife," 1:14:55.

62. Kathleen M. Blee, *Understanding Racist Activism: Theory, Methods, and Research* (New York: Routledge, 2018), 132.

63. Swain and Nieli, *Contemporary Voices of White Nationalism in America*, 246, 249.

64. Bre Faucheux, "How the Alt-Right Benefits Women," in Shaw, *A Fair Hearing*.

65. Darby, "The Rise of the Valkyries."

66. TheBlondeButterMaker, YouTube channel, https://www.youtube.com /channel/UCW9mamBv3maRhnCOFXf9d4A/feed, accessed October 24, 2018.

67. "Happy Homelands—Faith Goldy," YouTube video, posted by RamZPaul, June 30, 2018, https://www.youtube.com/watch?reload=9&v=sCGtH2Usoks& feature=youtu.be.

68. See tweets by @FaithGoldy on "Faith for Mayor," https://www.faithfor toronto.ca, accessed October 24, 2018; also see Brian Budd, "The Ominous Third-Place Finish of a White Supremacist in Toronto," *The Conversation*, October 24, 2018, http://theconversation.com/the-ominous-third-place-finish-of-a-white -supremacist-in-toronto-104816.

69. Jane Coaston, "Steve King Endorses a Bona Fide White Supremacist for Toronto Mayor," *Vox*, October 18, 2018, https://www.vox.com/policy-and-politics

/2018/10/18/17990718/steve-king-faith-goldy-white-supremacist-canada-iowa
-republicans.

70. Christopher Mathias, "Rep. King Goes Full White Nationalist in Interview
with Austrian Site," *Huffington Post*, October 20, 2018, https://www.aol.com/article
/news/2018/10/20/rep-king-goes-full-white-nationalist-in-interview-with-austrian
-site/23566828/.

CHAPTER 6: NORMALIZING NATIONALISM

1. See in particular the posts of James Lawrence on *Counter-Currents Publishing*: Lawrence, "The Kursk Strategy," *Counter-Currents Publishing*, July 3, 2018,
https://www.counter-currents.com/2018/07/the-kursk-strategy/; Lawrence,
"Thoughts on the State of the Right," *Counter-Currents Publishing*, June 28, 2018,
https://www.counter-currents.com/2018/06/thoughts-on-the-state-of-the-right/.

2. See "Radical Agenda: Live, Uncensored, Open Phones, Right Wing Talk
Radio," https://radicalagenda.com, accessed October 27, 2018.

3. See Zeskind, *Blood and Politics*; interview with Don Black in Swain and Nieli,
Contemporary Voices of White Nationalism.

4. Comment by David Duke, "Why I Support the New Stormfront Policy,"
Stormfront Blog, February 14, 2011, https://www.stormfront.org/forum/t779948,
accessed October 27, 2018.

5. Massanari, "Gamergate and the Fappening," 329–46.

6. Schlatter, *Aryan Cowboys*.

7. Heidi Beirich and Susy Buchanan, "2017: The Year in Hate and Extremism," *Intelligence Report—SPLC*, February 11, 2018, https://www.splcenter.org
/fighting-hate/intelligence-report/2018/2017-year-hate-and-extremism.

8. "The State of the Alt-Right Movement," *AltRight Radio*, March 2018,
https://altright.com/2018/03/02/the-state-of-the-alt-right-movement/.

9. Fróði Midjord, "Jared Taylor, Greg Johnson, F. Roger Devlin, Millennial
Woes & Marcus Follin to Speak at the Scandza Forum, Stockholm, April 7th,"
Counter-Currents Publishing, March 26, 2018, https://www.counter-currents.com
/2018/03/the-scandza-forum-april-7-2018/.

10. Greg Johnson, "Understanding the Pittsburgh Synagogue Massacre,"
Counter-Currents Publishing, October 29, 2018, https://www.counter-currents.com
/2018/10/understanding-the-pittsburgh-synagogue-massacre/#more-87176.

11. YouTube comment found at https://youtu.be/xe8u3pBHI2U, post has been
removed.

12. James Allsup as quoted in https://www.youtube.com/watch?v=_012Wmp
MrdQ; post has been removed.

13. "2018 American Renaissance Conference: Courage and Perseverance,"
American Renaissance, https://www.amren.com/2018-american-renaissance
-conference, accessed October 27, 2018.

14. Gregory Hood, "AmRen 2018: The Fire Taking Hold," American Renaissance, April 30, 2018, https://www.amren.com/features/2018/04/amren-2018-the
-fire-taking-hold/.

15. "About Us," Identity Evropa, https://www.identityevropa.com/about-us,
accessed October 27, 2018.

16. Beirich and Buchanan, "2017: The Year in Hate and Extremism."

17. "Membership Application," Identity Evropa, https://www.identityevropa.com
/apply, accessed October 27, 2018; Argyle, "My Weekend with White Nationalists."

18. See podcasts available on https://www.identityevropa.com/identitarian-action.

19. See Marcus Follin's YouTube channel, The Golden One, https://www.you tube.com/channel/UCN0-RRaxMgh86eOwndAklxw, accessed October 27, 2018.

20. Hood, "AmRen 2018: The Fire Taking Hold."

21. Hatewatch Staff, "Identity Evropa Holds Its First National Conference Setting Off a Dispute over Who Represents the Future of the Alt-Right," *Southern Poverty Law Center Blog*, March 15, 2018, https://www.splcenter.org/hatewatch /2018/03/15/identity-evropa-holds-its-first-national-conference-setting-dispute -over-who-represents.

22. Greg Johnson, "Budapest Conference Update," *Counter-Currents Publishing*, September 30, 2014, https://www.counter-currents.com/2014/09/budapest -conference-update; Keegan Hankes, "Eating Their Own: Several Feuds Erupt Among White Nationalists," *Southern Poverty Law Center Blog*, October 21, 2014, https://www.splcenter.org/hatewatch/2014/10/21/eating-their-own-several-feuds -erupt-among-white-nationalists.

23. Ramsey, "The Alt Right—What Went Wrong?" site has been discontin- ued. On Anglin, see Luke O'Brien, "The Making of an American Nazi," *Atlantic*, December 2017, https://www.theatlantic.com/magazine/archive/2017/12/the -making-of-an-american-nazi/544119/. Some in the alt-right believe that Anglin and the Daily Stormer are "controlled opposition," planted to ensure that the alt-right is associated with neo-Nazis, perhaps even as part of a grand Jewish plot. See "The Daily Stormer or Shtormer Is Controlled Opposition," Christogenea, https://boards.christogenea.org/forum/main-category/main-forum/american -nationalist-politics/49083-the-daily-stormer-or-shtormer-is-controlled-opposition, accessed October 27, 2018.

24. Casey, "Civil Unrest: America Is Coming Undone," 24:44.

25. Brett Samuels, "Richard Spencer Banned from 26 Countries in Europe," *Hill*, November 23, 2017, http://thehill.com/blogs/blog-briefing-room/361677 -richard-spencer-banned-from-26-countries-in-europe. Spencer discusses his brief detainment in Iceland on the podcast "Europtrip 2018!," *AltRight Politics*, July 2018, https://www.spreaker.com/user/altright/arg-sweden.

26. Wendling, *Alt-Right*.

27. April Glaser, "White Supremacists Still Have a Safe Space Online," *Slate*, October 9, 2018, https://slate.com/technology/2018/10/discord-safe-space-white -supremacists.html.

28. Casey, "Civil Unrest: America Is Coming Undone."

29. Jared Taylor, "Your Foremost Love Belongs to the Homeland," American Renaissance, September 27, 2018, https://www.amren.com/podcasts/2018/09/your -foremost-love-belongs-to-the-homeland; Greg Johnson, "Unite the Right 2 Couldn't Have Been Better," *Counter-Currents Publishing*, August 13, 2018, https:// www.counter-currents.com/2018/08/unite-the-right-2-couldnt-have-been-better.

30. "This Week on the Alt-Right with Mike Enoch," January 2, 2019, https:// www.youtube.com/watch?reload=9&v=Pq-SelBLOxc&feature=youtu.be, 5:00.

31. Johnson, "Unite the Right 2 Couldn't Have Been Better."

32. "The State of the Alt-Right Movement," *AltRight Radio*, March 2018, ps:// altright.com/2018/03/02/the-state-of-the-alt-right-movement.

33. Hawley, *Making Sense of the Alt-Right*; also see "Study: 11 Million White Americans Think Like the Alt-Right," *Vox*, August 10, 2018, https://www.vox.com /2018/8/10/17670992/study-white-americans-alt-right-racism-white-nationalists.

34. George Hawley, "The Demography of the Alt-Right," Institute for Family Studies, August 9, 2018, https://ifstudies.org/blog/the-demography-of -the-alt-right.

35. UVA Center for Politics, "New Poll: Some Americans Express Troubling Racial Attitudes Even as Majority Oppose White Supremacists," *Sabato's Crystal Ball*, September 14, 2017, http://www.centerforpolitics.org/crystalball/articles/new -poll-some-americans-express-troubling-racial-attitudes-even-as-majority-oppose -white-supremacists.

36. "Reuters/Ipsos/UVA Center for Politics Race Poll," *Ipsos Public Affairs*, September 11, 2017, http://www.centerforpolitics.org/crystalball/wp-content /uploads/2017/09/2017-Reuters-UVA-Ipsos-Race-Poll-9-11-2017.pdf.

37. Yascha Mounk and Roberto Stefan Foa, "Yes, People Really Are Turning Away from Democracy," *Washington Post*, December 8, 2016, https://www.washington post.com/news/wonk/wp/2016/12/08/yes-millennials-really-are-surprisingly -approving-of-dictators/?utm_term=.e8c448499e97; Amanda Taub, "How Stable Are Democracies? 'Warning Signs Are Flashing Red,'" *New York Times*, November 29, 2016, https://www.nytimes.com/2016/11/29/world/americas/western-liberal -democracy.html.

38. Maggie Astor, "Holocaust Is Fading from Memory, Survey Finds," *New York Times*, April 12, 2018, https://www.nytimes.com/2018/04/12/us/holocaust -education.html.

39. Karen Stenner and Jonathan Haidt, "Authoritarianism Is Not a Momentary Madness, but an Eternal Dynamic within Liberal Democracies," in Cass R. Sunstein, ed., *Can It Happen Here? Authoritarianism in America* (New York: William Morrow, 2018), 210. Also see Madeline Albright, *Fascism: A Warning* (New York: Harper Collins, 2018).

40. Stenner and Haidt, "Authoritarianism Is Not a Momentary Madness," 183.

41. Yascha Mounk and Roberto Stefan Foa, "The End of the Democratic Century: Autocracy's Global Ascendance," *Foreign Affairs* (May–June 2018), https:// www.foreignaffairs.com/articles/2018-04-16/end-democratic-century.

42. Roger Eatwell and Matthew Goodwin, *National Populism: The Liberal Revolt Against Democracy* (London: Penguin Books, 2018), xxvi–xxvii.

43. Alan I. Abramowitz, *The Great Realignment: Race, Party Transformation, and the Rise of Donald Trump* (New Haven, CT: Yale University Press, 2018), 126.

44. Abramowitz, *The Great Realignment*, 140.

45. Arlie Russell Hochschild, *Strangers in Their Own Land: Anger and Mourning on the American Right* (New York: New Press, 2016), 230.

46. Marisa Abrajano and Zoltan L. Hajnal, *White Backlash: Immigration, Race, and American Politics* (Princeton, NJ: Princeton University Press, 2015), 3.

47. Katie Rogers and Sheryl Gay Stolberg, "Trump Calls for Depriving Immigrants Who Illegally Cross Border of Due Process Rights," *New York Times*, June 24, 2018, https://www.nytimes.com/2018/06/24/us/politics/trump-immigration -judges-due-process.html.

48. Abramowitz, *The Great Realignment*, 125.

49. Abramowitz, *The Great Realignment*.

50. Olga Khazan, "A Surprising Reason to Worry About Low Birth Rates: They're Linked to an Increase in Populist Sentiments," *Atlantic*, May 26, 2018, https://www.theatlantic.com/health/archive/2018/05/a-surprising-reason-to-worry -about-low-birth-rates/561308; also see Boris Podobnik, Marko Jusup, Dejan

Kovac, and H. E. Stanley, "Predicting the Rise of EU Right-Wing Populism in Response to Unbalanced Immigration," *Complexity* (2017), https://doi.org/10.1155/2017/1580526.

51. Polakow-Suransky, *Go Back to Where You Came From*.

52. "James Allsup: Internet to Institutions—Leading Our People Forward 2018," YouTube video, posted by Identity Evropa, March 22, 2018, https://www.youtube.com/watch?v=_0l2WmpMrdQ.

53. Podcast on "Identitarian Action," *Identity Evropa*, July 14, 2018, https://identitarianaction.libsyn.com/make-america-beautiful-again.

54. Sabrina Tavernise, "Fewer Births Than Deaths Among Whites in Majority of U.S. States," *New York Times*, June 20, 2018, https://www.nytimes.com/2018/06/20/us/white-minority-population.html.

55. Dowell Myers and Morris Levy, "Racial Population Projections and Reactions to Alternative News Accounts of Growing Diversity," *Annals of the American Academy of Political and Social Science* 677 (April 2018): 221.

56. Greg Johnson, "White Extinction," *Counter-Currents Publishing*, February 14, 2014, https://www.counter-currents.com/2014/02/white-extinction/.

57. Alex Vandermaas-Peeler, Daniel Cox, Molly Fisch-Friedman, Rob Griffin, and Robert P. Jones, "American Democracy in Crisis: The Challenges of Voter Knowledge, Participation, and Polarization," *PRRI*, July 17, 2018, https://www.prri.org/research/american-democracy-in-crisis-voters-midterms-trump-election-2018/.

58. Maureen A. Craig, Julian M. Rucker, and Jennifer A. Richeson, "Racial and Political Dynamics of Approaching a 'Majority-Minority' United States," *Annals of the American Academy of Political and Social Science* 677 (May 2018): 208.

59. Farida Fozdar and Mitchell Low, "'They Have to Abide by Our Laws and Stuff': Ethnonationalism Masquerading as Civic Nationalism," *Nations and Nationalism* 21, no. 3 (2015): 524–25.

60. Ian Haney-Lopez, *Dog Whistle Politics: How Coded Racial Appeals Have Reinvented Racism and Wrecked the Middle Class* (Oxford, UK: Oxford University Press, 2014).

61. Quotes from Aviel Roshwald, "Civic and Ethnic Nationalism," in *The Wiley Blackwell Encyclopedia of Race, Ethnicity, and Nationalism, Vol 1: A-Con*, ed. John Stone et al. (Malden, MA: Wiley-Blackwell, 2016), 1–4; Farida Fozdar and Mitchell Low, "'They Have to Abide by Our Laws and Stuff": Ethnonationalism Masquerading as Civic Nationalism," *Nations and Nationalism* 21, no. 3 (2015), 524–25; Noah Pickus, *True Faith and Allegiance: Immigration and American Civic Nationalism* (Princeton, NJ: Princeton University Press, 2005).

62. Ibram X. Kendi, *Stamped from the Beginning: The Definitive History of Racist Ideas in America* (New York: Nation Books, 2016).

63. Nikhil Pal Singh, *Black Is a Country: Race and the Unfinished Struggle for Democracy* (Cambridge, MA: Harvard University Press, 2004).

64. Steven Levitsky and Daniel Ziblatt, *How Democracies Die* (New York: Broadway Books, 2019), Kindle ed.

65. Pickus, *True Faith and Allegiance*.

66. Greg Johnson as quoted in "R*ce, Culture, White Genoc*de."

67. Sidney Fussell, "AI Experts Say ICE's Predictive 'Extreme Vetting' Plan Is 'Tailor-Made for Discrimination,'" *Gizmodo*, November 16, 2017, https://gizmodo.com/ai-experts-say-ices-predictive-extreme-vetting-plan-is-1820505745.

68. https://www.youtube.com/watch?v=75uyObVKvng; post has been removed.

69. Mark Collett (@MarkACollett), "Five Ways Donald Trump Has Helped Nationalism," Twitter, July 20, 2018, 11:58 a.m., https://twitter.com/markacollett ?lang=en.

70. Caitlin Dickerson, "Detention of Migrant Children Has Skyrocketed to Highest Levels Ever," *New York Times*, September 12, 2018, https://www.nytimes .com/2018/09/12/us/migrant-children-detention.html; Lomi Kriel, "Longer Stays Leaves Record Number of Immigrant Children in Detention," *Houston Chronicle*, November 21, 2018, https://www.houstonchronicle.com/news/houston-texas /houston/article/Thanksgiving-in-immigration-shelters-as-number-of-13415048.php.

71. Leo R. Chavez, *Anchor Babies and the Challenge of Birthright Citizenship* (Stanford, CA: Stanford University Press, 2017).

72. "Patrick Casey: American Identitarianism—Leading Our People Forward 2018," YouTube video, posted by Identity Evropa, March 22, 2018, https://www .youtube.com/watch?v=QisDUMB6cIU.

73. Twitter account has been discontinued, https://twitter.com/PKsbpdl/status /1018693830303010818, retweeted by Paul Kersey.

74. Patrick Casey, "Reactionary Futurism: An Inauguration," *Reactionary Futurism Blog*, May 2, 2018, https://reactionaryfuturism.com/2018/05/02/reactionary -futurism-an-inauguration/.

75. "Finding Identity and a Home in Future White America," *Renegade Tribune Blog*, February 16, 2018, http://www.renegadetribune.com/finding-identity-home -future-white-america/.

76. Michael Ignatieff, *Blood and Belonging: Journeys into the New Nationalism* (New York: Farrar, Straus & Giroux, 1993), 10.

77. Counter-Currents Radio, "Alt-Tech & the Electronic Ethnostate with Louis Cypher," *Counter-Currents Radio Podcast No. 191*, August 30, 2017, https:// www.counter-currents.com/2017/08/counter-currents-radio-weekly-alt-tech-and -the-electronic-ethnostate.

78. Papacharissi, *Affective Publics*.

79. Brian Massumi, *Politics of Affect* (Cambridge, UK: Polity Press, 2015); Michel de Certeau, *The Practice of Everyday Life*, trans. Steven Rendall (Berkeley: University of California Press, 1984); Klein, *Fanaticism, Racism, and Rage Online*.

80. Letter from Iron Mitten to Austin , undated, received on July 30, 2018; shared with the author with permission to cite.

CONCLUSION: DECODING AND DERAILING WHITE NATIONALIST

1. For a classic example of such work, see Victor Klemperer, *The Language of the Third Reich*, trans. Martin Brady (London: Athlone Press, 2000).

2. There was much talk of imminent change and tipping points at the Scandza Forum on September 15, 2018. See "The Scandza Forum: Copenhagen 15.9.2018 part 1/2."

3. Janet Reitman, "U.S. Law Enforcement Failed to See the Threat of White Nationalism. Now They Don't Know How to Stop It," *New York Times*, November 3, 2018, https://www.nytimes.com/2018/11/03/magazine/FBI-charlottesville-white -nationalism-far-right.html.

4. Ryan Bort, "Trump Is Using a White Nationalist Conspiracy Theory to Inform Policy," *Rolling Stone*, August 23, 2018, https://www.rollingstone.com /politics/politics-news/trump-south-africa-714744/.

5. "FARMLANDS (2018) Official Documentary," YouTube video, posted by Lauren Southern, June 25, 2018, https://www.youtube.com/watch?v=a_bDc7FfItk; Tom Head, "Who Is Lauren Southern? Five Facts on the Far-Right Filmmaker," *South African*, March 27, 2018, https://www.thesouthafrican.com/who-is-lauren-southern-five-facts.

6. Tyler McBrien, "U.S. and Foreign Governments Should be Skeptical of AfriForum's Lobbying," June 12, 2018, https://www.cfr.org/blog/us-and-foreign-governments-should-be-skeptical-afriforums-lobbying.

7. Bort, "Trump Is Using a White Nationalist Conspiracy Theory to Inform Policy."

8. Charlie Nash, "Lauren Southern: South Africa Is a 'Human Rights Crisis,'" *Breitbart*, August 28, 2018, https://www.breitbart.com/politics/2018/08/28/lauren-southern-south-africa-is-a-human-rights-crisis.

9. Matt Pearce, "'This Is a White Supremacist Talking Point': Anti-Racism Groups Blast Trump's 'White Farmers' Tweet," *Los Angeles Times*, August 23, 2018, http://www.latimes.com/nation/la-na-white-farmers-20180823-story.html.

10. Farouk Chothia, "South Africa: The Groups Playing on the Fears of a 'White Genocide,'" BBC, September 1, 2018, https://www.bbc.com/news/world-africa-45336840.

11. Colin Dwyer, "Here's the Story Behind That Trump Tweet on South Africa—and Why It Sparked Outrage," NPR, August 23, 2018, https://www.npr.org/2018/08/23/641181345/heres-the-story-behind-that-trump-tweet-on-south-africa-and-why-it-sparked-outra.

12. Angry White Men, "Lauren Southern's 'Farmlands' Is Lazy, Dishonest, and Racist," September 9, 2018, https://angrywhitemen.org/2018/09/09/lauren-southerns-farmlands-is-lazy-dishonest-and-racist/.

13. Office of the UN Special Adviser on the Prevention of Genocide, "Legal Definition of Genocide (OSAPG) Analysis Framework," http://www.un.org/ar/preventgenocide/adviser/pdf/osapg_analysis_framework.pdf, accessed October 18, 2018.

14. Tracy Jan, "White Families Have Nearly 10 Times the Net Worth of Black Families. And the Gap Is Growing," *Washington Post*, September 28, 2017, https://www.washingtonpost.com/news/wonk/wp/2017/09/28/black-and-hispanic-families-are-making-more-money-but-they-still-lag-far-behind-whites/?utm_term=.fbc8b13d96d5; Johnson, *The White Nationalist Manifesto*, 23.

15. Eugene Scott, "Laura Ingraham Tries to Walk Back Her 'Demographic Changes' Monologue—but Doesn't Apologize," *Washington Post*, August 10, 2018, https://www.washingtonpost.com/politics/2018/08/10/laura-ingraham-tries-walk-back-her-demographic-changes-monologue-doesnt-apologize/?utm_term=.438a626bb8a2.

16. "Laura Ingraham Retweeted a British Neo-Nazi," *MediaMatters Blog*, January 7, 2018, https://www.mediamatters.org/blog/2018/01/07/laura-ingraham-retweeted-british-neo-nazi/218996.

17. Scott, "Laura Ingraham Tries to Walk Back Her 'Demographic Changes' Monologue."

18. Haley Britzky, "Go Deeper: Laura Ingraham's Demographics Backlash," *Axios*, August 10, 2018, https://www.axios.com/laura-ingraham-demographics-fox-news-4e169316-d912-40d8-b3b6-9666cc2d1af8.html.

19. Luke O'Neil, "Laura Ingraham Isn't an Outlier, She's the Mainstream," *Observer*, August 10, 2018, https://observer.com/2018/08/laura-ingraham-anti-immigration-rant-mainstream.

20. Erica L. Green, Katie Benner, and Robert Pear, "'Transgender' Could Be Defined Out of Existence Under Trump Administration," *New York Times*, October 21, 2018, https://www.nytimes.com/2018/10/21/us/politics/transgender-trump-administration-sex-definition.html.

21. Stanley, *How Fascism Works*, 137.

22. "The Genderbread Person," *Sam Killermann Blog*, November 2011, https://samuelkillermann.com/work/genderbread-person, accessed October 27, 2018.

23. German Lopez, "Gender Identity, Explained in an Adorable Infographic," *Vox*, March 10, 2015, https://www.vox.com/2015/3/10/8180533/genderbread-man.

24. "The Gnostic Genderbread Person," YouTube video, 0:55; 1:18, posted by RamZPaul, October 9, 2018, https://www.youtube.com/watch?v=89Kz82ZfVgo&feature=youtu.be.

25. "Jordan Peterson—Gender Identity," YouTube video, 1:18, posted by ManOfAllCreation, August 27, 2017, https://www.youtube.com/watch?v=bCIoAw5Z_pY.

26. Anne Fausto-Sterling, "Why Sex Is Not Binary," *New York Times*, October 25, 2018, https://www.nytimes.com/2018/10/25/opinion/sex-biology-binary.html.

27. "The Perils of Covering the Alt-Right," *On the Media*, August 31, 2018, https://www.wnycstudios.org/story/perils-alt-right.

28. Lisa Nakamura, "'Screw Your Optics: I'm Going In': Watching White Supremacy on Digital Video Platforms," draft article for *Film Quarterly*, forthcoming.

INDEX

abortion ban, 54
Abramowitz, Alan, 120
adopted children, nonwhite, 67
Adorno, Theodor, 24
A Fair Hearing, 108
affirmative right, 7
African Americans: disenfranchisement
  of, 48; enslavement of, 123; and white
  ethnostate, 52, 58. *See also* racism
"African boat people," 79
Africa Quarterly (magazine), 57
AfriForum, 131
"against time," 10, 35, 36, 37, 38, 42
age, 118
Aladdin (musical), 71
Alaska, 61
Alba Rising, 21
aliases, 8
Allsup, James, 62, 113, 124
Alpines, 2
"Alternative Culture Zone," 65
Alternative for Germany, 7, 52
Alternative for Sweden, 7
AlternativeRight.com, 30
alt-light, 5, 11–12, 19–20, 76–79, 135
alt-paternalism, 83
alt-right: demographics of, 117–18; lexi-
  con of, 4; origins of term, 2, 5; primary
  objective of, 23; use of term, 7
Alt-Right (Wendling), 73
Altright.com, 116
altruism, pathological, 80
AMA (Ask Me Anything) videos, 78
America First Media, 45
"American Dream," 46, 72
American Identity Movement, 7, 114,
  142n26
American National Election Survey
  (ANES), 118

American Nazi Party, 37
American Nightmare, 46
American Renaissance: and biological
  essentialism, 74, 77, 86, 88–89; and
  normalization, 113, 115; and vs. old
  white nationalism, 1, 3, 4; and red
  pilling, 31, 146n60; and timescape, 46,
  49; and traditionalism, 96; on white
  ethnostate, 55, 56, 60
American Society of Human Genetics, 91
American Thinker, 125
amnesia, alt-right, 44–49
ancestry, 100, 104–10
Ancestry.com, 91
ancestry testing, 91–92
ANES (American National Election
  Survey), 118
Anglin, Andrew, 15, 86, 116
Anti-Defamation League, 6, 131
anti-egalitarianism, 9, 28–29
anti-fascists (antifa), 63
anti-feminism, 72, 75, 76, 82, 84
antiliberalism, 40
anti-Semitism: and biological essentialism,
  86; and normalization, 125; and vs. old
  white nationalism, 5; and red pilling,
  31; and timescapes, 47; and traditionalism, 108; and white ethnostate, 57,
  68–69
anti-womanism, 84
archeofuturism, 36, 42–44, 125
Archeofuturism (Faye), 43, 44
"Arctic Cycle of the Golden Age," 41
Arditi, 30
Arendt, Hannah, 14
Arktos Media, 4, 22–23, 26, 35, 40, 86
Aryan Liberty Net, 30
Aryan Nations, 26, 30, 53, 63, 112–13
Asian Americans and white ethnostate, 65

Ask Me Anything (AMA) videos, 78
authoritarianism, 4, 10, 13, 119, 124
autocracy, 44
avatars, 8
Aztlán, 52, 60

Badiou, Alain, 23
Bannon, Steve, 39, 80
Belew, Kathleen, 98
The Bell Curve (Murray and Herrnstein), 20, 90
Benoist, Alain de, 25–26, 36
betas, 85
biological binary, 71, 79–87
biological determinism, 87
biological essentialism, 11, 71–92; alt-light and, 76–79; and feminism, 76, 78, 79–83; and homosexuality, 85–87; IQ and DNA of, 87–92; and masculinity, 83–85; Proud Boys and, 71–76
bioregion, 11, 60, 61
birth rate of whites, 54
birthright citizenship, 13, 54, 124
BitChute, 4, 95, 112
black(s). *See* African Americans
Black, Derek, 112
Black, Don, 112
black ethnostate, 54, 58, 65
Black Lives Matter, 67, 118
Black Panther (film), 52
black pills, 10, 17
Blee, Kathleen, 107–8
TheBlondeButterMaker, 101, 109
Blonde in the Belly of the Beast, 101
blue pill, 27
"Books Against Time," 10–11, 35
border policy, 54, 106, 120–21, 124–25, 133
Bowden, Jonathan, 37, 76
brain size, 90
Brave New World (Huxley), 60
Breitbart News, 23
Brexit, 20, 52, 107
The Brigade (Covington), 64, 132
British National Party, 124
Bronze Age, 38, 39
browning of America, 132–33
Buchanan, Patrick, 5
Buckley, William F., 149n6
Butler Plan, 53

"caged manhood," 84
Calexit, 61
California, 61
Callenbach, Ernest, 61–62

"A Call for Unity," 86
The Camp of Saints (Raspail), 80–81
Cantwell, Christopher, 111
Carlson, Tucker, 8, 99, 121, 127, 130–31
Cascadia, 51, 60, 61–65
Cascadia Independence Party, 61
Casey, Patrick: and normalization, 113, 117, 125; and old vs. new white nationalism, 142n26; and timescapes, 33–34, 36, 44, 49
catchphrases, 3
"Cat Ladies," 79
celibates, involuntary, 18, 78, 85
census data, 99, 121–22
Cernovich, Mike, 76, 77
Charlottesville, Virginia: and biological essentialism, 74, 75, 86; and normalization, 111, 116; and old vs. new white nationalism, 4, 7, 13; and red pilling, 22, 31; and traditionalism, 95
Chateau Heartiste blog, 17, 31, 81
children: expulsion of nonwhite, 125; nonwhite adopted, 67
Chinese Exclusion Act (1882), 123
Christian Right, 26, 98
citizenship: for African Americans, 123; birthright, 13, 54, 124; partial or minimal, 67–68; path to full, 68
civic nationalism: assault on, 123–27; and old vs. new white nationalism, 11, 13; and timescapes, 34; and white ethnostate, 51, 55; and white nationalist discourse, 133
civil rights march, 49
civil unrest, 49
Clinton, Bill, 20
Clinton, Hillary, 6
Coates, Ta-Nehisi, 55
Collett, Mark: and biological essentialism, 82; and normalization, 116, 124; and red pilling, 21; and traditionalism, 93, 94, 104, 109
community organizing, 28
conditions of possibility, 117–23
Confederate secession, 52, 95
The Conquest of a Continent (Grant), 2–3
Conte, Gregory, 21, 22–23
conversion. *See* red-pill conversion
Coulter, Ann, 48, 99, 121
Counter-Currents (webzine/book publisher): and biological essentialism, 77, 81–82; on metapolitics, 26, 27–28, 29, 30, 31, 32; and normalization, 113–14, 126; and old vs. new white nationalism,

3, 4, 10; on timescape, 35, 36, 37, 38, 40, 44; and traditionalism, 96, 99–100; on white ethnostate, 53–54, 66
Covington, Harold, 63–64, 132
criminality, race and, 35
Crispr, 91–92
"cuckservative" ("cuck"), 4, 21, 34, 73, 80
cultural dispossession, 72, 73–74
"cultural Marxism," 18, 24, 27
culture: and archeofuturism, 43–44; metapolitics and, 23–26, 28, 29–30, 32; red-pill conversion and, 21
The Culture of Critique (MacDonald), 80
Cumberland, 60
Cuomo, Andrew, 74
cyberspace, metapolitics and, 30–31
cyclic nature of time, 33–34, 36, 38, 41–42, 44–45

The Daily Shoah podcast, 117, 124
Daily Stormer: and biological essentialism, 75, 86; and normalization, 116; and red pilling, 15, 17, 30, 31; and traditionalism, 96
Damigo, Nathan, 33
Daniels, Jessie, 96
Darby, Seyward, 164n20
Dare, Howard, 18
Dark Age, 38, 39, 44
Dark Enlightenment, 44
Data & Society Research Institute, 17
dating apps, 82–83
Davenport, Charles, 89
decentralization, 5, 7
deep ecology, 37, 60
dehumanization, 57
democracy, 44, 124
Democratic Party, 28, 29, 76, 120, 122, 123
Democratic Socialism, 49, 132
demographic change, 132–33
demographics, 117–18
deplatforming, 4–5, 31–32, 96, 129
deportations, 54, 68, 121
desegregation, 52
detention, prolonged, 56
Devi, Savitri, 36–37, 42, 47
Devlin, F. Roger, 83
difference, 11
digital storytelling, 12
Discord, 117, 142n26
The Dispossessed Majority (Robertson), 57–58, 59
dispossession, 72, 73–74, 118, 133

dissident right, 7
diversity: and biological essentialism, 72, 84, 89; and normalization, 10, 26, 46, 49, 51, 122; and old vs. new white nationalism, 10; and red pilling, 26; and timescapes, 46, 49; and traditionalism, 101, 104, 105; and white ethnostate, 51
Dixie, 60
DNA of racial essentialism, 91–92
do-gooder leftists, 12
dog-whistle, 121
The_Donald subreddit, 73, 112
Donovan, Jack, 84–85
Donovan, Joan, 91
doxing, 93
Draper, Wickliffe, 59
drug addicts, 67
Dubiel, Matt, 20
Duke, David, 31, 57, 112, 133
Dune (film), 44
Dyck, Kirsten, 30

Eastern occultism, 36, 37
Eatwell, Roger, 119
eco-consciousness, 60
eco-fascism, 60
Ecotopia, 60, 61–62
Ecotopia: The Notebooks and Reports of William Weston (Callenbach), 61–62
"edge cases," 66–67
Edwards, James, 8
egalitarianism, 12, 43, 44, 46, 105, 125
Eichmann in Jerusalem (Arendt), 14
8chan, 4, 6, 31, 97, 112
electronic ethnostate, 126
"emancipation" of women, 41
emasculated men, 76
Empress Wife, 82
end-time, 42
"enforced monogamy," 78, 83
Enlightenment, 34, 42, 43, 47, 125
Enoch, Mike, 117
ENR (European New Right), 10, 22–27, 32, 36, 40
enrichment programs, 90
environmentalism, 3, 11, 60, 61–62
equality, 34, 72, 84, 88, 105
equity, 88
Estado Novo (Brazil), 39
Estonia, 52
"Eternal Return," 42
eternity politicians, 34
ethnic cleansing, 53, 54, 69
ethnic communities, 52

ethnocentric history, 2
ethnomasochism, 58, 80
ethnonationalism: defined, 57; and meta-
    politics, 26–27; and normalization, 112,
    121, 125–26; and old vs. new white
    nationalism, 7, 10, 11, 13; and red
    pilling, 15, 16; and white ethnostate,
    51, 52, 55, 57
ethnopluralism, 26
ethnoracial plurality, 34–35
ethnostate. *See* white ethnostate
*The Ethnostate: An Unblinkered Prospectus
    for an Advanced Statecraft* (Robertson),
    57, 58–59, 65
eugenic optimization, 11
eugenics, 3, 40, 59–60, 89
eugenic surveillance, 60
Eurocentrism, 2
European New Right (ENR), 10, 22–27,
    32, 36, 40
European races, 2
European Union (EU), 121
Europe Is Falling, 15–16, 31
Evola, Julius, 30, 36, 40–42, 44, 45, 47
evolutionary psychology, 18

Facebook: and biological essentialism, 73,
    74; and normalization, 116, 117; and
    old vs. new white nationalism, 13; and
    red pilling, 31; and traditionalism, 95
FAIR (Federation for American Immigra-
    tion Reform), 60
"family reunification" policies, 48
family separations, 56
the Farm, 52
Farmlands (film), 131, 132
fascism: and old vs. new white national-
    ism, 8, 9, 10–11; and timescapes, 37,
    38, 40; and transphobia, 134; and white
    ethnostate, 51
Fascist Crew Love, 29
Fash the Nation podcast, 17, 21, 53
"fashy," 21, 29
Faucheux, Bre (pseudonym): and old vs.
    new white nationalism, 12; and red pill-
    ing, 20, 21; and traditionalism, 93–94,
    97, 101, 104, 105, 108
Faye, Guillaume, 26, 36, 42–44, 79, 125
Federated Black States of America, 127
Federation for American Immigration
    Reform (FAIR), 60
female promiscuity, 83
feminism: and biological essentialism, 76,
    78, 79–83, 84–85; and Islam, 79; and

Jewish influence, 79–80; and red-pill
    conversion, 18–20; and traditionalism,
    103–4, 105, 108; and white ethnostate,
    52, 58
feminization, 41, 105
Le Figaro, 25
fitness, 115
Follin, Marcus, 115
4chan: and biological essentialism, 73, 77;
    and normalization, 112; and old vs. new
    white nationalism, 4, 6; and red pilling,
    31; and traditionalism, 97
Four Ages, 36–42, 44
Fourteenth Amendment (1868), 46, 115
Fourteen Words, 53
Fox News, 8, 13
France, 121
Frankfurt School, 22, 24, 27
Freedomain Radio, 19–20
French National Front, 52
French nationalist movements, 10
French New Right, 25, 26, 28, 79
French Revolution, 47
French Right, 24–25, 26
Friberg, Daniel, 86
frontier, taming of, 47
Fuentes, Nick, 116
futurism, 42–44; reactionary, 36, 44

Gab: and normalization, 112, 116; and old
    vs. new white nationalism, 4, 12, 13;
    and traditionalism, 94, 95
gamblers, 65
Gamergate, 97
"gangs," 84
Gariépy, J. P., 116
Gattaca (film), 59
gay-bashing, 85
gay pride marches, 80
gender binary, 11, 71, 79–87
GenderBread Person, 134–35
gender complementarity, 82, 108
gender differences, 84, 102–4
gender discrimination, 78
gender equality, 10, 102–4
gender essentialism, 9, 41
gender fluidity, 77, 134
gender nonbinariness, 77, 78, 134–35
gender politics, 94
gender pronouns, 78
gender roles, 18–20, 98, 164n20
Gender Unicorn, 134
gene editing, 91–92
general intelligence, 88

Generation Identitaire website, 29
Generation Z, 114
Generation Zyklon, 135
Genetic Ancestry Testing, 91
genetic determinism, 92
genetic modification, 91–92
genetics and intelligence, 87–92
genetic similarity theory, 90
genetic technologies, 43
genetic testing, 59–60, 91
geographical fragmentation, 62
geographical reshuffling, 65
Germany, 121
g factor, 90
G Factor, 88
Giroux, Henry, 13
globalism, 52, 58, 84, 107
globalization, 58
Goethe, Charles M., 3
Golden Age, 34, 36–42, 44, 112
Golden One, 115
golden ratios, 39
Goldy, Faith, 32, 75, 101, 109
Goodwin, Matthew, 119
Google Chat, 31
Gottfredson, Linda, 87, 88
Gottfried, Paul, 5, 7, 68
Gramsci, Antonio, 22, 25, 27, 32
Grant, Madison, 1, 2, 3, 4, 60, 89
The Great Realignment: Race, Party Trans-formation, and the Rise of Donald Trump (Abramowitz), 120
"The Great Replacement," 52, 75, 97
Green counterculture, 62
Green Party, 60
Griffin, Roger, 25, 38, 40, 51
Group for the Research and Study of European Civilization (GRECE), 25–26, 40
group solidarity, 55
Guénon, René, 36, 38–42, 44, 45
guerrilla country, 64
Gulflandia, 51, 61

Hailgate, 6, 7, 116
Haitian Revolution, 47
Happy Homelands, 116
Harry Potter series, 29
Hart-Celler Immigration Act (1965), 48, 127, 133
Harvard Educational Review, 90
Hatewatch blog, 17
Hawley, George, 117–18
Hayden Lake, 53
heavy-metal music, 29–30

hegemony, 25, 27–28, 29, 57
Heidegger, Martin, 35
Hellman, John, 26
Helping Euro-Americans Reclaim their Land and National Destiny (HEARTLAND), 65
heritability of intelligence, 87–92
Herrnstein, Richard, 20, 90
hierarchy(ies), 9; natural, 75, 78–79
Hinduism, 36, 39, 80–81
Hispanics, 11, 65, 120–21, 122
historical amnesia, 11
historical memory, 11
Hitler, Adolf, 36, 37
Hobbes, Thomas, 55
Hochschild, Arlie, 120
Holocaust, 47–48, 119
Holocaust denialism, 47, 57
homeland, 55, 58
home-schooling, 105, 109
homophobia, 73, 85–87
homosexuals, 65, 67, 85–87, 98
homosociality, 84, 98
Hood, Gregory, 46, 56
Hoppe, Hans-Hermann, 44
horizons, 45
Horkheimer, Max, 24
How Democracies Die (Levitsky and Ziblatt), 124
How Fascism Works: The Politics of Us and Them (Stanley), 134
Hufeland, Gottlieb, 23
Huffington Post (newspaper), 113
human biodiversity, 4, 26
Hungary, 52, 118
Huxley, Aldous, 60
hyperacceleration of time, 39, 45, 49
Hyperborea, 51
hyperfeminization, 80
hypergamy, 82, 83, 103
hypermasculinity, 71–72, 75, 82, 85, 87, 98

Identitarian Action podcast, 114–15
identitarianism: and biological essentialism, 81; and normalization, 112, 113, 114–15; and old vs. new white nationalism, 7; and red pilling, 22, 26–27; and timescapes, 33, 40; and traditionalism, 105
Identity Evropa: and biological essentialism, 79; and metapolitics, 32; mission of, 33; and normalization, 113, 114–15, 125; and old vs. new white nationalism, 7, 142n26; and timescapes, 33–35, 42,

48, 49; and traditionalism, 96; and white ethnostate, 69
identity politics, 5, 33, 40, 120
"If" (Kipling), 20–21
Ignatieff, Michael, 125–26
"illegal aliens," deportation of, 54
image makeover, 111–17
immigrants and immigration: and biological essentialism, 75; and environmentalism, 60; European policies on, 52; extreme vetting of, 13, 124; invasions by, 80–81, 100–101, 106, 121; Muslim, 114, 121; and normalization, 124–25; quotas for, 2, 48–49, 52, 59; and traditionalism, 104; unchecked, 80; undocumented, 69, 79, 120–21; welfare benefits for, 54, 106; and white ethnostate, 52, 53, 57
Immigration Act (1965), 48–49
Immigration Restriction League, 1
impotence, 72
incels (involuntary celibates), 18, 78, 85, 97
inclusion, 10, 51
income, 118
individualism, 34
inequality, 11
Infowars, 20, 30, 31, 76
Ingraham, Laura, 99, 132–33
initiation ritual, 71–72
Inner Traditions, 40
intelligence, race and, 19–20, 35, 87–92
internet, 6, 72–73, 93–98
interregnum, 44–45
Interregnum podcast, 22–23, 35
involuntary celibates (incels), 18, 78, 85, 97
IQ of racial essentialism, 87–92
Ireland, Sumner Humphrey, 57–60
Iron Age, 38, 39, 44
Iron Mitten, 126–27
Islamophobia, 79, 106, 131
Israel, 58, 65, 68
Italian Futurist Movement, 30
Italy, 52, 121

Japan, 52
Japanese Americans, internment of, 123
Jazzhands McFeels, 17
Jefferson (proposed state), 61
Jensen, Arthur, 90
Jewish hegemony, 57
Jewish influence, 79–80
Jewish Question (JQ), 7, 68–69, 75, 86
Jews: and biological essentialism, 75; and immigration policy, 48; at Temple of

Life synagogue, 113; and white ethnostate, 58, 65
John Birch Society, 98
Johnson, Greg: and biological essentialism, 77, 78, 83, 86, 90; and normalization, 113, 115–16, 117; and red pilling, 27–28, 32; and timescapes, 44, 45, 47–48; and traditionalism, 93, 99–100; on white ethnostate, 53–54, 56, 62, 69
Johnson-Reed Immigration Act (1924), 2
Jones, Alex, 5, 20, 76, 77
Jordan, David Starr, 3
JQ (Jewish Question), 7, 68–69, 75, 86

Kali Yuga, 38–42, 44–45, 49, 112
kalpa, 39
Kemp, Arthur, 1
Kendall, Ward, 47
Kennedy, Edward M., 48
Kersey, Paul, 49, 96, 116, 117
Kessler, Jason, 74
Killermann, Sam, 134
Kimmel, Michael, 72
King, Martin Luther, Jr., 48
King, Steve, 100, 109, 136
Kipling, Rudyard, 20–21, 29
Ku Klux Klan (KKK), 1, 5, 47, 74, 112

Lane, David, 53, 112
La Raza, 67
LARP (live-action role-playing) video games, 65, 114
Latina/os, 11, 65, 120–21, 122
law and order, 123
League of the South, 86
Leave It to Beaver (television show), 104, 109
leftism, 78
Lehmann, Claire, 135
Lenin, Vladimir, 23
Lenz, Ryan, 17
Leonard, John Bruce, 23
Levertov, Denise, 61
Levitsky, Steven, 124
Lewinsky, Monica, 20
LGBTQ community, 84, 98, 134
liberalism, 80, 84, 103–4, 105
Liberia, 52
libertarianism, 5, 28
The Lightning and the Sun (Devi), 36
linear temporality, 35–36, 43
live-action role-playing (LARP) video games, 65, 114
Lokteff, Lana: and biological essentialism, 75; and traditionalism, 93, 94, 100–102,

107–9, 164n20; and white ethnostate, 54, 63
Lombroso, Cesare, 38
London, Jack, 20
London Forum, 45
Lutheran Social Services, 107
Lynn, Lacey, 49, 94, 101, 104–5

MacDonald, Kevin, 47, 48, 80, 104, 114
majority-minority, 122–23
"Make America Great Again" (MAGA), 33, 46
Making Sense of the Alt-Right (Hawley), 117–18
male bonding, 71
male-centrism, 12
male dominance, 41
male narcissism, 83–84
male primitivism, 84
male victimhood, 73–74
Malkin, Michelle, 68
Manichaean worldview, 17, 19
Manifest Destiny, 47
Manifesto per una rinascita europea (Manifesto for a European Rebirth, Benoist), 25
manosphere, 10, 17–19, 84, 97, 99
man's man, 84
manvantaras, 39
Mao Zedong, 23
March of the Titans: The Complete History of the White Race (Kemp), 1
Marcuse, Herbert, 24, 27
Marxism, 23, 25, 106; cultural, 18, 24, 27
masculinity, 72, 82, 84–85
masculinization, 41
masculinized women, 76
The Matrix (movie), 10, 16, 19
McCarthy, Tara, 93–94, 97, 104, 163n3
McInnes, Gavin, 32, 71–72, 73–75, 77
McPherson, Tara, 95
media hosts, 8
Mediterraneans, 2
memes, 4, 14, 136
"men against time," 36–37, 42
H. L. Mencken Society, 5
Men Going Their Own Way (MGTOW): and biological essentialism, 82; and old vs. new white nationalism, 5; and red pilling, 17, 18; and traditionalism, 93, 94, 105
men's rights movement, 5, 82, 84
message boards, 4
messaging, 28

metamorphosis, 42
metanarratives, 42
metapolitics, 10, 21–22; American-style, 27–32; and culture, 23–26, 28, 29–30, 32; and cyberspace, 30–31; and European New Right, 22–27; and hegemony, 25, 27–28; importance of, 32; origin of, 23; as pre-political, 28; and white ethnostate, 66
Metapolitics (Badiou), 23
Metropolitan Republican Club, 74
"Mexican aliens," 108
MGTOW. *See* Men Going Their Own Way (MGTOW)
millennials, 114, 119
Millennial Woes, 16, 31, 56, 78, 104, 116
minimal citizenship, 67–68
Minority Relocation Act, 65
misogyny, 5, 12, 31, 41, 93, 97
mixed-race people, 65
modernization, 58
Molyneux, Stefan, 19–20, 77, 83, 87–88, 104, 131
monogamy, "enforced," 78, 83
Morning, Ann, 92
Morpheus Manfred, 18–19
multiculturalism, 10, 52, 56, 57, 89, 104
multiracialism and white ethnostate, 52, 58
Murray, Charles, 20, 87, 88, 90
music, 29–30
Muslims, 100, 106, 114, 121
Mussolini, Benito, 40
mythic past, veneration of, 10

narcissism, male, 83–84
National Alliance, 26
nationalism, civic vs. ethno- (racial): and normalization, 123–27; and old vs. new white nationalism, 7, 10, 11, 13; and red pilling, 15, 16, 26–27; and white ethnostate, 51, 55
National Policy Institute (NPI), 6, 21, 34–35, 116
national populism, 13, 136
National Review (magazine), 149n6
National Socialism (NS). *See* Nazism
national victimhood, 34
Nation of Islam, 60
Native Americans, 52, 60, 65, 68
nativist priorities, 59
natural hierarchies, 11, 78–79
Naturalization Act (1790), 46, 51, 67, 123
The Nature of Race (Morning), 92

Nazism: and metapolitics, 22; and normalization, 112; and old vs. new white nationalism, 5, 10–11; and timescape, 36–37, 40, 47
neoconservatives, 5
neo-folk music, 30
neo-Nazism: and biological essentialism, 74, 86; and normalization, 111, 112, 116, 117, 118; and old vs. new white nationalism, 8–9, 11, 12; and red pilling, 26; and timescapes, 38, 47; and traditionalism, 107–8; and white nationalist discourse, 130
neo-reactionaries, 5, 44
Nero, Dante, 73
the Netherlands, 121
"networked public," 95
New Albion, 51, 61
New Europa, 61
New Left, 24, 28
New Right, 22
New Right Versus Old Right (Johnson), 47–48
New York Forum, 45
Nietzsche, Friedrich, 35, 41, 150n38
Nixon, Richard, 123
nonlinear temporality, 35–36, 38, 41, 49
Nordics, 2
normalization, 12–13, 111–27; and assault on civic nationalism, 123–27; conditions of possibility and, 117–23; and identitarianism, 112, 113, 114–15; and image makeover, 111–17
"normie," 21
North Africans, 107
North Dakota, 106–7
Northwest American Republic, 63–64
Northwest Front, 53
Northwest Volunteer Army brigade, 64
Nouvelle École, 25
#NoWanks, 71, 72, 73
NPI (National Policy Institute), 6, 21, 34–35, 116
NS (National Socialism). See Nazism
Nyborg, Helmuth, 88

Obama, Barack, 120, 136
Ocasio-Cortez, Alexandria, 49, 132
Occidental Dissent, 86
The Occidental Quarterly, 28, 30, 47, 114
Old Left, 28
O'Meara, Michael, 42
one-drop rule, 67
Oneida Colony, 52
online community, 93–96, 126

the Order, 53, 63, 112
Ordre Nouveau, 25, 26
organic intellectuals, 25
Osborn, Frederick, 59
Ostara Publications, 1–2, 4, 35
overpopulation, 60
Overton window, 21, 45, 101
Ozarkia, 51, 60

Pacific Northwest, 11, 61–65, 84
paleoconservatism, 5, 28
palingenesis, 38, 39, 51
Palingenesis Press, 3
Palmgren, Henrik, 116
Panofsky, Aaron, 91
Papacharissi, Zizi, 95
"Parasite Class," 79
partial citizenship, 67–68
The Passing of the Great Race (Grant), 1, 2, 3, 60
paternalism, 83
patriarchy, 9, 12, 82, 98, 108, 134
Patriot Prayer, 74
Paul, Ron, 5, 20
PayPal, 32
Pepe the Frog, 6
Peterson, Jordan, 78–79, 88, 102, 103, 135
Pick Up Artists (PUA), 17, 97
Pioneer Fund, 59, 60, 90
Poland, 52, 118, 121
polarization, 49
polar origins of Aryans, 36, 41
Political Cesspool (radio show), 8
political correctness, 12, 101, 118
"Politically Incorrect" forum, 77
Pompeo, Mike, 131
populism, 13, 119, 136
pornography, 71, 85
Portaz, Maximine Julia, 36
Pound, Ezra, 29
preservationism, 60
primitivism, male, 84
"primordial state," 39, 42–43
prisoners, 67
The Prison Notebooks (Gramsci), 25
progress, 42–43, 44
progressivism, 104
promiscuity, female, 83
pronatalist policies, 54, 82, 99–102
propaganda, 28
The Protocols of the Elders of Zion, 80
proto-ethnostate, 62
protofascism, 40
Proud Boys, 32, 71–76, 87, 124

Proud Boys' Girls, 72
PUA (Pick Up Artists), 17, 97
Public Religion Research Institute, 122
purity spiral, 7
Purple Heart Foundation, 114

quality vs. quantity, 39
Quillette (webzine), 135
Quinn, Spencer J., 66–67, 68

race: and criminality, 35; and intelligence,
    19–20, 35; and political party, 120
race baiters, 111
race realism, 3, 45, 55, 77
race wars, 54, 64
racial degeneration, 11
racial differences, 58, 66
racial division, 120–21
racial essentialism, 9, 87–92
Racial Holy War (RaHoWa), 30
racial homogeneity, 1
racial hygiene, 40
racial identity politics, 75
racialists, 5, 60
racial mixing, 80
racial nationalism. *See* ethnonationalism
racial othering, 75
racial purity, 41
racial rebirth, 35, 38, 40
racial resentment, 120–21
racial separation, 59
racial state, America as, 123
racial superiority, 40
"racial vetting," 66–67, 68
racism: and biological essentialism, 72,
    73, 87–92; and normalization, 120–21,
    123; and traditionalism, 104; and white
    ethnostate, 59
Radical Agenda, 111
Radio 3Fourteen, 63, 100, 101, 104–7
Radix Journal, 4, 28, 29–30, 116
RaHoWa (Racial Holy War), 30
RamZPaul (Paul Ramsey), 5, 9, 81, 116,
    134–35
Raspail, Jean, 80–81
reactionary futurism, 36, 44
Reactionary Futurism (blog), 125
Rebel Media, 75
rebirth, 35, 38, 40
rebranding, 111–17
Reb Rebel Records, 30
Reddit, 4, 18–20, 73, 97, 102, 112
Red Ice TV: and biological essential-
    ism, 75, 77; and old vs. new white

nationalism, 8; and red pilling, 30, 32;
    and timescapes, 35; and traditionalism,
    93, 94, 100–101, 107; and white ethno-
    state, 54, 63
Red Pill 1965 (video), 104, 105
red-pill conversion, 9–10, 15–32; and
    American-style metapolitics, 27–32;
    and culture, 21; debut in *The Matrix of*,
    16; experience of, 15–16; feminism and,
    18–20; and metapolitics and European
    New Right, 22–27; overview of, 15–17;
    stories about, 17–22
Red Pill forum, 102
Red Pill Women (RPW), 102–4
Reeve, Elspeth, 136
refugee bans, 56
repatriation, 68
reproductive technologies, 43
Republican Party, 13, 28, 120–23
restorationism, 52
Return of Kings blog, 17, 31
Revolt (Evola), 41
The Revolt Against Civilization (Stoddard),
    3
Revolt Against the Modern World (Evola),
    40–41
Ride the Tiger (Evola), 44
Right Stuff website, 30, 63, 77, 117
*The Rising Tide of Color Against White
    World Supremacy* (Stoddard), 3
R/k theory of reproduction, 90
Robertson, Colin, 16, 31, 56, 78, 104, 116
Robertson, Wilmot, 57–60, 65
Rodger, Elliott, 97
Rogan, Joe, 78
Romanian Iron Guard, 39
Roosevelt, Theodore, 2
Roosh V, 97
RPW (Red Pill Women), 102–4
Rubin Report, 87–88
Ruby Ridge, 53
Rushton, Philippe, 90

"safe spaces," 19
Sailer, Steve, 121
Sanders, Bernie, 20, 79
Sargon of Akkad, 31
Scandza Forum, 7, 89, 96, 113, 117
scaremongering, 101
science, technology, and engineering
    (STEM) programs, 68
Second Vermont Republic, 61
self-determination, 55
self-sufficiency, 61

sexism, 72
sexual counterculture, 27
Sexual Utopia in Power: The Feminist Revolt Against Civilization (Devlin), 83
shadow-banning, 31
Shaw, George, 89
Sierra Club, 60
Silver Age, 38, 39
Singh, Nikhil Pan, 123–24
SJWs (social justice warriors), 12, 47–48, 72, 77, 101, 103–4
skateboarders, 29
Slack, 142n26
slavery, 123
snowflake, 4, 21
Snyder, Gary, 61
Snyder, Timothy, 13, 34
social justice warriors (SJWs), 12, 47–48, 72, 77, 101, 103–4
social media, 13–14, 93–95
sociogenomics, 92
"soft power," 28
Somalis, 107
South Africa, 114, 131–32
Southern, Lauren, 101, 131
Southern Oregon Proud Boys, 74
Southern Poverty Law Center: and biological essentialism, 74, 77, 84; and normalization, 113, 115; and red pilling, 17; and timescapes, 38; and white ethnostate, 63, 67; and white nationalist discourse, 136
"Southern strategy," 123
Southwestern borders, 69
Spencer, Richard: and biological essentialism, 77, 86; and metapolitics, 22, 31; and normalization, 115–17; and old vs. new white nationalism, 2, 3, 4, 5, 6, 7; and red-pill conversion, 15, 21; and timescapes, 34, 47; and traditionalism, 93, 104; and white nationalist discourse, 136
"sperm jacking," 83
sports and metapolitics, 29
Spotify, 31
spouses, nonwhite, 67
Stanley, Jason, 134
states' rights, 123
STEM (science, technology, and engineering) programs, 68
Stenner, Karen, 119
stereotypes, 3
Stewart, Ayla, 31, 75–76, 88, 100, 101
Stoddard, Lothrop, 3, 89

Stormfront, 4, 30, 31, 91, 112
storytelling, digital, 12
Students for Trump, 113
supermajority, 42, 69
"Surfing the Kali Yuga," 45
The Surrendered Wife, 102–3
sustainable communities, 55
Swain, Carol, 108
Sweden, 121
Swift, Taylor, 29

Taki's Magazine, 5, 28, 30
tattoos, 72, 114
Taylor, Jared: and biological essentialism, 77, 86, 89, 90; and normalization, 113, 117; and old vs. new white nationalists, 3, 5; and red pilling, 31, 146n60; and timescapes, 45–46, 49; and traditionalism, 96, 105; and white ethnostate, 68
technology, 34, 42–43
Temple of Life synagogue, 113
temporality. *See* timescapes
Teutonics, 2
Texas secession (Texit), 61
The Red Pill (TRP) subreddit, 18–19, 20
They Want You Dead White Man! (Lokteff), 101
Third Reich, 3, 36
This Week on the Alt-Right, 82, 93–94, 117
timescapes, 10, 11, 33–49; and alt-right amnesia, 44–49; and archeo-future, 42–44; and Kali Yuga, 38–42
time warps, 42
"toxic technoculture," 97
traditionalism, 12, 93–110; and ancestry, 100, 104–10; and biological essentialism, 75; and ethnostate, 52; and gender equality, 102–4; and gender roles, 98; and internet, 93–98; and metapolitics, 28–29; and timescapes, 35–36; and "toxic technoculture," 97; and "white baby challenge," 99–102; and Woman Question, 96–97
Traditionalist Worker Party, 86
"traditional spirit," 41
TradLife. *See* traditionalism
transformation, 9–10. *See also* red-pill conversion
transphobia, 12, 76, 77–78, 134–35
tribalism, 35–36
trolling, 28, 44
tropes, 4
TRP (The Red Pill) subreddit, 18–19, 20
True Cascadia, 63

Trump, Donald: and American metapolitics, 28; and biological essentialism, 73, 74, 80, 91; and European New Right, 22; and normalization, 113, 120, 124; and old vs. new nationalism, 1, 4, 6, 8, 13; and red-pill conversion, 20, 21; and timescapes, 45, 46, 49; and traditionalism, 95, 97; and transphobia, 134; and white ethnostate, 56; and white nationalist discourse, 129, 130–31, 134, 136
Truth, Justice, and a Nice White Country (Johnson), 77
Turner, Lisa, 108
The Turner Diaries, 132, 135
12 Rules for Life (Peterson), 78–79
27Crows Radio, 21, 93, 105
23andme, 91
Twitter: and biological essentialism, 74, 78, 82–83; and normalization, 116, 126; and old vs. new white nationalism, 4, 12, 13; and red pilling, 20, 31–32; and timescapes, 45; and traditionalism, 93–94, 95; and white nationalist discourse, 130
211 Boot Boys, 74

ultranationalism, 4, 34, 37, 38, 51, 55
"unadmissable minorities," 57
undocumented immigrants, 69, 79, 121; children of, 125
Unicorn Riot, 142n26
Unite the Right rallies: and biological essentialism, 74; and normalization, 111, 117; and old vs. new white nationalism, 6–7, 13; and red pilling, 31
universality, 12
University of Virginia, 118
US Border Patrol, 2
utopia, 61–62
utopian experiments, 52

Vargas, Getulio, 39
VDARE, 74, 96, 114
Vedanta, 39
Vertigo Politix, 31
vetting: algorithms for, 11, 66–67, 68; extreme, 13, 124
Vice, 20, 136
Vice Media, 71
victimhood, 9, 12, 34
Victoria (Hobbes), 55
video games, 85
virtual communities, 4
"virtue signaling," 80
Vishnu, 36

vlogs, 12
von Rotteck, Carl, 23
von Schlözer, August Ludwig, 23
voting rights, 108
Voting Rights Act (1965), 48
Vox Day, 31

Wakanda, 52
Waking Up from the American Dream (Hood), 46
war of position, 25, 28, 32
Warren, Elizabeth, 91
warriors, 41, 42, 64
watchdog groups, 136
Wayback Machine, 5
The Way of Men (Donovan), 84–85
The Way of the Right (Benoist), 26
welfare benefits for immigrants, 54, 106
Wendling, Mike, 73
West, lure of, 61–65
Western chauvinism, 72, 74
"The West Is the Best," 32, 71
westward expansion, 47
Whiggish histories, 37–38
"white baby challenge," 99–102
White Citizens' Council, 98
WhiteDate, 82–83
white demise, projection of, 10
"white dispossession," 58
white dominance, 52
white ethnostate, 11, 51–69; and archeofuture, 42; Cascadia and lure of the West for, 61–65; and civic vs. racial nationalism, 51, 55; determining whiteness for, 65–69; electronic, 126; emotional appeal of, 55; imagining, 57–60; implications of, 54, 55–56; Greg Johnson on, 53–54; mission of, 51; and old vs. new white nationalism, 4, 9; prototypes for, 52–53; reputed benefits of, 54–55; Donald Trump and, 56–57
white exceptionalism, 9
white extinction, 13, 99–102, 122, 132–33
#WhiteFamily messaging, 83
white genocide, 3, 52, 89, 99, 101, 130–33
"white guilt," 48
white identity, 118
White Identity: Racial Consciousness in the 21st Century (Taylor), 45–46, 89
white identity politics, 65, 112, 117
white liberals, 65
white majority, 54
white male victimhood, 9, 12
"The White Man's Burden," 21

white nationalism: new vs. old, 1–14; use of term, 8
white nationalist discourse, decoding and derailing, 129–37
whiteness, criteria for, 11, 65–69
white pills, 10, 17
white power extremism, 11, 12–13
White Republic: and biological essentialism, 76; and timescapes, 46, 48; and traditionalism, 97, 109; and white ethnostate, 54, 56
white solidarity, 118
white supermajority, 42, 69
white supremacy, 8–9
white tribal identity, 14
white victimization, 118
Whitey on the Moon (Kersey), 49
"Whitopia." *See* white ethnostate
Why We Fight: Manifesto of the European Resistance (Faye), 26
Wife with a Purpose, 31, 75–76, 88, 100, 101
Wilders, Geert, 100
Witoslawski, Alex, 45
Wolves nationalist, 84
Wolves of Vinland, 84
Woman Question (WQ), 7, 96–97
women: and gender equality, 102–4; and gender roles, 98; and internet, 93–98;

and "toxic technoculture," 97; and "white baby challenge," 99–102; white nationalist, 9
World Church of the Creator, 26, 108
World Wide Web, 30
WQ (Woman Question), 7, 96–97

xenophilia, 58, 124
xenophobia: and biological essentialism, 75, 80; and normalization, 119, 123; and old vs. new white nationalism, 2, 5, 13; and traditionalism, 104; and white nationalist discourse, 136

Yiannopoulos, Milo, 68, 76
YouTube: and biological essentialism, 74–78, 81, 82, 87; and metapolitics, 31; and normalization, 115, 116, 124, 126; and old vs. new white nationalism, 4, 12, 13; and red pilling, 15; and timescapes, 49; and traditionalism, 93–95, 97, 100, 104, 109; and white nationalist discourse, 130
yugas, 39
Yule web TV, 8, 94

zero-sum logic, 84
zero tolerance, 56
Ziblatt, Daniel, 124